CECILIA NORMAN'S MICROWAVE
COOKERY COURSE

Cecilia Norman was born in Chelsea, London and studied domestic science. After marriage and raising her two daughters she returned to teaching as a home economics teacher in secondary and further education.

Her interest in Microwave cooking started in 1969 when little was known about the domestic side of the subject in this country. Her first book was *Microwave Cookery for the Housewife* which became a best seller. Her other books on the subject are *Freezer to Microwave*, *Microwave cooking*, *The Colour Book of Microwave Cooking* and *Faster Cooking with Magimix to Microwave*. She founded the first Microwave School, which she still runs, in September 1980.

At Croydon College and the Polytechnic of North London she is currently lecturing in Recipe Development and the Preparation of food for Photography for third year diploma students.

She takes an active interest in the Association of Home Economists, of which she is a member, and the Charlie de Rotisseurs.

By the same author

Microwave Cookery for the Housewife
The Heartwatcher's Cook Book
Microwave Cooking
Freezer to Microwave
The Colour Book of Microwave Cooking
The Sociable Slimmer's Cook Book
The Crêpe and Pancake Cookbook (re-titled *Pancakes and Pizzas* for paperback)
Faster Cooking with Magimix to Microwave

CECILIA NORMAN'S

Microwave Cookery Course

A MAYFLOWER BOOK

GRANADA
London Toronto Sydney New York

Published by Granada Publishing Limited in 1981
Reprinted 1982

ISBN 0 583 13544 7

A Granada Paperback Original
Copyright © Cecilia Norman 1981

Granada Publishing Limited
Frogmore, St Albans, Herts AL2 2NF
and
36 Golden Square, London W1R 4AH
866 United Nations Plaza, New York, NY 10017, USA
117 York Street, Sydney, NSW 2000, Australia
100 Skyway Avenue, Rexdale, Ontario, M9W 3A6, Canada
61 Beach Road, Auckland, New Zealand

Printed and bound in Great Britain by
Cox & Wyman Ltd, Reading
Set in Times

Granada ®
Granada Publishing ®

Contents

Note
Both Imperial and metric weights and measures are given in this book. Either should give perfect results but they are *not* equivalents and therefore are not interchangeable. Do not mix Imperial and metric weights and measures in the same recipe. Use either one or the other.

Introduction

Thank you for picking up this book. I love cooking and trying out new ideas but, way back in 1969 when I was asked to write a book on microwave cooking, it took quite a bit of research even to *find* a domestic microwave oven. When I did, I had the enviable task of working out recipes. There were no British books on the subject so I had to start from scratch and the method I used was to try out basic conventional recipes. Mostly I was lucky but, of course, I had problems with overcooking – cakes that tasted like dried biscuits and fish that had shrunk to such an extent that they were bumpy all over.

Since my first book was published in 1974 I have continued my microwave work, improving recipes all the time and, with the introduction of variable control, so many more cooking processes are possible.

Now I have my own school and it is so rewarding to see my 'lady and gentleman students' showing the same enthusiasm and excitement for microwave cooking that I have always felt.

This book is called *Cecilia Norman's Microwave Cooking Course* because I have endeavoured to explain each process in detail, so that you can see whether or not you are on the right lines. A recipe is all very well but it is you, the cook, who is responsible for success or failure – provided, of course, that the recipe was a good one in the first place. In this book I give recipes for basics, so that you can make up your own dishes, using mine as a guideline. For example, on page 109 you will learn how to cook Dover sole; in chapter 9 there is a selection of sauces; add a little of this or that, garnish prettily, and ring the changes to suit yourself.

There will be times when you want to use all your appliances and there is no doubt that the mixer, food processor and liquidizer can do many of the tedious cooking jobs for you. Often you may wish to use both your microwave oven and the conventional oven to produce quick delicious dishes, so I also give some suggestions for dual cooking.

I have been more concerned with the techniques of microwave cooking than the conventional grouping of recipes – so look for recipes in the index as they may not be where you expect them to be.

I hope you will enjoy using this book and become a microwave cooking addict too.

The Advantages of the Microwave Oven

Perhaps you already have a microwave oven or are thinking about buying one. Maybe you have heard about them or seen them in the shops, but are not yet quite convinced. Have you been led to believe that all the microwaves will do is reheat or, on the other hand, that miraculous meals will instantly appear on the table without any effort at all?

The truth of the matter is that the microwave oven, or microwave cooker, as it is sometimes called, is an invaluable asset in every home. It will take 99% of the drudgery out of meal preparation; cook at less than quarter of the conventional speed; save up to 70% on the fuel bill; and reduce washing up by 80%.

Ninety-five percent of the dishes you are likely to cook can be done in your trouble-free microwave oven. It can be used instead of the hob for boiling, simmering, stewing and poaching. It can sauté in its own way – but it cannot fry. With the use of a special easy-clean browning dish you can sear and brown chops, steaks and sausages, although some models have a fitted grill. It will bake and roast but not brown and crispen, but is it worth that extra time in a conventional oven just to achieve a crisp and brown finish but with no difference in taste? In any case, the food can be flashed under a conventional grill if browning is required. The microwave oven will defrost and heat foods at remarkable speed and, in this age of convenience foods and the freezer, what is the point in buying fast foods if you cannot cook them fast? There is no point in filling up the freezer if it may take eight hours for the food to thaw out before you can cook it.

The microwave oven hygienically excludes airborne germs from coughs and sneezes and fly blows and will not make your kitchen hotter in the summer. Much of the food can be cooked covered with cling film and left to form a perfect seal, so that food that does not require immediate refrigeration can be left on the side to be reheated on demand. What is more, the speed of cooking aids vitamin retention. It will take you twenty seconds, rather than twenty minutes, to clean your oven, so that Sunday lunch needn't be followed by an afternoon's scouring session.

You can't move heavy conventional cookers around but the microwave oven is portable. It can be lifted by one strong or two weaker people. You can site it anywhere there is a 13 amp fused socket. You can cook while watching the television, have it on the floor beside you if you have to take to your bed or, using a suitably safe extension lead, use it as a back-up for the barbecue to cook the potatoes or reheat the burgers. You can even fix it in a marquee for summer parties. Take your microwave oven at weekends to your country cottage or on a very large boat with a sufficiently powerful battery. (The ordinary canal boat has only a 12 volt battery which is not suitable.)

The cost of a microwave is no longer astronomical and the rate of breakdown is almost nil. I should know – I have ten.

All this may sound too good to be true but it isn't. The microwave oven, expensive though it may seem at first, will pay for itself over and over again.

How the Microwave Oven Works

When you open the oven door you will be confronted by a cavity and you may wonder how on earth it is going to be heated. The answer is, it isn't. The only heat created is within the food itself which causes it to feel warm within the cabinet. When the microwave oven is plugged in and switched on, the electricity voltage which we know as 230/250 AC, passes through a power pack and is transformed into a very high voltage. The magnetron (the oven's heart) starts working and converts this voltage into a very high frequency (2,450 megacycles) generating microwaves down a channel into the cavity. These are distributed evenly around the cavity and deflect off the sides and base of the oven in a criss-cross pattern at a speed of 2,450 million times a second. These microwaves pass through the cookware and cause the food particles to agitate, rubbing them together to form heat and so cook. As the process continues, the food gets hotter and that is how cooking occurs. When the oven is switched off, the microwaves go away just as electricity disappears when you switch off the light. I could explain all this in more technical jargon but the process is complicated and how many clever cooks know how their gas or electric cookers work?

Don't look for the microwaves. They are invisible, but should not be confused with X-rays which are very short. When you have an X-ray, the radiographer disappears behind a screen. This is because the rays are ionic and there is a build-up effect in the body. Microwaves are non-ionic so this cannot occur. All ovens have a number of built-in safety devices which ensure that microwave leakage is almost non-existent, and all activity cuts out when the door is opened. Special safety standards are applied with which manufacturers should comply. From my experience leaks over the permitted level have never occurred. However, if there were to be a leak it would be strongest within 5cm (2 in) of the oven, gradually dispersing until it was only one-hundredth as strong at arm's length.

I would not expect to be unscathed if I put my hand on a heated electric ring nor prevent my hair from catching fire if I leaned over a gas flame. Stand at a reasonable distance from the microwave oven and I don't cook with my nose pressed up against the door and neither should you. An elbow's length away is a sensible distance from the oven and you can see better from this distance through the screen than if you were closer.

It is a good idea to have your oven regularly serviced to ensure it is giving its best performance. At the same time you can ask the engineer to check the door seals with his meter. Very little can go wrong with a microwave oven but it is best to let the professionals put in the new bulbs, and to remove any fiddly bits so that you can clean them. The magnetron has a very long life and, like our own hearts, slows down a bit in old age. Door seals should be kept very clean and grease-free at all times and abrasives must not be used in the oven.

As more and more new models appear in the shops a market in second-hand ovens will occur. Do not purchase one until you have had it checked, even if it has hardly been used. Little used televisions wear out from tube inactivity and so do magnetrons.

Types of Microwave Oven Available

The first domestic microwave ovens had only one power setting and were very simple to operate. Many are still in use and none the worse for wear. They will carry out all microwave cooking, but if you are a keen defroster you need to use different techniques to those used with more modern machines.

Most ovens now have a dual control so that you can either cook at full power or slow-cook and defrost at a low speed. The defrost control may either work on a low wattage or on a 'pulsing' system whereby the microwave energy is switched on and off at regular set intervals. If you listen carefully you can hear the difference in tone. It does not matter which method is incorporated as the end result is the same except in the case of soufflés.

Some ovens are fitted with push button or touch controls which give a choice of three or four powers; others work on a shift or cog system, allowing the user to turn the dial to the power required.

More sophisticated ovens include the electronic touch controls where just a brush of the finger will convey instructions to the machine. Many of these are capable of obeying combined orders – defrosting, resting and restarting, for example – and cooking perfectly without further guidance. This requires some practice and you will have to study the manufacturer's handbook.

Ovens with turntables are presently popular. Manufacturers of these claim that results are more even, since dish-turning is unnecessary. Anchor Hocking make a turntable that will fit into most ovens. Yet other manu-

Guide to Microwave Oven Settings & Symbols

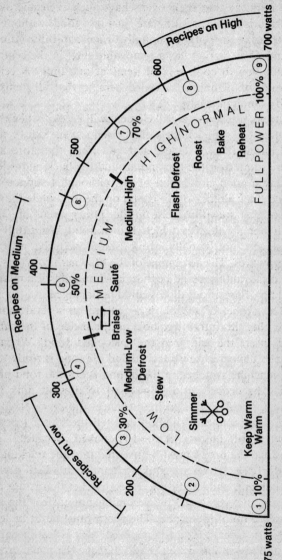

At least 150 watt difference is necessary before there is any significant change in the cooking or time patterns.

700 watts

Recipes on High

600

Recipes on Medium

500

Recipes on Low

400

300

200

75 watts

9 8 7 6 5 4 3 2 1

100% 70% 50% 30% 10%

FULL POWER 100%

HIGH/NORMAL

Roast
Bake
Reheat

Flash Defrost

MEDIUM

Medium-High

Sauté

Braise

Medium-Low

Defrost

Stew

LOW

Simmer

Keep Warm
Warm

facturers say that their ovens have such even microwave distribution that results are just as good without the necessity to turn either manually or mechanically. Another oven on the market has a removable shelf in the centre to enable you to cook several items at one time. A certain amount of planning is needed here so that all items are ready simultaneously.

Ovens fitted with a grill element will get hot when this is in use. On some models there is no space between the outside and inside layers and you must therefore allow more room over the top and around the back and sides to ensure a good circulation of air, although I suppose you could thaw a block of ice cream on the top, while the oven is cooking something else inside. Other ovens are fitted with hot air devices which brown food beautifully but these do not usually work simultaneously with the microwaves. The advantage of the browner is obvious, but the disadvantage could be that paper and plastic containers and non-flameproof dishes could be damaged.

The probe, or sensor, is a feature on several models. You plug this into a wee hole on the inside of the cabinet and insert the end into the uncooked food. When the correct temperature is reached and the food is ready to eat the machine switches to 'hold' and keeps the food piping hot. The probe can also be used to prevent milk from boiling over. In certain circumstances, however, the probe can give wrong information and tell the motor to switch down or off before the food is cooked. Because it is so sensitive the probe must be inserted into the thickest part of the food. If you are cooking items with a high sugar or fat content, and should there be a pocket that is not quite mixed, this part can, by becoming hot, affect the most sensitive tip of the probe. The probe must never be left in the oven when it is not being used. If it is left in without being fixed in its socket, it will damage the magnetron by causing sparking. If it is fixed in its socket but is lying in the oven, it will pick up the temperature in the cavity and not in the food so that there is no proper control. The plastic on the probe can also become distorted by misuse. Correctly used, the probe can be a very helpful implement.

One of my ovens has a humidity detector which automatically determines the correct cooking time and proceeds to cook the food perfectly, pinging when ready to serve.

More types of oven will be coming on the market over the years and there is even a gas-cum-microwave which has been mooted.

PROS AND CONS

You should give thought before purchasing since what is a pro to one person, is a con to another. You must choose the type of oven that suits your pocket and your lifestyle. At the moment a microwave oven could cost as little as £160 or as much as £450. At the lower end of the scale you will only be buying a 500 watt output oven which you will find somewhat slow really and at the top of the range are the super electronic wizards. Having decided on how much you can afford, the next thing to consider is the size of your family or the number of people for whom you will generally be preparing food. It really isn't practicable to cook for more than four people in a microwave oven simply because the time that it would take to cook something like 1.75 kg (4 lbs) of frozen peas would be longer than if you were to pop them in a saucepan of boiling water. If you are a complete microwave addict you will not want to use your conventional cooker at all, but planned cooking is much the best, so cook some of the items by microwave and others by conventional means. This applies to prime cooking as well as to just heating up convenience foods. For those people who like to keep a large stock of meat and poultry in the freezer, it is better to have a microwave oven with a defrost button, which is also useful if you are going to cook casseroles and stews. Buy an oven with variable control if you are going to do much in the way of egg and cheese cookery or embark on a big programme of cake-making. If your purpose is mainly to defrost, then a lower output and consequently a cheaper oven will suit you – the rating is likely to be 500 watts. For optimum cooking results, a 600/700 watt output should be your choice.

When you have decided what you want your microwave oven to do for you, you can choose the shape and design. Decide what size will fit into your kitchen and just how portable you really require it to be. Although you shouldn't stand things on top of the oven, the chances are that you will and if this is at all likely to be permanent, you must not purchase an oven which has an air outlet at the top, because this must not be covered. Look inside the oven and see if it is going to be easy to clean in the corners and around the light fittings. Can the 'ceiling' be removed for cleaning? Will the impeller (if there is one visible) get dirty? Is there a difficult grid with a light behind it? Are the shelves (or base plates) easy to get in and out and do you prefer to wipe up spills in the oven or remove the shelf for washing in the sink? Do you prefer a shiny or a matt finish?

All ovens operate on a time switch for there is no temperature control when the oven is not being used with a sensor. Have a good look at the controls and see if you like the way they work. On models with the electronic fascia you have to touch each required digit – for example, you would touch 1, then 0 followed by 0 for one minute. Read your instructions carefully because on some models the 100 counts down from 59 to 0. Thus, if you put in 99 it will work for 1 minute 39 seconds. If therefore you want to cook for 1¾ minutes (105 seconds), you must not make the mistake of dialling 1.75 because you will find you are actually cooking for 2 minutes and 15 seconds (1 minute plus 75 down to 60, then 59 down to 0).

There are ovens with a built-in base plate or shelf and those with a removable kind. On no account should you switch on the oven without the shelf in position, even though some manufacturers state that 'theirs' will absorb some of the microwaves to save damage to the magnetron if inadvertently switched on while the oven is empty.

Have a good look at On/Off and Cook controls before you decide which you like the best. In addition to setting the timer, there may be one, two or three other dials to press or flick before cooking can start. Some models have a separate power selector plus an On button, or you can have a power select, an On button and also a Cook button. Cooking cannot proceed until this latter is pressed, but you could be forgiven for forgetting this as there is a constant buzzing from the On button even if you have not pressed the Cook button.

Lighting also varies. The choice is of a separate switch to control the lighting quite independently of the cooking, or one which automatically comes on when the oven is in action. There is a further choice of having the oven illuminated until the control is switched to the Off position or where the light automatically comes on when the oven is in action and remains on until the door is opened. This can be disconcerting if the oven is sited in a dark corner of the room and, in any case, when you open the door you probably wish to see the cooking result.

Internal measurements should also be taken into account. If you like to use tall jugs or 'Dutch ovens', or you frequently cook an 8 kg (18 lb) turkey, an oven with a large cavity must be bought. Fishermen may prefer the non-turntable oven in which it is possible to stretch out a whole small salmon. Ovens fitted with a turntable have a certain amount of wasted space so far as the food is concerned (but not for the efficiency of the oven). There is one particularly efficient oven which has a rectangular shelf but this causes problems when similar shaped dishes are given a 90° turn.

Doors open either right-handed or drop down. Site the oven with this in mind. Doors should not be leaned on, distorted, or forced in any way. The drop-down door on one oven is said to be strong enough to use as a shelf while on another this could be considered dangerous. If you have young children it may be better to choose a side opener so there is no chance of the machine being pulled over. The side openers open either by deflecting a switch on the fascia or by gently pressing a catch concealed behind the handle. Some doors must be smartly snapped shut while on others a protruding lever must be pushed either up or down. Whichever you choose you can be sure that the oven will not operate unless the door is secure.

Timing devices also offer a choice of a single selector, twin turn-round dials and, as mentioned previously, the touch-sensitive panels. Watch for devices which start immediately the door is closed if the cycle has been interrupted. Most ovens are fitted with a pinger which rings when cooking is finished. On some machines the pinger may even be operated without using the microwave so that it can be used for all cookery and preparation times.

Throughout this book I have given instructions for settings on High, Medium and Low and if you are in doubt about the relevance to the settings on your own oven, refer to the chart on page 16. Generally speaking I used High for fish, vegetables and liquids; Low (30% power) for egg and cheese dishes, milky foods, casseroles and reheating dishes when no stirring is possible; Medium (50% power) for when fast cooking combined with extra tenderizing and development of flavouring is required.

Note: The Consumer Appliance Section of the International Microwave Power Institute is working on standardization of the common settings for the various makes of ovens. The settings proposed are 100% (High), approximately 70% (Medium-High), 50% (Medium), approximately 30% (Low) and approximately 10% (Warm). Your oven may differ from these percentages and the chart can only therefore be a helpful guide for conversions. As a very quick guide, if for any reason you prefer to cook on Low rather than High, multiply the given times on High by 2½, double the times for Medium and if you decide to cook half on High and half on Low, multiply the *second half* of the cooking period by 2½.

If you wish to halve the quantities of a recipe you should halve the cooking time and add a fraction more time. If on the other hand you want to double the quantities you need to allow time and three-quarters.

The recipes in this book have been calculated on a 650 watt oven.

Every week a new and more splendid machine attracts us – but, before you commit yourself, give a thought to your washing machine. How many of its programmes do you use? Regard your microwave oven in this light. Whatever you decide you will have made a good purchase – the microwave oven is like having a third arm.

COOKING TIMES CHART

600-700 Watt Machines				450-550 Watt Machines			
High 100%	Med-High 70%	Medium 50%	Low 30%	High 100%	Med-High 70%	Medium 50%	Low 30%
1 min	1½ min	2 min	2½ min	1¼ min	1¾ min	2½ min	3 min
2 min	3 min	4 min	5 min	2½ min	3½ min	4¾ min	6 min
3 min	4½ min	6 min	7½ min	3½ min	5¼ min	7¼ min	9 min
4 min	6 min	8 min	10 min	4¾ min	7¼ min	9½ min	12 min
5 min	7½ min	10 min	12½ min	6 min	9 min	12 min	15 min
6 min	9 min	12 min	15 min	7¼ min	10¾ min	14½ min	18 min
7 min	10½ min	14 min	17½ min	8½ min	12½ min	16¾ min	21 min
8 min	12 min	16 min	20 min	9½ min	14½ min	19 min	24 min
9 min	13½ min	18 min	22½ min	10¾ min	16 min	21½ min	27 min
10 min	15 min	20 min	25 min	12 min	18 min	24 min	30 min
12 min	18 min	24 min	30 min	14½ min	21½ min	29 min	36 min

The Four Uses of the Microwave Oven

1. THAWING

You can use your microwave oven for gentle defrosting or complete thawing. There are three ways of accomplishing these: give repeated short bursts of microwave energy at full power, followed by a resting time of equal or more length; or give a short burst of microwave energy on full power, followed by completing the thawing process in the refrigerator or at room temperature; or thaw by using the defrost control at the lowest setting. For the best results, stir or reposition the food as soon as softening begins and repeat frequently.

It is best to thaw food completely before cooking, except where it has been partially cooked or blanched, as in the case of frozen vegetables. (More information on this is given in the specific chapters.) For blocks of frozen cooked food – stews, casseroles, soups and vegetables – turn the block ice side up in a dish that will be large enough to fit the food when it is spread out and thawed. Switch on the oven for three or four minutes, then open the door and have a look. You should see some softening of the block on the outside. Give it a prod with a fork and, if it is soft enough, gently break away lumps from the sides. Continue microwaving for a few more minutes, then repeat the process. If the block consists of lumps of food, you must be careful not to mash, so it might be an idea to change to a wooden spoon at this stage. Soon you will find yourself with several large semi-frozen lumps surrounded by almost hot liquid – at times this can be boiling. Now is the time to push the lumps towards the outside of the dish, but not to the very edge – if they protrude beyond the rim the thawed liquid will spill over and make a mess. The maximum microwave energy will affect the perimeter and so, for the most efficient thawing, you should try to break up the central block as soon as possible. A problem with liquid-based frozen foods is that the ice particles act as containers and allow the microwaves to pass through them without them becoming thawed.

I haven't mentioned 'covering' up to now because if you use cling film, it is difficult to replace after stirring. Greaseproof paper may blow off and any ceramic or glass lid will slow down the thawing or cooking process. However, as soon as the food can be spread or stirred easily, loosely cover with cling film. The heat and steam created will be trapped inside as microwaving continues and this will hasten the thawing process. Provided the cling film is loosely applied you should be able to press your fingers on to the food and feel if it is hot. Leave for a few moments before carefully removing the cling film – the jet of steam that escapes can scald you.

For cooked or uncooked frozen food that cannot be stirred, such as pies, if they are shallow they will thaw more easily than if they are deep. Microwaves are at their strongest for the first 4 cm (1½ in) or so of penetration and this applies to the sides as well as to the top and bottom. The signal then becomes weaker and that is why the centre is the last part to heat. If you try to thaw in one long burst of full power, the outside will not only thaw, but overcook, while the bit in the middle is still frozen. Switch off the oven for one minute then give the dish a quarter turn and repeat three times. Now leave the dish to stand for two minutes so that the heat from the outside part will gradually transmit to the inner part. Repeat the process until the middle of the food is hot. Test with a skewer or feel the underside of the dish.

Only cover this type of dish if its contents are to be kept

moist on top. Pastry and crisp toppings will become soggy as the condensation drops back on to them. Deep dishes will take longer and it is more difficult to tell when they are just right.

For large masses of food, such as frozen chicken and meat joints which may either be cooked or raw, you should turn the food over rather than turning the dish after each minute of microwaving. Allow a resting time of ten minutes in between each four-minute cycle otherwise the outside will cook and the inside remain raw.

Delicate foods such as egg custards and cheese dishes do not easily respond to thawing on High. However, there are ways of converting a high setting into a lower one quite simply. (See page 28-29.) If you accept that at any one time there can only be a set amount of microwaves at work and these are distributed between that work-load, it must follow that the more items there are in the oven, the less attention each will receive. If you put a jug of water or even a few glasses of water into the cavity at the same time as the delicate food, the heating time will be lengthened. So, to defrost delicate items on High, put them in the oven with other foods – the more frozen the better. You must, of course, split the bursts of energy and resting times as before.

All these remarks have referred to defrosting on the high control, but if you have a defrost button the thawing will take about 2½ times as long and you can forget all about the special instructions.

DEFROSTING CHART

This chart must be taken only as the roughest possible guide to defrosting times. The reasons that specific times cannot be detailed are many. How cold is your freezer?

How long has the item been in the freezer? How big are the lumps? How efficient is your oven? But I have had so many requests to give some guide on defrosting timings that I feel the chart on pages 28-29 may be of some help.

2.   COOKING

Cooking processes are explained later in the book. As a rule, cover when you wish to keep the contents moist and soft, and leave uncovered for a crisper result. Reposition or turn over food of uneven shape such as chops, chicken on the bone and large items including joints, whole duck or chicken. All solid items cooked in a minimum of liquid, if more than 2½ cm (1 in) thick, should be turned over and, whenever possible, make a well or leave a space in the centre of the dish. Wherever stirring is permitted without disturbing the appearance of the food, it will not be necessary to turn the dishes, but otherwise give the dish a quarter turn for each quarter of the estimated cooking time. *This is not necessary if you have an oven fitted with a turntable or guaranteed efficient microwave distribution.* You can test this for yourself. Place several identical glasses or undecorated cups, evenly spaced on the oven shelf. If they all boil at once you have perfect microwave distribution. If those in the centre are slower, this is less important, but if, for example, you note that one corner is particularly slow, then food in this oven must be turned.

By now you will not need to be told that food doesn't brown very well. Microwave cooking is a moist and not a dry form. When you switch on a conventional oven, the air in the cavity is heated and affects the food as soon as it is put in, some items requiring a more intense heat than others. The heat turns liquid content into steam, as does

Item	Quantity	On Defrost (30% power)	On High (100% power)	Comments
Bread	1 large loaf	5 mins	2 mins	Wrap in kitchen paper or place on roasting rack
Cakes, fruit plain	400 g (14 oz)	2½-3 mins		Uncovered on kitchen paper
	400 g (14 oz)	3-4 mins		
Cream	150 ml (5 fl oz)	4-5 mins		Covered, first removing the original lid, stirring occasionally
Egg whites	4 eggs	3 mins		Uncovered. Remove before all lumps have melted – these break up when whisked
Fish, whole fillets and steaks	per 500 g (1 lb)	8-12 mins	3 mins	Covered, but exercise great care not to commence cooking
	per 500 g (1 lb)	6-8 mins	2 mins	
Fruit	275 g (10 oz)	4-6 mins	1-1½ mins	Covered
Made-up dishes, stirrable	4 servings	15 mins	6 mins	¾ covered. Do not need turning but break off lumps
non-stirrable	4 servings	20 mins	8 mins	Covering depends on whether crispy or soft finish required. Must be turned

Meat, joints	per 500 g (1 lb)	6-9 mins		Uncovered
chops	per 500 g (1 lb)	5 mins		Uncovered
steaks	per 500 g (1 lb)	6-8 mins		Uncovered
Pasta	350 g (12 oz)	8-10 mins	15 mins	Covered
Pastry, quiche	23 cm (9 in) flan	10 mins		Uncovered
jam & fruit fillings	23 cm (9 in) flan	2 mins		Uncovered – watch for jam, which gets hot very quickly
Poultry, whole chicken	per 500 g (1 lb)	6 mins		Uncovered
chicken pieces	per 500 g (1 lb)	5 mins		Uncovered
Rice	350 g (12 oz)	12 mins	5 mins	Uncovered, breaking up the lumps
Sauces, basic	600 ml (1 pt)	10 mins	4 mins	Covered, stirring as soon as possible.
emulsion	600 ml (1 pt)	6 mins	2 mins	Uncovered. Must be thawed very gently
Soups	600 ml (1 pt)	10 mins	4 mins	Covered, keep ice side up
	1 serving	5-8 mins	2-3 mins	Covered. Bubbles round edge no indication of complete thawing. Stir before tasting

If 10% = defrost setting on your microwave oven, the above Low times will need to be, say, doubled.

If there is only a High setting available, where the above chart does not give a High time (as it is so much preferable to thaw those items on Low) give short bursts of cooking with 10-minute rests between. Most composite dishes that can be stirred can be thawed on High.

the friction in a microwave oven. As food rises the heat also causes hardening, then browning. In a conventional oven the food is entirely cooked by conduction, each hot layer heating the next.

In a microwave oven, however, heat is engendered solely by friction, the most powerful action being in the first 3-4cm (1¼-1½ in) depth and width and the remaining food is heated by conduction. As the microwaves penetrate, the extreme outer layer cools and you will often see a soft covering and because it is moist it does not brown. However, greater heat does accumulate in the hot air in the upper part of the cabinet, so that food on the shelf, or tall items nearest to the magnetron, are more likely to brown. In the case of a joint, prolonged cooking causes the fat on the outside to burn and to brown the escaping mineral salts.

Sugar attracts the microwaves like moths to the light. All food can burn whichever method of over-cooking you use but, whereas in conventional cooking the burning appears on the outside, in the case of microwaves it starts in the centre. So high sugar content foods, such as cakes, burn first in the centre. After the outer layers are cooked, the middle holds on to the microwaves and, enclosed in its own cocoon, the sugary middle browns and burns. Jam for example is a great microwave attracter, so take care when reheating jam doughnuts – you could burn your tongue badly. Sugar in conjunction with a liquid is an ideal mixture for microwave cookery, so syrups and preserves are quickly made.

Fat is the other great microwave attracter and that is why it is better to draw off accumulations during roasting. As the meat juices drop into the fat there could be some spattering. Also, energy is wasted on surplus fat when it could be better used to cook the meat.

A browning dish is invaluable for searing and browning steaks, chops, sausages and chicken. Use salted butter in the dish because, as salt burns easily, it will act as a natural browner. Do not put salt directly on to food as this will draw out the moisture and cause toughening.

If the browning dish gets burnt-on deposits, do not use an abrasive to remove them. A soft cloth and a paste made with bicarbonate of soda will remove every trace.

3. REHEATING

Glorious trouble-free meal-times, coffee on demand, a bigger variety of food to almost restaurant proportions and practically total elimination of left-overs, saving the microwave owner time, money and trouble, not to mention temper.

Before you had your microwave oven, do you remember listening for the click of the front door as various members of the family turned up late or very late and there you were praying that the dinner hadn't got cold? You either had to keep it hot in the oven or over a pan of water and neither way was totally satisfactory. You dared not let food get completely cold because it would take ages to heat up and dinner would be served around midnight.

When reheating by microwave, food tastes as good and as fresh as it did when first cooked. It doesn't dry up as in a conventional oven and it doesn't go soggy as in a steamer. Reheat only the quantity that you require and leave the rest in the refrigerator for the next arrival. Because heating is so rapid less precious vitamins are lost.

With a microwave oven you are free to cook whenever the fancy takes you or when you have the most spare time, but since I am talking here about reheating, *not* thawing and reheating, this would not be more than a few hours in advance, depending naturally upon the nature of the food. Vegetable dishes like ratatouille improve with keeping for a day or two, but I wouldn't store cooked meat dishes for more than a day. Cook each dish separately, preferably in the serving container, and cover in cling film to keep out the germs. If the food has been cooked within the hour it need not be refrigerated, so microwave reheating time is decreased. Line up the dishes on the work surface and reheat the denser foods first, progressing to those with less heat-retentive properties. Sometimes I find I have to boost the reheating of these while I am carrying plates to the table.

It is a good idea to have really hot plates, a job which the microwave oven won't do. If you are serving a substantial meal with several dishes you should reheat by microwave. Light the conventional oven at a low temperature and pop in the hot dishes, at the same time warming the plates – but this should be for a matter of minutes only. Cling film will not disintegrate if the oven temperature is below 150°C (300°F) and the food will not deteriorate in such a short time.

When only a couple of dishes are being reheated you will not need to use the conventional oven. To heat the plates soak them in a bowl of very hot water, then dry, stack and wrap in a thick towel or an old-fashioned oven glove – the long kind, not a 'mitt'. When you have a means of plate-warming, food will stay hotter for longer. If all the courses are hot ones, the main course can be reheated while the soup is consumed and the dessert put into the microwave oven as the dishes are cleared. Only reheat such food as is going to be eaten at that meal for, marvellous as microwave is, it doesn't do food any good to be heated and cooled several times over. The goodness will be completely destroyed, leaving only the roughage value.

The shape of food, the density and the size all affect heating times, so it doesn't follow that all the food on a plate will heat at the same rate. Gravy and sauces become hot in seconds while potatoes are notoriously slow. Therefore, put the slower heating items around the edge of the plate and the thinner pieces in the centre. A pile of peas will heat more quickly and evenly than if they are spread out, for each pea is very small and little lonely ones will dehydrate. The pockets of air trapped in a mound will conserve the heat as it is generated and so speed the heating process. Plated foods heat best when all is of about the same depth. Always cover anything that needs to be kept moist, and make the gravy or sauce slightly thinner, diluting with water, wine, stock or milk.

For even reheating of large dishes, such as casseroles, stir and turn as you would for cooking. Do not over-reheat or the result will be overcooked. Individual portions should be heated on the smallest possible plate or dish either singly or stacked, according to the time at your disposal. When reheating plated meals in stacks, it is important to stagger the different foods so that all will be ready simultaneously. For example, on plates containing potatoes, peas and meat stew, arrange the slower-heating potatoes so that they are above the peas on the plate underneath and below the meat on the plate above, so that there is a vertical mixture. Polypropylene stacking rings are ideal for separating the plates and only the top plate needs to be completely covered. Check that the rings and plates are a good match so that the ring rims fit just inside the plate edge or else stacking rings will be dripping with food when removed.

When reheating in an oven with a raised shelf, stagger the food so that the plates are not directly over one another. If you don't object to squashed food cover each plate with cling film and stack the plates on top of one another. Each plate should be covered with cling film and interleaved with greaseproof paper to prevent the film from sticking to the plate above. This method makes for slower reheating, as no current of hot air can pass between the layers.

In common with conventional methods, reheating times in the microwave oven depend upon the starting temperature of the food, the longest being when reheating from frozen. Dishes at room temperature reheat the fastest and this may influence your choice of meal – for example, cooked meats, poultry and shellfish should not be left for long in an ambient temperature, as this is the one in which bacteria thrive.

4. QUICK AIDS

All the small tedious washing-up-producing jobs will be done at a moment's notice, using the high setting on your microwave oven. All these speedy but essential operations help to make cooking so much easier.

Cake-making often requires that butter and sugar be creamed together. Butter taken straight from the refrigerator is normally too hard to use, but if you put the measured quantity on an undecorated saucer for a few seconds in the microwave oven on High it will be soft enough to use. If melted butter is required, use a low setting so that there is an even texture as soft as you wish. Sandwiches can be rapidly prepared using melted butter applied with a pastry brush.

Cold eggs cause curdling in cakes and mayonnaise. Take courage and pop them in the oven on High while you count 1-2-3 while the chill is taken off. They should be balanced carefully on the oven shelf to prevent them rolling about.

Chocolate should be removed from its wrapping and be placed in a small bowl on High to ensure even melting. This process takes only a minute or two.

Warm oil briefly for guaranteed mayonnaise success for

which all ingredients must be at room temperature. Yeast mixtures require warm conditions and it is a good idea to warm the flour and stir in before adding the other ingredients.

Refresh salted peanuts on a paper-lined dish and just before serving, remove the paper and add a sprinkling of fresh salt.

Gelatine, which is generally tricky, blends easily when dissolved in the microwave oven.

Use a microwave oven to boil small quantities of water. When using an electric kettle the element must be covered and this might require a half pint thereby wasting energy.

Take the chill off baby's milk but remember to shake the bottle well and test before giving it to the child, so that there are no pockets of very hot liquid.

Put a piece of bread or apple in a packet of lumpy sugar and microwave on High for just a few seconds to make the sugar easier to manage.

Use a microwave oven to refresh coffee beans, roast almonds, soften chestnuts for easy peeling, and dry flowers after quickly dipping in silicone gel.

Soften lumpy marzipan in the oven, but be careful as the high sugar content can cause the centre quickly to become too hot to handle.

Both oranges and lemons will yield juice more easily when placed for a few seconds in the microwave oven, and rolls and stale bread can be quickly refreshed with a few seconds on High. This can be done in a wooden serving basket if you wish, provided there are no metal staples.

Yoghurt pots may not be microwave-proof because of their low heat resistance, but if you want to make decorative pots for children to play with, half-fill with water and cook on High, keeping a close watch so that the pot can be taken out when they have become the shape you want. You can also make 'play-dough'.

Candles melt easily for reshaping provided they are placed in a wax container, otherwise the mess will counteract the advantage. You can even restore old shoe polish provided it is taken out of the metal tin before warming.

Despite what you may have read elsewhere do *not* attempt to use the microwave oven to dry tea cloths – I have tested this and nearly had a fire.

Every time you reach for a small saucepan think whether it would not be easier to use the microwave oven. You will be surprised how often this is the case.

Cooking Containers and Utensils

You will find that most of the casseroles, dishes and bowls that you already have are suitable for microwave oven use as glass, pottery and china allow the microwaves to pass through to cook the food they contain. Since it is possible to cook and serve or eat from the cooking container, you won't have to transfer the food. It is not feasible to warm plates in the microwave oven because they will absorb only minimal microwave energy. Turning food out of a hot pan into a cold dish or plate makes the food cool more rapidly, but if the food is served from the dish in which it is cooked, which by conduction becomes hot itself, the problem does not arise. Because microwaves cannot pass through metal there is little point in using this type of dish even if it is substantial enough to eliminate 'arcing' so obviously you cannot use saucepans or saucepan lids.

The Metal Story

All ovens are metal-lined – even the door has a fine mesh – and some are fitted with metal racks, so it is understandably confusing to be told not to use metal in the microwave oven. These solid metal parts are reflective but do not cause arcing. It would not be possible to have a solid metal shelf because the microwaves would be unable to reach the lower section of the oven.

Much depends on the kind of metal you want to use. Most stainless steel and foil dishes are probably acceptable, provided they are full of food and the metal does not touch the oven walls. The problem is mainly that the microwaves cannot penetrate the metal and the food will not heat properly. If the dish is also covered with metal even the chill will not be taken off.

Aluminium foil is a boon to microwave users because of its capacity both to shield and hold in the heat. It may only be used in small pieces in the microwave oven to cover or shield thin or cooked parts and must not be allowed to blow about in the oven nor to touch the walls otherwise pitting of the aluminium may occur. Instructions about this are given in the recipes. Foil is also ideal to wrap up joints, baked potatoes or any other foods to keep them at serving temperature after being removed from the microwave oven. In fact, since cooking continues during standing time, you can save even more on fuel costs.

Totally forbidden in the microwave oven is the thin silver paper such as is wrapped around chocolate or foil butter wrappings because it sparks badly. Also in the forbidden category are metal tags normally used to seal polythene bags. Silver, gold or metallic decoration on china will spark, causing arcing, and will go black under these conditions. Examine the underside of your china and if there is silver or gold printing these items too are unsuitable.

Metal skewers can be left in kebabs, although they should be turned over during cooking to prevent the skewer forming a barrier. And one or two skewers can be left in a large chicken or turkey.

Metal is not always visible. I thought my microwave oven must have gone wrong when I tried to heat Long Life milk in its carton. I found out later that this was because the carton was lined with insulating silvery paper.

Heavy iron pots, such as those manufactured by Le Creuset and Copco, which are often covered in a coloured vitreous enamel, may appear to be pottery, but are not. Some ceramics have a metal content mixed in during manufacture. The dishes do not cause arcing but they do become very hot and may suffer damage. To test if dishes are suitable, put them in the microwave oven with a glass half-filled with water. Switch on for two or three minutes, then feel the water then the dish. The water should be hotter than the ceramic container.

Paper and Plastics

You have a wider choice of cooking containers for microwave use than for conventional cookery. Not only can you use glass, pottery, china and ceramics, but now you may cook in paper, cardboard and even some plastics. There are many different kinds of plastic, most of which are microwave proof, and some have a very long life. Others have a limited life and some are suitable for use in the conventional oven as well. Use them for freezing and for initial thawing of foods of low fat the sugar content. If a container is dishwasher-proof it means it can resist to just under boiling point, so it would behave very well if used for reheating under microwave conditions, but not for boiling.

Some of the specially produced containers are very well designed and are suitable for cakes and breads. They are reasonably priced and do not distort, unless used in prolonged cooking. Even better are the polypropylene bowls which are normally used for steamed puddings though subject to slight damage if used with syrup in the base. However – they are as long lasting as the white pottery basins – which are also ideal in the microwave.

While the Tupperware Company, because of their ten-year guarantee, do not recommend their products for use in the microwave oven, I have been exceedingly pleased with their cake shaped, rigid – coloured polypropylene canisters. Although they cannot be used for sugar syrups, jams or sautéing, I have used them for reheating and for cake-making, where I found that no greasing was necessary. Of course you must not cook with the lid seals in position, but these are useful for turning out the cakes on to. The softer Tupperware containers can only be used in the microwave oven for loosening blocks of frozen food that have been stored in them.

Polythene bags are available in two densities, but the thinner kind is never suitable for freezer storage so it is unlikely to be used in the microwave oven. It is inadvisable to cook in either of the types of bag, as the plastic softens when heat is applied and the hot contents would burst out when the bag was lifted and holes will appear if left in the oven too long. There are boilable bags, though, which are totally satisfactory. Provided the metal tag is removed, initial thawing may be done with the contents still in a freezer bag. I find it a good idea to fold back as much as possible and invert the frozen pack in a dish, leaving the bag on top as a covering. It can be removed easily when the food is thawed. Cellophane is also suitable for covering, particularly if you wish to inspect the food without removing the cover.

Plastics tend to stain so I would not advise their use for highly coloured foods such as tomatoes, carrots or rich red sauces. Some plastics, like melamine, absorb microwaves, which makes them get hot and increases the likelihood of distortion. However, you can test plastics to some extent by using the water method. Half fill a glass with cold water, place it in the oven next to the empty plastic container, switch on for fifteen to twenty seconds, then feel the container, which should be cool. Empty yoghurt pots, cream pots and the like are not microwave-proof merely because their heat resistance is low. Foam dishes are only acceptable if they are used for brief heating of foods which are not fatty or sugary and these dishes must not be covered.

At best they distort, and at worst they melt so that the gooey plastic strands stick to the food making it inedible.

Wooden bowls can be used for instant heating of rolls, but wood, being a natural substance, is absorbent and so will become hot and could crack. Straw baskets, provided they have no metal staples, can be used for warming rolls or similar items, but not for cooking. Wooden spoons may be left in mixing bowls for a few seconds but they may become very hot. Plastic spatulas can also be left in food for the same time, although I have trained myself to avoid this in case I forget and leave them in too long or absent-mindedly put in a fork which could be disastrous.

See-through roasting bags are recommended (without the metal tag of course), but they must not be completely sealed or they will split or burst. Use them for joints or vegetables. Elastic bands will soon dry out and crack and so break. Paper plates and dishes can be used for reheating or cooking small items, but if food is too wet the paper will become waterlogged and soft. If too dry, the paper will stick to the food. Some paper dishes are waxed, making them more moisture-resistant. Deeko make a paper dish which is specially treated so that, not only is it suitable for use in the microwave, but it can also be placed in the conventional oven at temperatures below 200°C (400°F, Gas 6), and the freezer.

Although glass is one of the most versatile microwave containers, since it can be used for mixing, cooking and serving, you must not use any glass with a metal content. This means that you cannot use crystal, which contains lead. If you decide to serve a microwave heated dessert or drink in a stemmed glass, do not use a good one, unless it is being reheated only.

Foil tartlet cases can be used for brief reheating of, say, mince pies, fruit pies and other commercially produced tartlets – but without the lid, of course.

Glue is not microwave safe so do not use cups with glued-on handles.

I have used the rounded tops of dishwasher powder cartons for shortbread and flan rings and chocolate boxes for cakes and the like. Waxed paper is used widely in America but less in the United Kingdom and this makes a good wrapping for fish cooked whole.

Cling film is obtainable in different degrees of clinginess and is an indispensable microwave aid. It absorbs no microwaves so does not slow down the cooking as a conventional lid will do. It also makes a perfect seal, keeping in all the moisture and odours, but keeping out germs. Try it with kippers and see what I mean. Two important points to remember: do *not* stretch it as you put it over the dish, and be very careful as you remove it or you may be scalded. Cling film may be used to partially cover food – and I would recommend this when stewing fruit or cooking with milk or other ingredients that can boil over – so that you can slide the spoon in the gap to stir. Do not try to peel back cling film for stirring as it is practically impossible to reposition. The heat causes its edges to twist and curl, resulting in your loss of temper. If you are careful, you can facilitate draining vegetables by peeling back an inch of the cling film and tipping the dish while supporting the vegetables through the cling film with the oven glove to drain away the liquid. If in doubt about removing cling film prick through before removing it. Use cling film to line cake, bread and biscuit dishes, particularly the cardboard kind. Cling film cannot support heavy weights so don't try to lift food out while holding the edges. If you are going to freeze cooked food, line a serving dish with cling film leaving a generous border, pour in the cooked food, fold the loose edges over the top of the food, pop the whole into a polythene bag when cool, and place in the freezer. When frozen, you can then remove the food in the cling film from the container so that the container is not out of use during the storage period. When you want to reheat for serving, put the wrapped food back into the original serving dish and microwave just long enough to remove and discard the cling film before continuing thawing.

Use kitchen paper towels for covering greasy foods, like sausages, or under jacket potatoes to absorb escaping moisture. Non-stick paper is ideal for all sugary or sticky mixtures – use it for lining cake bases. Greaseproof paper is a useful covering for preventing spattering of food over the oven.

Cardboard boxes such as chocolate and candy boxes make useful cake shapes, so don't throw them away after you have consumed the contents. They are not suitable if they are silver or gold though. Cut out circles from a piece of cardboard to fit paper tartlet cases then cakes will keep their shape better. Make sure, however, that there are no metal staples in the cardboard.

The effect of containers on cooking

The shape and density of food and also the shape and material of its containers all have a relationship with the speed and method of cooking. All dishes absorb some microwaves and those with even a small proportion of inbuilt metal will to some extent shield the food, although the heat build-up in the dish conversely speeds the cooking.

High-sided dishes are good, because food is less likely to boil over, but on the other hand cooking will be slower. Shallow dishes are the most efficient and food well spread out in them receives more equal microwave attention. Highly glazed pottery may craze but dishes such as Denby are ideal. Corning (Pyrex) also produce some useful shapes. Straight-sided dishes are better than curved or slanted dishes and a soufflé dish is just right for cakes. Savarin rings, because of the microwave cooking pattern, produce good even results when the food doesn't need stirring.

If you decide to use a loaf shape you may find, particularly with heavy dense mixtures such as bread, that the middle third is decidedly undercooked, but this may also occur with plastics of similar shape. Large rectangular shapes are about the poorest choice, as over-cooking will take place in the corners. Although round or square shapes cook more evenly, it is perfectly satisfactory to cook in an oval shape if food is to be stirred. Always choose a dish that just takes the contents unless it is a liquid or a very wet mixture, e.g. stewed fruit. If you are a freezer enthusiast you will find this advice useful, because as defrosting occurs, any seepage of liquid around the edges tends to cook while the centre of the food is still frozen.

Although not essential, here is a list of useful shapes:

Large shallow dish = 18 × 28 × 3.5 cm (7 × 11 × 1½ in)
Large deep dish = 20 × 28 × 7.5 cm (8 × 11 × 3 in)
Small shallow dish (oval) = 15 × 20 × 3.5 cm (6 × 8 × 1½ in)
Small casserole (deep dish) = 1.2 litres (2 pints)
Large casserole (deep dish) = 2.25 litres (4 pints)
Oblong loaf shape = 23 × 10 cm (9 × 4 in)
Oblong plastic shape = 18 × 10 × 7.5 cm (7 × 4 × 3 in)
Round soufflé dish = 15 cm (6 in) diameter
Round deep dish = 18 cm (7 in) diameter
Round shallow dishes = 18 cm (7 in) and 23 cm (9 in) diameter
Square shallow dish = 20 cm (8 in)

Set of glass jugs or measuring cups = 300 ml (½ pint) or
    600 ml (1 pint) or 1.2 litres (2 pints)

Set of individual ramekins or custard cups, browning
    skillet, savarin or ring mould 1 litre (1½ pints)

Set of glass heatproof bowls up to 2.8 litres (5 pints).

Timing the Cooking

Approximate timings only can be given for microwave cookery, but that is often the case with conventional cookery. Two ovens operating on the same power will not necessarily cook at the same speed. Don't run away with the idea that microwave cooking is a precise science. Although less attention is required it must receive some care. Under-cooking should be the rule as you can always cook a little more. Remember also that the tremendous heat mounting up inside the food will cause cooking to continue after removal from the microwave oven. Since microwave cooking is so very quick, you have the time to test, stir and allow the food to rest, in between your other jobs in the kitchen. However, it is not a good idea to run upstairs to make the beds for anything less than a long slow defrosting.

There are many influences on the cooking time. Density and shape of food affect the cooking times. The more solid items, e.g. a joint of beef, will take longer than a cake with its open texture. Even shapes cook more easily than irregular ones and a leg of lamb will cook more rapidly at the bone end. To overcome this problem, however, the bone can be shielded with foil as soon as this part is cooked.

Starting temperatures also affect the length of cooking. Food from the freezer will obviously take longer than food from the refrigerator. Fresh food at room temperature will be faster and if food is cooked in water, timings will be even shorter if you start with hot rather than cold water.

If you wish to cook different commodities in the oven at

one time, you will find that one dish may be ready before another. Therefore, choose foods of similar shape and density if you expect simultaneous cooking.

Quantity also governs cooking time to a large extent.

You must follow the advice given in your manufacturer's handbook regarding general cooking times, maintenance and safety factors as these will vary from appliance to appliance.

Liquid	*Quantity*	*Approx Time on High*
Water	150 ml (¼ pt)	1¾ min to boiling
	300 ml (½ pt)	3 min to boiling
	600 ml (1 pt)	5 min to boiling
	250 ml (8 fl oz)	1½ to 2 min to steaming
Chocolate	1 glass	1 min (2 min on Medium)
Cocoa	1 cup (6 oz)	1½ to 2 min
Coffee	(See separate coffee chart on p.293	
	1 cup	2½ to 2¾ min
Milk	150 ml (¼ pt)	1½ min to boiling (3 min on Medium 3¾ min on Low)
	300 ml (½ pt)	2½ min to boiling (5 min on Medium 6¼ min on Low)
Soup (thick)	200 ml (7 fl oz)	3½ to 4½ min on Medium
(diluted)	200 ml (7 fl oz)	2½ to 3 min
Tea	1 cup	1¼ to 1½ min

Liquids Heating Times

Liquids should be heated to 60°-65°C (140°-150°F).

Because oven temperatures vary, heat for the lower period, then test.

If reheating, fill the receptacle; if to be boiled, leave a space above the liquid.

Water-based liquids will reheat best on High. Where the proportion of milk is great, watch very carefully or microwave on Medium or Low instead.

To prevent boiling over, before microwaving smartly tap the base of the jug or glass on the worktop to stabilize the air distribution.

If several cups are being reheated at the same time, place them in a circle in the oven.

Liquids should not be heated in a tall bottle such as a milk bottle.

Small amounts of liquid should be reheated uncovered.

Trouble-shooting

YOUR QUESTIONS ANSWERED

Q. Why don't microwaves penetrate the see-through door?
A. The door screen consists of perforated metal or sometimes metal wires inlaid in plastic. These holes are so small, in relation to the wavelength of the microwaves, that the light comes through without the microwaves escaping. You will find you will be able to see more easily into the microwave oven if you stand an arm's length away.

Q. Can you tell me more about the workings of the microwave oven?
A. I am not a technical expert being only concerned with the cooking results. The manufacturer should be able to enlarge on the basic details I have given in the introduction.

Q. What is a defrost button and how does it work?
A. The defrost button reduces the total microwave energy. On some ovens it is done by changing the wattage and on others by pulsing to interrupt the full power. If you are only using the defrost setting for a short length of time, make certain that the microwaves are active during that period.

Q. What is variable control?
A. It provides a choice of setting from Very Low to High.

Q. Where does 'simmer' come on the range of settings?

A. This is not in the same position on all models. I do not regard 'simmer' meaningful in the microwave sense, but check with the chart on page 16.

Q. Why do cooking times vary?
A. Ovens vary in their output, suffer from voltage fluctuation and are as different from one another as conventional ovens. Each has its own idiosyncrasies.

Q. Can I deep fry?
A. No. There is insufficient control of temperature and the oven could catch fire.

Q. Why doesn't the food brown?
A. Some foods do brown – for example, joints of meat – when the hot fat bursts through and burns the surface. Syrups brown and will burn if over-cooked. Generally speaking, microwaves will not brown because there is no dry heat generated.

Q. Should I buy a second-hand oven?
A. Only if you have had it checked by a microwave engineer.

Q. Will microwaves affect a pacemaker?
A. Normally pacemakers are fitted with a shield to prevent 'interference' but you must check with your doctor.

Q. Why is a glass of water sometimes recommended to be put in the oven during cooking?
A. To reduce the cooking power.

Q. What will happen if my oven is switched on without anything in the cavity?

A. It could damage the magnetron. Always leave a glass of water in the cavity as you never know who may fiddle with the switches.

Q. I made a mistake and left a metal decorated cup in the oven and when I switched on I saw terrible flashing. Will I have damaged the magnetron?
A. Very unlikely for such a short period, but try not to do it again. In any case you may have spoilt the cup.

Q. Why if foil is recommended for covering tips of chicken legs, etc. is metal not suitable in the microwave oven?
A. Experts are still arguing about this but, provided the metal is solid and does not touch the sides of the oven and is very small in proportion to the mass of food, no damage should result.

Q. Why do microwaves cook more round the edge than in the middle?
A. Because the edges get the full microwaves from all directions and the centre only gets a weaker signal from the top.

Q. Why do some foods cook quicker than others?
A. This is because they have different densities, different shapes and different starting temperatures. As a rough guide food will take 5-7 minutes per pound to cook.

Q. How can I tell if my microwave oven is cooking as fast as it should?
A. Put 450 ml (¾ pt) water into a 1 litre (1½ pt) glass bowl or jug and take its temperature. Microwave on High for 1 minute and take the temperature again. Work out the difference, multiply by 17½ and that should give the

wattage of your oven. Do this test three times to provide an average and if the wattage comes out correctly your oven is properly set.

Q. Can I tell by looking if food is over-cooked?
A. Not usually because the over-cooking takes place under the surface, but you will know when you eat it. Meat, fish and poultry and egg and cheese dishes will be tough and cakes will be burnt inside.

Q. Can I use conventional recipes?
A. Yes, mostly. Add liquid to fast cooking items and reduce the liquid in foods normally simmered or casseroled.

Q. What is the reason for covering food during cooking?
A. To keep in the steam and prevent the food from drying out.

Q. Should food be covered during the heating?
A. Not invariably, but gravies will dry out if reheated without covering.

Q. What can I do to ensure even reheating of a plated meal?
A. Put the slower heated items towards the edge. This particularly applies to potatoes.

Q. How can I tell if all the food on the plate is reheated?
A. By feeling through the cling film covering and also underneath the plate.

Q. Should I pierce the cling film?
A. Only after cooking to release the steam and avoid burning the fingers when peeling it away.

Q. Why does cling film balloon?
A. Because you have stretched it over the dish too tightly. Cling film rarely bursts as it is slightly porous. If it does burst it is due to contact with very hot or sugar mixtures, or you stretched it truly beyond its endurance.

Q. How much standing time must I allow.
A. As a rule of thumb 3 minutes for quick cooking items and 10-15 minutes for slower cooking foods such as joints of meat and pastry.

Q. Why does a large quantity of food take proportionately less time than a small quantity?
A. Conduction assists the microwave activity.

Q. Why do I need to turn or rearrange foods?
A. To obtain even cooking. You turn foods which are not stirrable but stir foods which are.

Q. What is the good of a microwave oven if because I must keep stirring and turning I can't go and make the bed?
A. You won't have time to make the bed because miraculous microwaves will have the dinner ready for you while you are laying the table.

Q. Do I have to be fussy about cleaning the microwave oven?
A. Yes. A dirty oven slows down the cooking time and, if food sticks around the door seals and is not cleaned off, there could be a risk of leakage.

Q. Which shape is best for casseroles?
A. Food in round dishes cooks more evenly, but if stirring is to take place, this is not of vital importance.

Q. Are the size and shape of dishes relevant in determining cooking times?

A. Yes. High-sided dishes may shield the microwave energy. All dishes absorb some microwave energy and the size and material of the dish will therefore affect cooking times.

Q. You have said in your other books that foam dishes cannot be used but I have been told they can.

A. They can, but be careful not to use sugar or fat ingredients and do not cover with cling film. Because of the tremendous heat build-up it exceeds the temperature the foam can stand. It is only therefore suitable for brief reheating and not for cooking.

Q. Why must I prick shiny skins?

A. To prevent them bursting and spattering all over the oven. Enormous heat builds up inside the fruit or vegetable and, without piercing, the skin does not allow the steam to escape, so it bursts.

Q. Why can't I boil eggs in my microwave oven?

A. Because the shells cannot be properly pricked and they explode.

Q. Why is it inadvisable to salt most foods before cooking?

A. Salt attracts microwaves and draws the moisture out of food causing dehydration.

Q. What do you mean by carry-over standing time?

A. Heat builds up in the food and causes cooking to continue or carry-over after microwaving finishes. If this is likely to continue for very long a standing time is recommended. Heat equalizes during the standing time so that there will be no hot and cold spots.

Q. Why does milk boil over?
A. It only does if you microwave on High and the container is too small. The protein in the milk forms a lid which is pushed off by the gathering steam.

Q. Can I fry onions?
A. No, but they will appear fried as continual heating causes them to brown.

Q. Why must I turn a block of icy frozen food upside down to thaw?
A. To spread the incidence of the microwaves. If the food is dry inside the icy block, it could over-cook before the ice thawed. Ice allows the microwaves to pass straight through rather like glass, so that when the microwaves reach the food the friction caused by the molecules melts the ice next to it. Ice takes 25 times as long to heat as water.

Q. What does 'stir occasionally' mean?
A. Two or three times during cooking, but more if the cooking period is lengthy and the food is microwaved on High.

Q. What do you mean by 'stir frequently'?
A. At one-quarter intervals through the cooking time on fast cooking items and at one-eighth intervals through the cooking time on longer cooking dishes.

Q. Why should sauces be stirred with a whisk?
A. To separate the particles so that lumps don't form.

Q. Why do cakes have a gungy base?
A. When the container is buttered and floured, or when the container is shiny inside, or when the cake is baked in a tall container, or when the cake is under-cooked.

Q. How can I improve the flavour of my cakes?
A. Microwave for part of the time on Low and add a few drops of dairy butter flavouring (Langdales make it).

Q. How can I make my cakes more moist?
A. Add 1 teaspoon of golden syrup to the mixture and use half white and half soft brown or all brown sugar.

Q. Why does reheated pastry become soggy?
A. Because it was over-heated. Give pastry minimal reheating time.

Q. Why did the pie filling burn my tongue when the pastry was just at the right temperature?
A. High sugar content fillings quickly reach very high temperatures.

Q. How many people can I cook vegetables for at one time?
A. Anything above 4 servings should be cooked conventionally unless you have plenty of microwave time.

Q. Can food burn in the microwave oven?
A. Yes indeed *and* set fire to your expensive oven if left too long. Take especial care with sugary items.

Q. I was in the middle of eating my dinner when the phone rang. How long should I reheat it?
A. 45-60 seconds, covered if possible.

Q. Can I heat up baby's milk in the microwave oven?
A. Yes, but since the heating is uneven you must shake the bottle vigorously before testing the temperature.

THE COURSES

1

Meat

Tender cuts of meat require no additional treatment when cooking by microwave but tougher cuts should be tenderized before cooking. In casseroles and stews dice to the size of sugar lumps and cook on Low or frequently interrupted High, stirring often and giving the dish a ten-minute rest every ten minutes. It sometimes helps to cook these for five to ten minutes before adding other ingredients. Whether or not you use Low or High, total cooking time will be the same. Lamb, pork, beef and bacon casseroles will be succulent but beef will be only tooth-tender. If you are in a hurry, you may prefer to use the pressure cooker for beef stews or even the crock-pot both of which are fuel-saving. But it is often convenient to use the microwave oven and you will find the flavour improves if the cooked dish is stored in the refrigerator and reheated on Low, stirring from time to time.

BUYING TIPS

Beef at its best should be a bright red colour with a marbling of fat among the lean; the fat should be creamy and not dense and yellow. So much depends on your butcher – how he purchases and his skills in butchering and experience of hanging times. It certainly pays to be a regular customer. If you buy casually you will probably select from ready-cut pieces displayed in the window. Beef soon darkens after cutting but if it is a dark reddy brown with a dried-up appearance, this is an indication of meat from a tired old animal.

Examine frozen beef closely and if it has a grey appearance don't purchase. The flavour and texture would be like chewed-up cardboard. Frozen beef should be thawed completely before cooking, and although you may buy from a perfectly satisfactory supplier the best frozen beef is the kind you freeze for yourself.

Suitable cuts for microwave cookery are those that you would normally buy for frying or grilling. Rump, fillet or sirloin are naturally more tender, but cheaper frying cuts are better for casseroling, as in any case the fat must be cut away. Thus a lean frying steak will work out cheaper than heavily trimmed stewing steak. Mince, the great international stand-by, can be made into meat loaves, burgers or used in sauces.

Veal has very little fat or gristle and the bones produce a rich jellied stock which is best prepared conventionally. Fresh veal is a pale pink colour and the keeping qualities of uncooked veal are poor so you should freeze it immediately or cook within a few hours of purchase. Leg or shoulder is good for roasting and escalopes and chops cook efficiently, using the browning dish.

The colour of lamb depends on the breed and the country of origin. The quality is usually constant and the flesh should be firm to the touch and not sticky. The fat should be dense, white and clean-cutting. Shoulder or top end of the leg are suitable for roasting and, provided the bone end is not allowed to over-cook, this too is satisfactory. Lamb fillet can be cut into cubes for kebabs, and loin, chump or best end are cut into chops.

Pork flesh should be pale pink with a slight graining of firm white fat. Grey fat and browning flesh indicate staling. The prime cuts are leg, loin, spare ribs and belly and all are suitable for microwave cooking.

Ham, gammon and bacon cook satisfactorily in the microwave oven. Stickiness is an indication of staleness.

Salted bacon tends to be brittle, and sugary bacon browns at the edges but may stick to kitchen paper if you choose to cook it in this way.

Kidney, liver and sweetbreads should be cooked absolutely fresh and other offal such as tongue and hearts, are only suitable for more gentle microwave cooking (40 to 50 minutes per ½ kg [1 lb] on Low). All offal must be thoroughly washed in cold water and trimmed where necessary. Frozen offal should be thawed as gently as possible on a Defrost or Low setting.

Separately wrap chops and steaks before freezing, then pack in sealed bags or boxes. It will then be easier to separate the pieces while they are still frozen. Try to avoid crushing them together, for this produces odd shapes. To defrost put in the microwave oven in the plastic wrap, either in a dish or a folded sheet of kitchen paper, and thaw on Defrost until the wrappings can be removed. You can then wipe or wash the meat as you wish before continuing to thaw. When thawing more than one piece, arrange in an even thickness and reposition from time to time. Shield any vulnerable thin sections with a small piece of aluminium foil. To make sure the foil does not touch the sides of the oven do not use a plate, but choose a shallow dish so the raised sides will lessen the risk of this happening.

All meat should be removed from its original wrappings before storing. Put on a plate in the refrigerator and cover loosely with greaseproof paper.

ROASTING

Choose even-shaped joints if possible or try to reshape them yourself by a bit of judicious pummelling or restringing. Joints with a bone, such as leg of lamb, cannot be reshaped, so the thin end should be shielded for the first half of the cooking period. Cover this part with a small piece of aluminium foil and use a wooden cocktail stick to hold it in place so that the foil cannot touch the oven walls. Do not salt beef, veal or lamb before cooking, as this has a drying effect and also increases the shrinkage. All joints shrink by about one-third when roasted conventionally, but microwave is a little kinder and shrinkage should only be one-quarter. Pork crackling, however, should be slashed and liberally sprinkled with salt.

For a glossy brown finish, brush the joint with gravy browning or a mixture of tomato purée and Worcestershire sauce or home-made browner. Natural browning takes place only after a minimum of ten minutes' cooking and is more noticeable if the joint is well-marbled with fat. As the interior of the meat becomes hot, small beads of hot fat will break through to the surface and start to burn, causing browning. You can assist the process by dabbing the top surface of the joint with kitchen paper to remove moisture as condensation forms in the oven. Browning is also hastened by siting the meat in the top half of the oven. Some models have a built-in rack, but if not you can achieve the same effect by standing the dish or the dish containing the microwave roasting rack on a stacking ring or similar object. The roasting rack raises the joint so that the surplus fat can be collected in the dish. Spoon this away as it forms so that you will have less spattering and quicker cooking. Cooks who have no time to fiddle around will prefer to put the joint directly in the dish and this is perfectly all right if browning is less important to you.

Another roasting method is to rest the joint on an undecorated upturned saucer, which should be removed at the same time as the joint, so that it won't subsequently weld itself to the base of the dish.

Many people prefer to use roasting bags which seal in all the juices. Do not use the metal tag provided but fix loosely with a rubber band or string. Put the bag in a dish so that it will be easier to remove from the oven when cooking is finished. Roaster bags produce a more tender but less crisp finish. Slit the bag to remove the joint otherwise you risk getting a nasty burn and dropping the meat on the floor as you try to remove it through the neck of the bag.

Joints should be turned frequently during cooking so that all parts are evenly cooked but rotating is only necessary if no turntable is used. (Anchor Hocking make a turntable that will fit into most ovens).

Use the microwave roasting rack and do not turn the joint if some of your family prefer rare meat. For the most even result brush the raw joint with softened butter, preheat the browning dish in the microwave oven and quickly roll the joint over the heated base to seal the juices, then continue roasting in the uncovered dish. Remove the surplus fat as it accumulates. Rotate the dish four times during cooking and turn the joint over halfway through cooking (for a small joint) or cook it for one-quarter of the cooking time on each of the four sides. Roasts cooked in the browning dish should be cooked entirely on High and will take a little longer. There is a carry-over or standing time of fifteen minutes for a 1.75-2.25 kg (4-5 lb) joint and ten minutes for a smaller one. Always weigh the joint before cooking to calculate the correct time. The meat should not be carved before the standing period unless you prefer an underdone centre. To retain the heat evenly, tent the joint in foil during the standing time.

Should you prefer a really crispy brown joint, finish it under a hot grill during the standing period or pop it into a heated conventional oven if this is also being used for other items at a similar temperature.

For perfect results, use a *special* microwave oven thermometer or probe. The temperature will rise during the carry-over or standing time. Preferably cook on Medium but if you only have a High (600 watt or over) maximum setting, cook on High, giving a five-minute rest halfway through cooking.

ROASTING CHART
TIMES, TEMPERATURE AND MINUTES PER POUND/450 g

	Minutes per 450 g (1 lb) on High	Minutes per 450 g (1 lb) on Medium	Temperature before standing	Temperature after standing
Beef,				
rare	6-7	11-13	50°C (120°F)	60°C (140°F)
medium	7-8	13-15	55°C (130°F)	70°C (160°F)
well-done	8½-9	15-17	70°C (160°F)	75°C (170°F)
Lamb	8-10	11-13	75°C (170°F)	80°C (175°F)
Veal	8½-9	11-12	70°C (160°F)	75°C (170°F)
Pork	9-10	11-15	70°C (160°F)	80°C (175°F)

STEAKS

Steaks can only be successfully cooked in a microwave oven in the browning dish. A microwave oven is not a dry form of heat and so cannot seal in the juices.

Preheat the browning dish to the maximum the manufacturer recommends, adding a tablespoon of vegetable oil or preferably salted butter during the final thirty seconds. Quickly press the steaks flat over the outer area of the dish and, as soon as browning occurs, allowing ten seconds maximum, flip the steaks over. I find kitchen tongs the best for this. Close the oven door and quickly switch on again for the required time.

Usually steaks look the same on both sides but if there is a better side, brown this first. Check when dishing up and put on the plates browner side up. However, steaks will not be so brown if three or four are cooked at the same time.

Steaks cook very quickly and you will get the best results if you do two at a time. Wipe out the surplus fat with kitchen paper, taking care not to burn your fingers, then without further cleaning, reheat the browning dish for one to two minutes, add a further tiny piece of butter and repeat for the next steaks. Since steak is so expensive, always under-cook – you can't retrieve a dried-up portion. Always cook steaks on High and trim away surplus fat before cooking. In keeping with other foods a tender steak will cook tender and a tough one tough.

CHART FOR 2.5 cm (1 in) THICK STEAKS

| | *Minutes on each side after sealing* | | | |
	1 steak	*2 steaks*	*3 steaks*	*4 steaks*
Rare	1	1½	2	2½
Medium	1¼	1¾	2¼	2¾
Well-done	2	2½	3	3½

CHOPS

Pork or lamb chops may be cooked in an ordinary dish but they will look grey when cooked. It is quite in order to cook them without pre-sealing if all the surfaces are brushed with a colourful sauce diluted with an equal quantity of water. Choose from tomato ketchup, soy sauce, a fruity sauce (such as HP or OK) or a not too chunky chutney. Add a teaspoon of lemon juice or Worcestershire sauce for extra zip.

Select chops or cutlets of an even thickness – about 2 cm (¾ in) is best. Brush with the browning mixture and three-quarters cover with greaseproof paper. Microwave on Low or Medium with the bones towards the centre, giving the dish a quarter-turn three times during cooking, unless a turntable is used. A carry-over or standing time of five minutes should be sufficient, leaving the covering in position. Season with salt and pepper just before serving.

I prefer to use a browning dish for 'straight' chops. Chops should be taken directly from the refrigerator for cooking. Trim away the excess fat, then brush with vegetable oil or spread both sides with softened butter. Prepare all the ingredients before starting so that no heat is lost from the browning dish during the initial cooking. When no sauce is to be added, a browning tray without raised sides is more effective as the fats are channelled away. Heat the browning dish to the maximum time allowed and, as soon as it is ready, put in the chops uncovered, bones towards the centre. Alternatively, do not grease the chops, but add a walnut-sized piece of salted butter during the last 30 seconds of heating the browning dish. Move the chops rapidly over the browning butter.

Microwave on High for 1 minute, then flip the chops over, repositioning them at the same time. Lamb chops should be cooked on High before reducing to Medium, but pork chops may be cooked for the whole time on High. They should continue cooking until the flesh is no longer pink inside, and the juices run clear if prodded with a sharp-ended knife. Leave for three minutes before serving.

Always serve chops on heated plates as the fat will congeal on cold plates and look unattractive. Present with the brown sides uppermost.

PORK AND LAMB CHOP CHART
(To be treated as a guide only)

A) USING ORDINARY DISH ON LOW OR MEDIUM

1 average chop will take 6-8 mins
2 average chops will take 10-12 mins
3 average chops will take 14-18 mins
4 average chops will take 18-20 mins

B) USING PRE-HEATED BROWNING DISH

Lamb chops

1 average chop will take	1-1½ mins on High, then
	1½-2½ mins on Medium
2 average chops will take	1½-2 mins on High, then
	2½-3½ mins on Medium
3 average chops will take	2-2½ mins on High, then
	3½-4-½ mins on Medium
4 average chops will take	3-3½ mins on High, then
	5-6 mins on Medium

Pork chops

1 average chop will take 4-4½ mins on High
2 average chops will take 5-5½ mins on High
3 average chops will take 6-7 mins on High
4 average chops will take 6½-8 mins on High.

VEAL ESCALOPES

Veal escalopes should be beaten flat and can then be microwaved in several ways. Season with pepper, lemon juice and if you like the flavour a sprinkling of ground cloves. Place side by side in a greased dish, cover with greaseproof paper and microwave on High for about 2 to 3 minutes depending on size. Alternatively prepare and cook in the same way as Quick Chicken Schnitzel (see page 94).

Crumbed or floured and seasoned escalopes brown nicely when microwaved in 15 g (½ oz) salted butter in the pre-heated browning dish. After sealing, quickly flip the pieces over and then microwave on High until cooked. Drain on kitchen paper.

MINCE

Buy good quality mince or mince the meat yourself. Beef is the fattiest and it is no saving to buy the cheapest as the proportion of lean meat will be lower. But if you are using fatty mince it will certainly taste better cooked in a microwave oven. In a frying pan, as the fat oozes, the immense heat causes the fat to break down into fatty acids and give off a characteristic odour, which somehow clings. Mince cooked in a microwave oven discards the liquefied fat and it is easier to remove this as it accumulates. To draw off fat easily before cooking, put the meat on a microwave rack over a dish. Although it tastes good, microwaved mince will look grey unless it is disguised in some way. Here are some examples:

Make burger shapes, mixing in the seasoning thoroughly. Thicker patties should be depressed in the centre for even cooking. Microwave in a pre-heated browning dish, on the base of an ordinary dish or, if fatty, on a microwave roasting rack. Allow one to two minutes for each and reposition if several are cooked at one time.

Cook meat balls in a tomato or brown sauce or brush with diluted gravy browning or home-made browner. A marginally better colour and some crispness is obtained when the meat is cooked in a pre-heated browning dish or tray. Mince may be cooked on High but will be even more tender cooked at lower speeds. It cooks well because the chopping process tenderizes, allowing so many more broken surfaces to face the microwaves. Make the balls fairly slack as solid ones turn out a bit like cricket balls.

A meat loaf that takes 1½ hours to bake in a conventional oven can be cooked in the microwave oven in 15 to 20 minutes. The timing depends upon the content of the meat loaf, wetter mixtures taking longer than drier ones. If you are using fresh meat you will have to allow longer than when using minced cooked meat. Much depends on the shape and depth of the mixture, and the only way to be sure that the meat loaf does not over-cook is to test it three-quarters of the way through the given cooking time, by skewer, or is firm to the touch. Because the mixture is so dense, cooking will continue after the meat is removed from the microwave oven during a standing time of 5 to 10 minutes. For the very best results, use a ring mould but since this is not the traditional shape, the family may find it less attractive. The problem with the traditional loaf shape is that it tends to overcook in the corners. To overcome this microwave on High for half the cooking time and then, allowing twice as much time, finish the cooking on Medium or Low. The meat loaf baked in a ring mould will take half to two-thirds of the cooking time required in a loaf shape.

If you want to convert a favourite conventional recipe reduce the liquid by half and add an extra egg to the mixture. Meat loaves containing ham should be very well-mixed particularly if they are sweet-cured as this attracts the microwaves and causes uneven cooking.

Mincing or chopping is a natural way to tenderize, but all cheaper cuts of meat should be tenderized before microwaving to achieve an acceptable result. This is not to say you can't cook a casserole on High, but you must expect the texture to be chewy. Diced meat covered and cooked on Low and periodically stirred, will be tender in 1½ to 2 hours, but is it really worth doing, if you have a pressure cooker or slow cooker? It would not take much longer to cook in a covered saucepan or casserole in the conventional oven.

To tenderize meat a) beat with a rolling pin or cleaver, b) sprinkle with tenderizing powder, c) marinate in oil and an acidy liquid, such as lemon juice or wine or d) mince or chop finely.

CASSEROLES

Tenderize tough meat before cooking, otherwise choose lamb, veal or pork rather than beef and either seal the cubes of meat in a frying pan on the conventional cooker or use the browning dish for small quantities only. Another method is to microwave the meat dry for a quarter of the total cooking time before adding the other ingredients. A favourite method of mine is to seal the pieces (*not* taken straight from the refrigerator) in a thin brown roux (see page 180). When the roux is very hot toss in the meat, stir briefly, and cook for three to four minutes before adding the other ingredients and stock. Use oven gloves but do not remove the casserole to mix in the meat, as the base will be tremendously hot and could crack if rested on a cold or wet surface. Always cook casseroles covered and remember to stir from time to time or you will find dried-up sauce or burnt meat sticking around the sides. An average casserole, other than kidney or liver, cooked on High, takes about 35 minutes. Casseroles other than beef will take about 1½ hours on Medium and 1¾ hours on Low.

BACON

To thaw a pack of bacon microwave on Low for a few moments by which time the rashers should be easy to separate.

After much testing, I have come to the conclusion that the easiest, least smelly, way to cook bacon is to put the rashers on a plate, overlapping the fat and lean. Cover with cling film and microwave for 30 seconds per rasher, giving the dish a half-turn half way through cooking. Immediately peel away the cling film carefully and drain away the accumulated fat and moisture or transfer to a warm plate. You can cook bacon rashers on, between or covered with sheets of kitchen paper, which absorb the fat and produces a crisp result, but as there is sugar in the curing, the bacon often fuses to the paper, making it difficult to separate.

It is not worth getting out the bacon rack for a few rashers, but I would recommend it when cooking over 225 g (½ lb). Overlap the rashers on the rack, set in a large dish to catch the drips, cover with kitchen or greaseproof paper and microwave on High for 12 to 14 minutes per 450 g (1 lb).

For really crisp bacon (six or more rashers only) try the browning tray or browning dish. Put a few scraps of bacon fat in the dish while it is pre-heating so that the lean rashers will not stick. Quickly put in the bacon in a single layer and turn over at once. Microwave on High for ½ minute per rasher.

SAUSAGES

Take care not to over-cook sausages since they do not brown and if you do over-cook them the inside will shrink into a fibrous coil. Sausages are better cooked in a pre-heated browning dish but this might not be convenient at busy times. For cooking in an ordinary dish or plate choose thick sausages rather than chipolatas. Prick them thoroughly and arrange them in a circle for several or side by side for two. Reposition them half way through cooking and at the same time give the dish a half-turn, unless your oven is fitted with a turntable. Leave to stand for 1 to 2 minutes before serving and be sure that pork sausages are no longer pink inside. A better colour will be obtained if you pre-brush the surface with diluted gravy browning or similar food colouring.

Sausages should not be refrigerator-cold for cooking. To take off the chill microwave on High for a few seconds.

For nice crispy sausages prick thoroughly, then pre-heat the browning dish to maximum, adding a small knob of salted butter during the last 30 seconds. Using tongs, quickly put in the sausages and turn them over after 2 or 3 seconds and swoosh them around to brown all over. Try to arrange the sausages around the outside of the dish and turn them over halfway through the cooking period. Remove and drain on kitchen paper, leaving them to stand for 2 to 3 minutes before serving, so that the inside heat can equalize.

It is unrealistic to heat a large browning dish for just one sausage but if you are able to seek out a small round browning dish, this will only need a 2 to 3 minute pre-heat period. For more than 4 sausages spoon away the excess fat from the dish and reheat the browning dish for 1 to 2 minutes before cooking the remainder. It will not be necessary to add extra butter.

Number	Time	Setting
1 thick	1-1½ mins	Medium
2 thick	1½-2 mins	High
4 thick	3-3½ mins	High

Add 1 to 2 minutes standing time.

Using the browning dish.

2 thick	2½ mins	High
4 thick	4 mins	High

Bacon and Sausage Twirls in Tomato and Pimiento Sauce

This recipe, which is shown on the front cover, is a combination of three separate dishes – pasta, sausages and bacon, and a sauce. Use the microwave oven to cook them all or cook one or two parts conventionally. Make the sauce in the browning dish if you wish, but this must be wiped clean before using for the sausages.

225 g (8 oz) ribbon noodle
300 ml (½ pint) tomato pimiento sauce (see page 193)
8 large sausages
16 rashers streaky bacon, rinds and bones removed
15 g (½ oz) butter

Cook the noodles in a large casserole (see page 44).

Without covering, microwave on High for 6 minutes, then cover with a lid and leave to stand for 8 minutes to finish cooking before draining.

Meanwhile cook the sausage twirls.

Wrap two bacon rashers tightly around each sausage.

Pre-heat the browning dish to maximum, adding the butter during the last 30 seconds.

Using tongs, quickly put in 4 of the sausages and microwave on High for 2 minutes. Flip the sausages over, pushing them to the sides of the dish and microwave on High for 2 minutes.

Remove from the dish, drain on kitchen paper and cover lightly to keep hot.

Spoon away surplus fat and reheat the browning dish for 1-2 minutes only. Maximum time is not required as the dish will have retained some of the heat.

Cook the remaining 4 sausages.

To assemble, pour the noodles into a round serving dish or use the browning dish or the dish in which the sauce is cooked.

Arrange the sausage twirls on top and fork the noodles into clusters in between. Pour over the sauce. The vegetables will separate allowing some of the sauce to flow around the sides. To make sure the food is hot enough, microwave on High for 2 minutes giving the dish a quarter-turn every 30 seconds.

Serves 4 to 6

Variations
Use any variety of pasta. Use freshly chopped red pepper instead of the canned pimiento. Add a teaspoon of basil to the sauce while cooking. Sprinkle the finished dish with grated Parmesan cheese and garnish with a few black olives.

Beef and Liver Terrine

A stand-by dish which may be garnished with strips of crispy bacon or thatched with Duchesse potatoes for a more formal meal.

 350 g (12 oz) lean beef
 350 g (12 oz) calves liver
 1 small onion
 1 slice bread
 1 large egg
 3 tablespoons milk
 1 tablespoon tomato purée
 Salt
 Pepper
 1 garlic clove, crushed
 2 bay leaves

Wash the liver in cold salted water, removing any gristle, and dry on kitchen paper.

Mince the beef, liver, onion and bread into a mixing bowl.

Beat the egg, milk and tomato purée together, then season with salt and pepper to taste, and stir in the garlic.

Pour the mixture into the minced meat and stir well to blend.

Turn the mixture into a greased 23 × 13 cm (9 × 5 in) loaf dish.

Press down well and place two bay leaves on the surface.

Cover with non-stick or waxed paper.

Microwave on High for 8 minutes, giving the dish a quarter-turn every 2 minutes.

Microwave on Medium for 6 to 12 minutes or until the meat loaf is fairly firm.

Give the dish a half-turn halfway through the second cooking period.

Remove the dish from the oven and leave to cool before turning out.

Serve in slices with French bread and a tossed green salad.
(Left-over slices can be individually wrapped for freezing.)
Serves 6

Variations
Add chopped mushrooms, chopped green peppers and
flavour with marjoram, sage or chopped thyme. Substitute
75 g (3 oz) cooked ham for some of the beef or for a
smooth texture substitute sausage meat. Mix in canned
crushed pineapple and curry powder for an Eastern
flavour.

Cabby's Dinner

A no frills Englishman's dinner of liver, bacon, onions and
tomato.

    450 g (1 lb) lamb's or calf's liver, sliced
    3-4 tablespoons flour, seasoned with salt and pepper
    1 large onion, thinly sliced
    12 rashers streaky bacon, trimmed and chopped
    3 tomatoes, sliced
    1 teaspoon Bovril

Coat the liver with the seasoned flour and shake off the
surplus. Put the onion and bacon in a casserole dish and
microwave on High for 5-6 minutes, stirring occasionally
until the onion is soft and the bacon nearly cooked.
Add the liver slices one at a time, turning so that they are
evenly coated with the bacon and onion.
Top with the sliced tomatoes.
Blend the Bovril with 4 tablespoons hot water and pour
over the top.
Cover tightly and microwave on High for 8 minutes giving
the dish a quarter-turn every 2 minutes.
Reduce the setting and microwave on Low, continuing to

turn the dish, for 10-14 minutes until the liver is just pink inside. Do not over-cook.

Under-cooking can be rectified but over-cooking will result in leathery liver.

Serves 4

Country Pork Casserole

If no browning dish is available brown the chops first in a frying pan. Melt 25 g (1 oz) butter in a large casserole dish before microwaving the potatoes. Continue according to the recipe.

> 4 thick pork chops, surplus fat trimmed away
> Salt
> Pepper
> Flour
> 25 g (1 oz) butter
> 225 g (8 oz) potatoes, peeled and diced
> 1 bunch spring onions, trimmed and thinly sliced
> 225 g (8 oz) carrots, scraped and thinly sliced
> 1 × 427 ml (15 oz) can ready-to-serve cream of mushroom soup

Season the chops with salt and pepper and dust sparingly with flour on both sides.

Pre-heat a large browning dish to maximum, adding the butter during the last 30 seconds. Quickly add the chops, turning them to brown on both sides.

Remove the chops and set aside.

Reheat the browning dish in the microwave oven on High for 1 minute.

Add the potatoes and onions and microwave on High for 4 minutes, tossing occasionally so that all the sides are lightly browned.

Add the carrots and pour in the soup and 150 ml (¼ pint) water.

Arrange the chops on top, the tails towards the centre.
Cover with the lid and microwave on High for 25-30
minutes, giving the dish a quarter-turn every 5 minutes
until the vegetables and meat are cooked and much of the
liquid absorbed.
Serve from the browning dish.
Serves 4

Variations
Use lamb or veal chops. Substitute cream of chicken or
celery soup. Stir soured cream into the vegetables before
serving and garnish with paprika for a special appearance.

Lamb Curry

Preferably cook 'casserole cuts' of meat on Low, allowing
2½ times normal cooking periods on High. The secret of a
good curry is in the cooking of the spices before the meat is
added. Improve the texture and flavour of curries by
storing in a *cold* place for 24 hours before reheating. Cool
rapidly in a bowl of cold water after standing time before
refrigerating or freezing.

450-750 g (1-1½ lb) cubed leg of lamb
3 tablespoons vegetable oil
2 large onions, finely sliced
1 rounded tablespoon curry paste (or 1 teaspoon each
   powdered coriander, cumin, turmeric, and cardamom)
1 level teaspoon salt
½ teaspoon pepper
150 ml (¼ pint) beef stock
2 or 3 tablespoons tomato purée
2 tablespoons lemon juice
2 medium potatoes, peeled and quartered
100 g (¼ lb) okra (ladies' fingers), topped and tailed
   (optional)

Combine the oil and onions in a large deep dish.

Microwave on High for 8-12 minutes, stirring occasionally until the onions start to brown.

Stir in the curry paste, salt and pepper and continue to microwave on High for a further 2 minutes.

Stir in the lamb and microwave on High for 2 minutes, then remove from the oven and leave to stand while heating the stock for about 1¾ minutes on High.

This standing time is essential for tenderizing the meat.

Stir the tomato purée and lemon juice into the stock and pour over the lamb.

Add the potatoes and okra.

Cover and microwave on Low for 35-50 minutes until the meat is tender. Stir occasionally during cooking, adding more water if required. Leave to stand for at least 5 minutes before serving.

Serves 4 to 5

Variations

Substitute chicken for the lamb and reduce the cooking time by one-quarter. Substitute beef and increase the cooking time by one-quarter. Increase the curry paste or spices and add a pinch of chilli powder for a stronger curry. Vary the okra with cauliflower, sliced green beans, canned chick peas, carrots and peas.

Stir in 2 tablespoons of natural yoghurt or coconut milk for a creamy flavour.

Sliced Fillet of Beef Chasseur

Double the recipe if you wish but cook each batch separately, wiping the browning dish with kitchen paper and reheating for 1 minute between each session.

    225 g (8 oz) fillet steak, sliced thinly
    1 tablespoon vegetable oil
    Glazed carrot barrrels (see page 154)

Pommes Parisienne (see page 158)
Sauce Chasseur (see page 189)

Pre-heat a browning dish to maximum. While the dish is heating, brush the steak on both sides with the oil.
As soon as the dish is hot, add the steak slices and toss quickly.
Microwave on High for 2-3 minutes, turning the meat over once during cooking. Do not over-cook as steak continues cooking during the standing time and these slices should be very thin.
Transfer to a heated serving dish and pour the warmed sauce over the top. Garnish with carrot barrels and potato balls.
1 recipe serves 2
Double recipe serves 4

Variations
Use home-made or commercial burgers instead of fillet steak.

Vitello in Rollato

If you do not wish to use the browning dish, use one of the cooking methods for veal escalopes given in the Introduction to this section.

4 veal escalopes, beaten thinly
Black pepper
4 slices Parma ham
Beaten egg
Golden cooking crumbs
Grated Parmesan cheese (use 1 tablespoon for each 6 tablespoons crumbs)
25 g (1 oz) salted butter
100 ml (4 fl oz) sweet white wine
5-6 sage leaves, chopped

Sprinkle the veal with black pepper and lay the ham on top. Divide each sandwich into two. Roll up each sandwich and carefully coat in the egg and crumbs. Secure with cocktail sticks.

Pre-heat a large browning dish to maximum, adding the butter during the last 30 seconds.

Quickly place the 'rolls' in the browning dish, moving them around in the butter.

Microwave on High for 4 minutes, turning the dish once during cooking.

Reposition the rolls and turn them over.

Pour in the wine and add the sage leaves.

Microwave on Medium for 6-8 minutes or on Low for 8-12 minutes or until cooked, basting the meat occasionally.

Transfer the rolls to a serving dish.

Microwave the wine and pan juices until boiling and pour over the meat.

Serves 4

Variations

Use beaten chicken breast instead of veal. Use cooked instead of smoked ham. Omit the cheese and flavour the crumbs with mixed herbs. Roll an asparagus tip inside the ham.

2

Poultry and Game

Poultry is available at reasonable prices throughout the year because so many chickens are factory-farmed and the bulk is frozen. The flavour of frozen birds varies very little since they are all similarly fed. These chickens are often impregnated with preservatives making them retain large amounts of water. This makes them weigh more but they only yield an average quantity of meat. Some capons are specially over-fattened and this results in very fatty birds which shrink considerably during cooking and which exude a great deal of fat, which is not very good in microwave cooking.

All poultry may be thawed and cooked appetizingly by microwave except a boiling fowl, which is old and tough and will turn out leathery. Whether cooked conventionally or by microwave, frozen poultry will taste the same, so if you are changing to cooking by microwave continue to use the brand to which you are accustomed. A young fresh chicken has soft resilient flesh.

Turkeys are at their best when the weight is about 5 kg (11 lb). The flesh should be soft and white with plenty of breast meat.

Duck should also have a pliable breast bone and the breast should be plump. Duck is fatty and therefore serves fewer than a chicken of similar weight. An averagely sized duck weighs 2½ kg (5½ lb) and serves four.

Goose is also fatty and can be purchased frozen all the year round.

Fresh game must be hung for the flavour to develop and the flesh to soften. A bird is ready for cooking when the feathers close to the tail are easily plucked. The butcher will usually pluck and draw for you. Game is easy to cook and is most suitable for cooking by microwave but you must be careful that there is no metal shot in the bird as this may upset the magnetron. Game should not be over-cooked so be sure to weigh the bird first as there are considerable variations in size.

Rabbit may be cooked by the same methods as for chicken.

PREPARATION

Fresh chicken is naturally the most flavoursome and tender but fresh chilled chicken is excellent and is obtainable from the large grocery chains. Unwrap the chicken immediately you get it home, remove the giblets and wash the cavity well with cold salted water. Giblets are excellent for stocks and soups but cook best in a pressure cooker or saucepan. The flavour should be drawn out slowly and a constant simmering temperature maintained to kill off any lurking bacteria.

THAWING

Frozen poultry must be completely thawed before cooking and the giblets removed as soon as possible and cooked separately as bacteria multiply rapidly at warm temperatures. If parts nearest to the bone are not quite thawed, during cooking the temperature remains at a warm level for a fair length of time before becoming thoroughly hot, but if the poultry has sufficiently thawed right through, this warm level is passed more rapidly. Remove the wrappings and put the frozen chicken in a dish. If your oven has a High setting only, or you require the oven space to cook other items at the same time, microwave on High for 1 minute for every ½ kg (1 lb), then put into a bowl of cold water for 10 minutes to equalize the heat. Turn the chicken over and repeat the process. Then repeat on the remaining two sides. Check from time to time and if some spots seem too warm to the touch, give a longer resting time, as this is a sign that the poultry is beginning to cook.

To thaw on Defrost set the timer for 6 minutes per 450 g (1 lb). Turn the chicken over and rotate the dish about four times while the oven is switched on. A 1½ kg (3 lb) chicken will take about 18 minutes to reach the stage when the little bag of giblets should be well and truly loosened. To pull out the giblets, feel inside the chicken and when just a few ice crystals remain, the giblets can be removed. To quickly complete defrosting, run under the cold tap or immerse the bird in cold water. At no time should cooking immediately follow thawing, as all poultry must be rinsed in between. All timings are approximate as so much depends on how frozen the poultry was when it was put in the microwave oven.

Chicken pieces take about 5 minutes per 450 g (1 lb) to thaw on Defrost and should be turned over at the halfway stage. If the edges of small pieces become opaque and start to cook, finish thawing at room temperature as you must not shield a small volume of food with foil.

Slow thawing is best for a large turkey and could take at least three days in the refrigerator. A combination of refrigerator thawing and microwave thawing will maintain texture and flavour and is safer than a complete thaw by microwave.

Use a similar method as for chicken but give a rest of 20-30 minutes between each burst of microwaving and shield any warm parts with small pieces of foil secured with a wooden cocktail stick. When the turkey is half thawed finish the process in the refrigerator.

Allow 10-12 minutes per 450 g (1 lb) on Low. Put the turkey, still in its wrapping, directly on the oven shelf. Switch on for one-quarter of the calculated time then turn the turkey round and microwave for another quarter of the thawing time. Remove the wrapping over the sink so that you don't get drips everywhere and put the turkey into a dish that will fit into the oven. If your oven is fitted with a turntable this may have to be removed and substituted with an inverted shelf dish or roaster rack. If the revolving shelf works on a motor it is inadvisable to stop the moving parts. Give the turkey a rest for about half an hour before proceeding. Any parts that are now thawed should be shielded with foil (always making sure that this is secure and doesn't touch the oven walls). A large turkey with a plump breast may nearly touch the oven ceiling so take care, although this will be the area most likely to thaw first. Microwave on Low for a further quarter of the given time and turn the bird over. Rotate the dish and microwave for the final period. Remove the giblets and immerse the turkey in cold water to finish thawing.

To combine the methods, thaw for half the time in the microwave oven and finish in the refrigerator overnight.

Thaw other poultry and game in the same way, taking special care with pheasant, which is dry and bony.

ROASTING

Roasting chicken by microwave is the best way, but accustom yourself to the fact that it will brown very little. A 1.65 kg (3½ lb) chicken will take 20-30 minutes on High. Quite the easiest way is to put it in a dish, cover with a piece of greaseproof paper secured with a wooden cocktail stick and cook for half the time breast-side down, and half breast-side up, rotating the dish from time to time. Cook on High if you are in a hurry, otherwise on Medium.

Other roasting alternatives are to stand the chicken on an upturned undecorated saucer or a roasting rack in a dish for easy removal of fat accumulation. Season the cavity with salt or insert a halved onion for added flavour. If you prefer your chicken to look brown, brush before cooking with a) gravy browning and butter, b) paprika and butter, c) any barbecue or fruit sauce, d) turmeric and butter or d) your own home-made liquid browner (see page 195).

Roasting the chicken in the upper part of the microwave oven will help it to brown or you could put it under the grill after cooking. Remove the fat as it accumulates in the dish and wrap the wing and leg ends with foil as soon as they are cooked to prevent them from burning, making sure that the foil does not touch the oven walls.

Use a microwave thermometer to test which should register 82°C (180°F) in the thickest part of the thigh or cook using a probe as directed by your oven guide book. Chicken continues cooking for at least 10 minutes after it is removed from the oven, when the correct serving temperature should register 90°C (190°F). Experience will teach you when the chicken is ready as tests with a knife cannot be decisive until after the standing time. Insert the tip between the thigh and the body. If the juices are clear (not pink) and the flesh opaque as far as the bone, the chicken is ready. Cover with a tent of foil during the standing time for even heat distribution.

For a moister result, cook the chicken in a roasting bag breast-side up and add a few tablespoons of salted water. Partially close the bag end above the chicken, using a rubber band or string. By putting the bag into the dish before inserting the chicken, it is easier to manage. You can't easily remove accumulated fat from the bag nor is it possible to turn the bird over, so frequent rotation is important. Microwave on Medium or Medium High, allowing 8-10 minutes per 450 g (1 lb), and leave to stand in the bag for 10 minutes. Slit the bag down the middle and transfer the chicken to a heated serving dish, or grill for added browning if you wish.

Chicken pieces, which must first be thawed, are popular and easy to cook. Brush with browning, arrange the thinnest pieces towards the centre of the dish and turn over halfway through cooking. Cover with greaseproof paper or loose cling film and rotate the dish at equal intervals during cooking.

CHICKEN ROASTING CHART

Size	Time on Medium	Time on High
1 kg (2 lb)	18-20 mins	12-16 mins
1.25 kg (2 lb 12 oz)	24-27 mins	16-22 mins
1.5 kg (3 lb)	27-30 mins	18-24 mins
1.65 kg (3½ lb)	31-35 mins	21-28 mins
1.75 kg (4 lb)	36-40 mins	24-32 mins
1 piece	—	2½-3½ mins
2 pieces	—	3½-5½ mins
3 pieces	—	4½-6½ mins
4 pieces	—	6-9 mins

Poultry can be cooked stuffed but do not try to reheat with the stuffing inside, as it may not be hot enough when the chicken is ready. Take stuffing into account when calculating cooking times by adding to the net weight.

It stands to reason that you can only roast a turkey in the microwave oven if the cavity is big enough. If you have decided to roast it this way remember to measure the turkey before you buy it. Remember that you will probably only cook a large turkey three times a year so this should not influence your choice when buying your oven. Some ovens will take an 8 kg (18 lb) turkey but the choicest birds are only about 5 kg (11 lb) in weight. Don't put turkey on a roasting rack as it will almost reach the oven ceiling when put into a dish. Stuff the cavity and neck as you wish and use string or wooden cocktail sticks to secure the flap. You can use one or two metal skewers provided they are pressed well in and do not stick out like antennae.

Dry the surface of the turkey with kitchen paper, otherwise the butter and browning will not adhere to the bird. Roast in a similar way to chicken or, if you prefer, in an ordinary large brown paper bag (still in a dish, of course). Cook on Medium allowing 11-13 minutes per 450 g (1 lb). Shield the breast and wing tips as soon as they are cooked. Do be careful with turkeys with a high protruding breast (which should be covered with the foil *before* putting into a roaster bag, because of the danger of 'arcing' damaging the magnetron). A large turkey could take 2-3 hours to cook and you might prefer to three-quarter cook in the microwave oven, transferring to a hot conventional oven for the remaining time. This way you get the best of both worlds, less spatter and more crisping.

Tent the microwaved turkey with foil during a minimum standing time of 20 minutes.

Roast capon, duck and goose in the same way, allowing about 10 minutes to 450 g (1 lb), but never give additional time unless you are sure, because over-cooking results in dry, chewy meat and *not* a more tender bird as you might imagine.

Roast pheasant whole in a roaster bag or cut it in half and cook as a casserole.

Chicken Breasts Teriyaki

4 to 6 medium chicken breasts, washed and dried
150-300 ml (¼-½ pint). Teriyaki sauce (see page 192)

Put the chicken breasts in a shallow dish and pour over the
Teriyaki sauce.

Cover tightly with cling film and leave to soak for at least 2
hours. Baste or shake the dish from time to time so that the
chicken is well impregnated.

Microwave on High for 7-12 minutes or until the chicken is
cooked, giving the dish a quarter-turn three times during
cooking.

If the chicken is on the bone, turn the pieces over halfway
through the cooking.

Drain and serve hot on a bed of rice.

Serves 4 to 6

LEFT-OVER COOKED POULTRY

Turn left-over chicken or turkey meat into delicious supper
dishes by combining with any savoury sauce. Make sauces
of coating consistency, using half chicken stock. Heat the
chicken or turkey in the sauce thoroughly.

Sherried Turkey

In this recipe, which goes well with freshly heated rice or
creamed potatoes, the sauce is used as a topping.

   25 g (1 oz) butter
   1 small onion, finely chopped
   3 rashers bacon, derinded and finely chopped
   15 g (½ oz) flour
   50 g (2 oz) mushrooms, sliced
   2 tablespoons sweetcorn kernels
   300 ml (½ pint) turkey or chicken stock
   1 tablespoon tomato purée
   4 tablespoons sherry
   350 g (12 oz) cooked turkey, cubed

Put the butter in a large shallow dish and microwave on High for 1-1½ minutes or until melted.

Stir in the onion and bacon and microwave on High for 3-4 minutes until both are cooked. Stir occasionally to ensure that the bacon cooks equally.

Mix in the flour, then add the mushrooms, sweetcorn, stock, tomato purée and sherry. Microwave on High for 2-3 minutes or until the sauce thickens, stirring once.

Season to taste with salt and pepper and cover with a lid.

Place the turkey on a dish, cover with cling film and microwave on High for 2½-4 minutes until the turkey is thoroughly hot, shaking the dish once during cooking.

Leave for 2-3 minutes while briefly reheating the sauce on High, then carefully remove the cling film and pour the sauce over the turkey.

Serves 4

PÂTÉ

Pâté is so easy to make. Serve on biscuits or toast as canapés, wrapped in pastry en croûte or try vol-au-vent cases filled with pâté.

The microwave oven can make pâté preparation easy. Use any tried and trusted recipe but let the microwave do the cooking.

Here are two pâtés using chicken livers which you can buy fresh or frozen usually in 200-225 g (7-8 oz) packs.

Chopped Liver and Egg Pâté

40 g (1½ oz) butter or clarified chicken fat
100 g (4 oz) onions, chopped
225 g (8 oz) chicken livers, roughly chopped
Salt
Black pepper
2 hard-boiled eggs

Put the butter in a large shallow dish and microwave on High for 1-1½ minutes until melted.

Stir in the onions and microwave on High for 3-4 minutes until the onions are soft but not coloured.

Stir in the chicken livers, cover with greaseproof paper so that the paper does not protrude beyond the edges of the dish. Microwave on High for 4-5 minutes, stirring occasionally until the livers are no longer pink. Do not over-cook or they will turn out like little bullets.

Season to taste with salt and pepper, then chop the mixture very finely and press through a sieve. Roughly chop the hard-boiled egg and stir in lightly. If you are using a food processor, add the eggs after the meat and onions are coarsely blended and then switch on and off rapidly 3 or 4 times to prevent the yellow and white specks disappearing altogether. The pâté should be on the coarse side.

Use within 1 or 2 days.

Serves 4

Brandied Cheese and Liver Pâté

    25 g (1 oz) butter
    100 g (4 oz) chicken livers, chopped
    100 g (4 oz) raw chicken, cut into ½ in dice
    4 sage leaves, snipped into strips with scissors
    100 g (4 oz) curd cheese
    4 tablespoons brandy
    Salt
    Pepper
Topping
    25 g (1 oz) unsalted butter

Put the butter in a large shallow dish and microwave on High for 1-1½ minutes until melted.

Stir in the chicken livers, raw chicken and sage. Microwave

on High for 4-6 minutes, stirring occasionally until cooked.

Drain away the surplus butter, cover the chicken and cool rapidly.

Blend the cold chicken and sage with the curd cheese and brandy in the liquidizer or food processer, adding salt and pepper to taste.

Spoon into a dish and smooth with a palette knife leaving ½ in head space.

Put the unsalted butter in a small bowl and microwave on High for 1½-1¾ minutes until melted and just clear.

Pour evenly over the pâté through a tea strainer.

Refrigerate until required.

Use within 1 or 2 days.

Serves 4

Oriental Roast Chicken

This is a way of adding flavour and giving colour to microwaved chicken. You may have to search around but you can obtain fresh ginger from continental type grocers and larger branches of Tesco.

1 × 1½ kg (3½ lb) roasting chicken, cleaned
2 tablespoons sherry
7 tablespoons soy sauce
Small clove garlic, peeled
2½ cm (1 in) piece fresh ginger
1 teaspoon sugar
¼ teaspoon salt
¼ teaspoon pepper

Pinch and pull the chicken skin all over to help loosen it from the flesh. Starting at the neck, separate the skin from the flesh, including the drumsticks if you can. It may be better to begin with a long spoon handle and take over with your fingers.

Put the sherry, soy sauce, garlic, ginger, sugar, salt and pepper in the liquidizer and blend at high speed for 1 minute – or crush the garlic and mince the ginger separately before stirring into the liquid.

Spoon the mixture under the chicken skin, rubbing it well into the flesh.

Leave to stand for 15-20 minutes for the flavour to permeate.

Roast in the usual way, starting breast-side down.

Halfway through the cooking time, turn the chicken over and spoon away surplus juices.

Serves 4

Variations

Use the same sauce for duck or turkey.

Add 1 tablespoon tomato paste and 1 teaspoon Worcestershire sauce to the sauce.

POULTRY CASSEROLES

Chicken and turkey casserole exceedingly well in the microwave oven and you will be pleasantly surprised when you discover just how tender the meat becomes. The cooking times are relative to the other ingredients included and these may be slower cooking items in themselves. When a large quantity of liquid is included it is best to microwave on High but casseroles using a minimum of thick sauce should be microwaved on Low. Roughly speaking, allow 30-40 minutes for 1.5 kg (3 lb) cut-up chicken plus other ingredients.

Browning and sealing are not always necessary and, although it adds colour, there is no purpose in sealing in the juices. But if your recipe recommends this, use either the browning dish or, better still, the frying pan. Casseroles will be less fatty if the poultry is skinned.

This microwave recipe leaves you with a wide choice of options to enable you to produce many different chicken casseroles.

Chicken Casserole

   1 × 1.5 kg (3½ lb) oven-ready chicken
   2 medium onions, finely chopped
   1 clove garlic, crushed
   1 tablespoon vegetable oil
   25 g (1 oz) flour
   150 ml (¼ pt) wine or stock
   350 g (¾ lb) ripe tomatoes or 1 × 225 g (8 oz) can
      tomatoes
   100 g (4 oz) mushrooms, sliced
   1 level tablespoon freshly chopped parsley
   Salt
   Pepper
   1 tablespoon lemon juice

Skin the chicken and cut into 8 or 12 pieces.
Combine the onions, garlic and oil in a deep casserole dish and microwave on High for 3-4 minutes or until the onions start to brown.
Stir in the flour, then add the remaining ingredients.
Cover with a lid and microwave on High for 25-35 minutes, repositioning the chicken twice during cooking.
Leave to stand 10 minutes before serving.
Add extra liquid when repositioning the chicken if the casserole seems too dry. If at the end of the cooking time the sauce is too thin, stir a blend of 1 or 2 teaspoons cornflour and 3 tablespoons cold water and microwave on High until boiling.
Serves 5 to 6

Variations

Brown the chicken pieces before adding to the casserole for
a deeper colour. Use red or white wine, cider, Pomagne or
tomato juice. Omit or increase the quantity of,
mushrooms. Add thinly sliced carrots, green peppers,
quartered potato or canned vegetables. Vary the herbs
using ½ teaspoon dried or 2 level tablespoons fresh basil,
thyme or rosemary or 2 bay leaves.

Quick Chicken Schnitzel

Use 'Shake 'n' Bake' which, though expensive, is an
effective coating and can be used without the egg dip.

  4 boned chicken breasts, skinned
  Salt
  Pepper
  1 egg, beaten
  Few tablespoons golden crumbs
  2-3 tablespoons vegetable oil

Beat the chicken breasts to flatten. Season with salt and
pepper.
Dip in beaten egg and coat with the crumbs, pressing them
well in with a palette knife.
Put the oil in a large shallow dish and microwave on High
for 2-2½ minutes.
Place the chicken pieces in the dish, cover with greaseproof
paper and microwave on High for 1 minute for each piece.
Turn over the chicken breasts, replace the paper and
microwave on High for 1-1½ minutes per piece, depending
on the size.
Leave to stand for 1 minute before serving, then test with
the tip of a round-bladed knife.
Drain and serve hot or cold.
Serves 4

Roast Duck / Goose

Duck can be simply roasted, stuffed or garnished with a sauce. Prepare and clean duck or goose in the usual way. Tuck the wings and legs close into the body so that these bony parts cannot over-cook. Place breast-side down in a shallow dish on a rack or upturned undecorated soup plate.

Microwave covered for the first half of the cooking time, then turn the duck and complete the cooking without a cover.

Give the dish a quarter-turn 3 times during cooking and spoon away the surplus fat if more than 1 cm (½ in) gathers in the base of the dish. When the duck is just cooked (microwave thermometer should register 82°C (180°F)) tent with foil or a large brown paper bag and leave to stand for 15 minutes, when the temperature reading should rise to 90°C (190°F).

Duck may be cooked in a roasting bag loosely secured with string. More browning will occur but it is less easy to turn the bird over and remove the surplus fat – unless you use a suction baster.

Preferably microwave on Medium allowing 9-11 minutes per 450 g (1 lb) or microwave on High allowing 6-8 minutes per 450 g (1 lb). Calculate the cooking times to include the weight of stuffing and reckon on 450 g (1 lb) duck (including bone) per person.

Duck à l'Orange

Duck à l'orange is a favourite recipe because the sharp fresh orange not only contrasts with the flavour, but also counteracts the richness, of the duck meat.

2-2½ kg (4-6 lb) duck, cleaned
5 oranges

1 level tablespoon cornflour
. 1 generous tablespoon three-fruit marmalade (see page 258)

Slice one orange thinly and set aside for garnish. Peel and segment 2 oranges, removing all the membrane. Grate and squeeze the juice from the remaining 2 oranges.

Place the orange segments into the cavity of the duck, pushing them well inside so they will not tumble out.

Roast the duck and prepare the sauce during standing time.

Blend the grated orange rind and juice with cornflour in a large ovenglass measuring jug.

Add the marmalade and the de-fatted duck juices and make up to 300 ml (½ pint) with water. Stir thoroughly.

Microwave on High for 2½-3½ minutes or until the sauce thickens, stirring frequently to avoid lumps.

Pour over the roast duck and garnish with the orange slices.

Serves 4 to 6

Stuffed Chicken Breasts in Cream Sauce

Cook the chicken in an ovenglass dish if possible and then you will be able to see through the base when the chicken is cooked. Calculate the cooking times as if the weight were all poultry. Take care when reheating the sauce as cream curdles easily.

   4 boned chicken breasts, skinned
   25 g (1 oz) butter
   1 rounded tablespoon flour
   150 ml (¼ pint) single cream
   150 ml (¼ pint) water
   ¼ chicken stock cube, crumbled
   Freshly chopped chives

Salt
Pepper
8 wooden cocktail sticks
Watercress to garnish

Stuffing
4 artichoke hearts, chopped
50 g (2 oz) Cheddar cheese, grated
2 tablespoons fresh breadcrumbs
Salt
Pepper

Flatten the chicken breasts with a cleaver or rolling pin. This is easier if you first cover the pieces with cling film.

Put the butter in a medium bowl and microwave on High for ½-1 minute until melted.

Stir in the flour and microwave on High for ½ minute.

Gradually add the cream and water, stock cube and chives and season to taste with salt and pepper.

Microwave on High for 3-4 minutes, whisking once or twice until the sauce thickens.

Whilst the sauce is cooking, mix the stuffing ingredients. If you have a food processor substitute a slice of bread and blend the ingredients together.

Spoon a quarter of the stuffing on to the centre of each chicken breast. Form into parcels, securing with cocktail sticks. Put the chicken packets in a shallow dish, seam sides up. Cover with cling film and Microwave on High for 4-5 minutes giving the dish a half-turn halfway through cooking. Carefully remove the cling film and mix any surplus juices with the reserved sauce.

Remove the cocktail sticks and turn the chicken parcels over.

If the undersides are still pink, re-cover and microwave on High for a further 2 minutes.

Pour over the sauce and, without covering, microwave on High for 1-2 minutes to enable the sauce to reheat.

If you are concerned about curdling, reheat on Low or Defrost for 4-5 minutes instead.

Garnish with sprigs of watercress.

Serves 4

Variations

Substitute canned celery hearts or asparagus for the artichokes and flavour the sauce with fresh rosemary or thyme leaves.

3

Fish

All fish cooks exceptionally well in the microwave oven and, unless you like it crisply fried, forget about other cooking methods. Only in the microwave oven do you avoid sticky grill pans, the white scum left after poaching, or over-baked, dried-out cutlets. Although cooking results are perfect, they can only be so if you have bought good fresh fish in the first place. The flesh should be firm and resilient to the touch and there should be no strong odour. The fish is stale if the scales are coming off. Fillets should be white and, if there is yellowing or what looks like dirty patches on the flesh, don't buy them. Don't expect the microwave oven to improve poor quality foods.

Fish stock cooks well in a microwave oven and, if you are making a sauce, you might like to skin the fish or indeed fillet the fish yourself and use the bones as well. Frozen fillets are a devil to skin, so for those who dislike eating the skins or in dishes where they may look unattractive, you could start with fresh fish and let the fishmonger do the gutting and trimming for you.

SEPARATING FROZEN FISH

To separate a few fillets of fish from a pack, place the frozen pack (provided it is not covered with foil) in the microwave oven and switch on High for ½ minute for a 225 g (8 oz) packet. Turn the package over and microwave on High for a further ½ minute. Allow one minute on each side for a 500 g (1 lb) pack. The fish should snap away cleanly. Do not exceed the times given or you will find that the fish starts to thaw in parts, and over-thawing will result in cooking around the edges. Arrange the fish fillets in the dish, overlapping the tails to maintain a uniform thickness.

THAWING FROZEN FISH

All fish should be fully thawed before cooking or the outside edges will be fully cooked before the centre panel has thawed. Put the fish on a plate and cover with the plastic wrappings it was bought in. Microwave on Low allowing 6-8 minutes to 450 g (1 lb). To defrost on High, microwave for 15 seconds only, then rest for 2 minutes. Turn the fillets over and repeat as necessary.

Whole fish responds best to thawing on Low, as there is less chance of the tail end cooking. Put the fish on a dish and cover with greaseproof paper, tucking the paper under the dish on either side so that it doesn't blow off. Flat fish, such as plaice and sole, will take 6-8 minutes per 450 g (1 lb). Halfway through, turn the fish over and if the tail is thawed, cover this portion with a small piece of foil, holding it in place with a wooden cocktail stick.

Whole round fish, e.g. haddock, hake, cod, turbot, brill, red mullet, salmon trout and salmon, need slightly more thawing care. First you must make sure that they will fit into the oven without bending. Follow the same thawing rules as for flat fish but allow 8-10 minutes per 450 g (1 lb) on Low, depending on the thickness of the fish. Cover the tail with foil as soon as it is thawed, fixing with a cocktail stick, and make sure the foil does not touch the sides of the oven. Turning the fish over twice during defrosting improves the result. Should gutted fish still have ice crystals in the middle a quick douse in cold water will soon complete defrosting. It is better to divide into the required sizes, separating before freezing or cutting through before defrosting, for well-shaped darnes (cutlets). If after freezing fish in one piece you decide that you wish to thaw part only, defrost on the lowest setting, covering the centre section with foil. Cut off the top and bottom as soon as they are ready. Replace the frozen piece in the freezer. Do not try to wrap one half of a large fish with foil, as you will run the risk of the foil touching the oven walls and causing damage to the walls and the magnetron.

Shellfish must be absolutely fresh. Molluscs including oysters, scallops, mussels and clams have hinged shells, which when tapped should snap shut or be completely closed. If the flesh is soft and smelly, they are bad. Frozen scallops are obtainable throughout the year. They may appear to be whiter than the fresh ones because they tend to change colour during the freezing process.

Shellfish is open-frozen before packing, so separation should be unnecessary and you will only need to take out the number required.

Crustacea have jointed shells. Well-known types are crawfish, crayfish, abalone, lobsters, crabs, prawns and shrimps. Whether fresh or frozen take care that the shells are light and hard. Crabmeat is obtainable frozen as light and dark meat, and shelled prawns and shrimps are sold in different sizes.

Lobster can be cooked in the microwave oven but must be killed first. Live lobster is a blackish-blue colour and becomes bright red when cooked. Frozen cooked lobster in the shell will be red and the flesh opaque. Thaw by microwave on Low allowing 7-8 minutes per 450 g (1 lb).

COOKING FISH

Fish cooked in its own juices with a squeeze of lemon juice and a dab of butter and a judicious sprinkling of salt and pepper maintains maximum flavour. If no other ingredients are added and the fish is at room temperature allow 4 minutes to the pound and cook on High. Thin pieces may be eaten immediately but since there is a carry-over of cooking of one-third the cooking time, thicker pieces or whole fish should be left to stand for this period before serving.

Arrange fillets of fish either with the tails overlapping for even thickness or with the tails towards the inside when cooked in a round dish. Small pieces of fish should be gently stirred during cooking so that they are repositioned. Cutlets that are no more than 2½ cm (1 in) thick need not be turned over, but should be repositioned except when only one is being cooked.

Put large cuts such as a 450 g (1 lb) or 900 g (2 lb) piece of salmon skin-side up and turn once halfway through cooking. Slash the skin in two or three places to prevent bursting. The centre bones of cutlets fill with hot air and are inclined to pop causing immediately adjoining flesh to splatter. To help prevent this brush around the bones with lemon juice, white wine or water, and cover with greaseproof or waxed paper. Tuck the sides of the paper underneath the cooking vessel. Do not cover with cling film unless you are prepared to allow a standing time. I discovered this when I saw someone pull back the cling film too soon and the fish spattered in her face.

Very large fish may not fit into a dish so, provided they will fit into the oven cavity, cook them directly on a lipped shelf, wrapped in non-stick paper or placed in a large roaster bag sealed loosely with an elastic band so that air can escape and the bag does not balloon up and split. Turn the fish over halfway through cooking and, if possible, give it a half-turn once during cooking. This will not be necessary if your oven is fitted with a turntable. However, if the fish is longer than the diameter of the turntable, it is better to remove the turntable and replace it with a shelf.

Naturally this must not rest directly over any moving parts and microwave roasting racks do this job most efficiently.

The tail ends of large fish will cook more rapidly than the thicker parts, so it will be necessary to shield this portion as soon as it is cooked. Make sure that this end is easily accessible, particularly if cooking in a roaster bag, and insert a small piece of foil over the cooked part – but inside the bag, for if the foil touches the oven walls damage will occur. If in any doubt at all, overwrap with cling flim to hold the foil in place.

For crisper, drier results, lightly cover with greaseproof paper. Covering may not always be necessary but the eyes of whole fish, as well as the skin and bone, may pop. Although it is easier to use a loose paper cover when fish must be turned over, if you require quicker cooking and a moist juice-retaining dish, cover loosely with cling film. Although all types of cling film look alike some are more 'clingy' than others and once removed when the food is hot, may coil up and it is then impossible to reposition. If in any doubt cover very loosely, leaving a gap at one end.

Soft fish really does need turning and it is easy to baste by simply shaking the dish gently. Another useful and flavoursome covering is spring cabbage or lettuce leaves, but some varieties become bitter when cooked, so use the outer leaves only and discard later. Save the outside leaves from lettuce and cabbage and freeze them – when thawed they will be nicely limp for easier wrapping.

Fish can be cooked stuffed or in a sauce but this will slow the cooking time. If time is of the essence, pre-cook the sauce and pour over the fish for reheating. Flavours improve if a combination is used and combination dishes are even better if refrigerated for a few hours before reheating.

For cold dishes, cook the fish in a court bouillon or marinate before cooking and leave to cool in the liquor.

Court bouillon is a well seasoned liquor made with water and wine or water and vinegar plus a piece of carrot, onion and herbs.

When cooking with butter try to spread this evenly as soon as it is soft. Fat attracts microwaves and the parts of the fish under any particularly large lump will cook more slowly.

SMOKED FISH AND BOIL-IN-BAG FISH

Put whole smoked haddock, cod fillet, kippers, etc. in a dish and cook covered loosely with cling film, leaving this intact until ready for eating so that smells won't escape. Remove the cling film carefully so that you don't scald your fingers. If the fish is to be reheated don't uncover until required. Boil-in-bags should be slashed and always put on a plate as escaping juices may flow over.

Keep scallop shells and use them as cooking containers. They are easy to wash and can be used time and time again. You can also cook in lobster shells but these are more delicate.

ROES

Fish roes should be covered tightly as they tend to splatter during cooking. Cooking times are the same as for other fish.

STORAGE

Prepared fish dishes can be stored for up to 8 weeks in the freezer. Those which include left-over cooked fish should be consumed within 4 weeks. Raw fish has a freezer storage life of 6 months.

To summarize, generally cook fish on High, thaw on Low and reheat on Medium or Medium High. Cook for 4-

5 minutes per 450 g (1 lb) and include in this weight any other ingredients. Try to ensure an even thickness, overlapping the thinner pieces. Turn over thick cuts halfway and reposition small pieces during cooking. Slash the skins of whole fish and shield thinner, quick-cooking tails with foil after sufficient cooking has taken place. Over-cooked fish becomes tough and dry due to shrinkage of the protein. Allow for a carry-over cooking time, taking especial care if the fish is to be reheated later.

Avocado, Prawn and Haddock Scallops

Choose large, deep scallop shells and do not over-fill or the potato will topple off when reheating. The sauce should be very thick to start as it will thin down when the other ingredients are mixed in.

225 g (8 oz) fresh haddock
Salt
Pepper
35 g (1¼ oz) butter
35 g (1¼ oz) flour
150 ml (¼ pint) milk, or milk and fish stock mixed
3 tablespoons double cream, slightly beaten
1 medium avocado
25 g (1 oz) peeled prawns
350 g (12 oz) cooked mashed potato
15 g (½ oz) dried breadcrumbs
4 deep scallop shells

Put the fish on a plate, season lightly, cover with cling film and microwave on High for 2-2½ minutes until the fish is just cooked.
Test by pressing with your fingers through the cling film.
Put the butter in a medium bowl and microwave on High for ½ minute or until melted.

Stir in the flour and microwave on High for ½-1 minute until the mixture puffs up.

Stir in the milk and stock and microwave on High for 2½-3½ minutes, whisking frequently after the first minute until the sauce thickens.

Stir in the cream, and season to taste.

Scoop the flesh from the avocado and mash into the sauce.

Flake the fish, removing any bones, and mix into the sauce with the fish juices, then carefully add the prawns.

Divide the mixture between four scallop shells and pipe a decorative border of mashed potato around the edges.

Sprinkle breadcrumbs over the fish, then brown under a pre-heated grill.

To reheat, microwave on Medium allowing 1 minute per scallop. If you are reheating them all together microwave on High for 2-3 minutes, turning the dishes from time to time.

Serves 4

Variations:

Substitute smoked haddock and cooked sweetcorn kernels or canned salmon and cooked peas for the fish and avocado.

Barbecued Halibut

When I was visiting Haines in Alaska which is renowned for its halibut fishing I was invited to a halibut barbecue. They serve huge portions which we could never afford, so here is my scaled-down recipe. If you prefer, you can cook the fish in an ordinary dish and brown it under the grill after cooking.

   25 g (1 oz) salted butter
   4 × 175 g (6 oz) halibut steaks
   Flour seasoned with salt and pepper

Sauce

   150 ml (¼ pint) tomato ketchup
   Juice of half lemon
   1 teaspoon brown sugar
   1 tablespoon Worcestershire sauce
   ½ teaspoon paprika
   ½ teaspoon French mustard,
   Squeeze garlic powder

Mix all the sauce ingredients together.

Pre-heat a large browning dish to maximum, adding the butter during the last 30 seconds.

While the dish is heating, dip the fish in seasoned flour and shake off the surplus. Quickly place the fish, loop ends towards the middle, in the browning butter and turn over at once to seal.

Cover with greaseproof paper and microwave on High for 3 minutes, giving the dish a half-turn after 1½ minutes.

Pour the sauce over the fish and using a pastry brush, spread evenly and work the sauce into the flesh.

Microwave on High for 1½ minutes, then turn the fish over and microwave on High for a further 1½ minutes or until the fish is cooked.

Serves 4

Variations

Use cod or haddock steaks and add a few capers to the sauce, or use the sauce with pork chops.

Salmon Steaks

Cook as for Barbecued Halibut. Dip in seasoned flour and cook in sizzling butter in the browning dish, turning over the fish. Microwave on High for about 4 minutes per 450 g (1 lb) after browning. Cover with greaseproof paper to prevent splattering.

Fish steaks may also be simply cooked on a plate covered loosely with cling film.

Boiled Salmon

This is usually cooked in one piece. Because there is a large volume of liquid the fish will cook gently on High. Once the liquid boils there will be little appreciable difference in the cooking times for 450 g-1 kg (1-2 lb) of fish.

  1 whole piece salmon 0.5 to 1.25 kg (1-2½ lb)

Court Bouillon
  600 ml (1 pint) water
  2 tablespoons wine or vinegar
  1 small onion, quartered
  1 small carrot, sliced
  1 clove garlic, bruised (optional)
  1 clove
  1 cm (½ in) piece celery
  Small bunch fresh herbs or bouquet garni
  1 teaspoon salt
  1 bay leaf
  6 crushed black or white peppercorns

Combine the court bouillon ingredients in a large dish that will fit the salmon and the liquid.

Microwave on High for 3-4 minutes, stirring occasionally until the liquid reaches boiling point.

Lay the salmon in the liquid (court bouillon), cover with a lid and microwave on High for 3-4 minutes until the liquid bubbles.

Turn the fish over and microwave on High for 1-2 minutes or until the flesh can be easily separated from the bone and is opaque in the centre.

Replace the lid and leave to stand until cold.

Drain and remove the skin and bone if desired.
Allow 100-175 g (4-6 oz) salmon per person.

Variations

Cook any large pieces of fish this way. You will be
surprised how much more flavour white fish such as hake
or delicate bream will have.

Dover Sole

Dover sole is conventionally cooked with or without its
head, but when microwaving, it is better to remove it. To
remove the skin, make a cut across the skin at the tail end
and insert your thumb between the skin and the flesh close
to the outside edges and push up. It will then be easy to rip
the skin off from tail to head. Cook the fish 1 or 2 at a
time.

  2 × 350 ml (12 oz) prepared Dover sole
  15 g (½ oz) soft butter
  Salt
  Pepper

Spread both sides of the dish sparingly with butter and
sprinkle with salt and pepper to taste.
Arrange the fish side by side, head to tail on a large
shallow dish.
Cover loosely with cling film and microwave on High for 5
minutes, giving the dish a quarter-turn every minute.
Before giving additional cooking time press through the
cling film on to the thickest part of the fish and, if this
gives easily, the fish is nearly cooked.
Leave covered for 3 minutes for the fish to finish cooking.
Remove the cling film carefully.
Serves 2

Variations

Use the same method for whole plaice removing the black skin only and cooking skin-side down. Cook lemon sole similarly but sprinkle with lemon juice as the flavour of this fish is somewhat bland. Allow 4 minutes to every 450 g (1 lb) but test ahead of time as drier fish cooks more quickly than watery fish.

Haddock Provençale

In this recipe the vegetables are combined and cooked together before adding the fish fillets. It is a variation on the ratatouille theme.

1 tomato
1 small onion
1 green pepper
2 sprigs of parsley
175 g (6 oz) button mushrooms
Clove garlic
2 sprigs marjoram
2 tablespoons vegetable oil
1 tablespoon lemon juice
Salt
Pepper
450 g (1 lb) fresh haddock fillet, skinned
1 tablespoon tomato purée
2 tablespoons sweet red wine

Chop the tomato, onion, green pepper and parsley and slice the mushrooms. Crush the garlic between cling film or greaseproof paper with a powerful smash of a rolling pin.
Strip off the marjoram leaves with kitchen scissors.
Stir all these ingredients into a large shallow dish with the oil and the lemon juice.
Three-quarters cover with cling film and microwave on

High for 4-7 minutes, stirring occasionally until the
vegetables are tender.
Season to taste with salt and pepper.
Remove the cling film.
Season the fish and arrange on the vegetables, placing the
thinner parts towards the centre.
Brush the surface of the fish with the tomato purée and red
wine.
Cover with greaseproof paper and microwave on High for
4-5 minutes until the fish flakes easily with a fork, giving
the dish a quarter-turn 3 times during cooking.
Serves 4

Variations

Use any white fish fillet or cutlet. Substitute sliced
courgettes, aubergines, okra, green beans for the
mushrooms.
Use red pepper and vary the herbs. Add more tomatoes
when they are cheap. Sprinkle the fish with grated cheese
and brown briefly under the grill. Pipe mashed potato
whirls around the edges of the dish. Sprinkle with crushed
potato chips just before serving.

Kedgeree

Smoked haddock on the bone can't be beaten for flavour
but in a kedgeree smoked cod or haddock fillet will do as
well. Put the fish skin-side down in a shallow dish, cover
loosely with cling film and allow 4 minutes to every 450 g
(1 lb).
The rice, fish and eggs can be prepared well ahead of time.
Frozen fish and rice should be thawed separately by
microwave on High before mixing.

75 g (3 oz) butter
2 tablespoons milk

225 g (8 oz) smoked haddock, cooked and flaked
350 g (12 oz) cooked rice
White pepper
2 hard-boiled eggs, whites separated from yolks (whites
    chopped, yolks sieved)
1 tablespoon freshly chopped parsley
¼ teaspoon Cayenne pepper

Put the butter and milk in a deep serving dish and microwave on High for 1½-3 minutes until the butter is melted.
Stir.

Mix in the flaked fish and rice and season with the white
pepper.

Without covering, microwave on High for 2-3 minutes,
stirring occasionally until the mixture is hot.

Stir in the chopped egg whites.

Clean up the edges of the dish to remove any unruly food
particles.

Mix the sieved yolk and parsley and Cayenne lightly
together and sprinkle over the dish.

Serves 4

Variations
Use fresh fish or canned salmon or tuna.

PREPARING LOBSTER

It takes about half an hour to prepare a lobster so choose a
time when there are likely to be no interruptions, otherwise
you are continually having to wash your hands. First twist
off the claws and the feelers, crack open and remove the
flesh. The shells break easily when tapped with a cleaver or
rolling pin and a skewer is useful for poking out the flesh.
Split the lobster down the back lengthways and open out.
Pull out the top black vein, the spongy-like fingers and the

stomach sac located near the head and throw these away. Remove the flesh and keep undamaged claws for garnish. Lobster shells can be frozen for later use.

Lobster Newburg

1 cooked lobster
40 g (1½ oz) butter
1 tablespoon brandy
4 tablespoons single cream, day old
1 egg yolk
Salt
Pepper
Dash paprika
175 g (6 oz) cooked rice
Lobster claws and watercress leaves for garnish

Cut up the lobster meat.

Put the butter in a large shallow dish and microwave on High for 30-60 seconds until melted. Stir in the lobster meat and microwave on High for 1½-2 minutes, turning the pieces occasionally to add flavour and heat the meat. Pour over the brandy and stir once more.

Blend the cream and egg yolk in a large bowl and microwave on Low for 1-1½ minutes, beating every 15 seconds until the sauce just coats the back of a spoon. Be careful not to over-cook or you will have scrambled egg instead.

Mix in the lobster meat and season the sauce with salt, pepper and paprika.

Without covering, reheat the rice in the microwave oven for 1-2 minutes on High, fluffing up with a fork before serving.

Serve the lobster on a bed of rice and garnish with the claws and watercress leaves.

Serves 3 to 4

Variations

Serve the lobster in the shells and garnish with fried bread-crumbs.

Substitute scallops cut into quarters and sauté for 4 minutes per 450 g (1 lb) or until cooked.

Shrimp and Salmon Mousse

Fish mousses are very simple to make in the microwave oven since the fish is easy to cook, the sauce easy to prepare, the mayonnaise ingredients are assisted by warming and gelatine can be easily dissolved.

Do not make mousses too stiff or it spoils the texture. A good mousse is spongy yet wobbly on the plate.

> 225 g (8 oz) fresh salmon
> Béchamel sauce (page 186) made from 300 ml (½ pint) milk, 15 g (½ oz) butter, 15 g (½ oz) flour
> 6 tablespoons mayonnaise (page 188)
> 6 tablespoons double cream, half-whipped
> 2 tablespoons dry white wine
> 2 level teaspoons powdered gelatine
> 75 g (3 oz) peeled shrimps, chopped
> 1 egg white
> 4 or 5 whole prawns for garnish
> 1¾ litre (1½-2 pint) mould, rinsed in cold water or 4 to 5 individual ramekin dishes

Put the salmon in a dish, cover with greaseproof paper and microwave on High for 2-3 minutes or until cooked.

Remove the skin and bones and flake the flesh.

Make the sauce in the microwave oven in a large jug or bowl.

Prepare the mayonnaise and blend in the cream.

Put the wine in a small bowl.

Sprinkle on the gelatine and microwave for 30-60 seconds until dissolved.
Stir and set aside until clear.
Add the fish, mayonnaise and shrimps to the cooled béchamel sauce.
Pour in the dissolved gelatine from a height and stir thoroughly.
Whip the egg white until stiff peaks form.
Stir in 1 tablespoon of the beaten egg white and fold in the remainder evenly.
Pour the mixture into the prepared mould or ramekin dishes.
Smooth the surface with a damp palette knife and refrigerate for 2-3 hours or until set.
Do not freeze.
Garnish with the prawns.
Serves 4 to 5

Variations
Substitute canned salmon or tuna for the fresh salmon, and lobster or crab for the shrimps.
Add a tablespoon of tomato paste to the white sauce.
Substitute 350 g (12 oz) cooked flaked smoked haddock instead of the fish and shellfish.
Add a few cooked green peas for colour.

TROUT

Whatever size or type, trout can be garnished, flavoured or sauced in a number of ways and all of them are excellent when cooked by microwave. Frozen trout, provided it has been gutted before freezing, is suitable for programmed microwaving on machines which defrost, followed directly with higher setting cooking.

Score the skin in two or three places to prevent bursting and cook lightly, covered with greaseproof paper so keeping the oven clean. Cook trout with or without stuffing and calculate cooking times as for whole fish. Additional ingredients lengthen the cooking times and when an egg and cream sauce is used reduce the setting to Low.

Trout Almondine

    75 g (3 oz) butter
    75 g (3 oz) flaked almonds
    4 small trout
    Salt
    Pepper
    1½ tablespoons fresh lemon juice
    200 ml (⅓ pint) single cream

Put the butter in large shallow dish and microwave on High for 30-60 seconds until melted.

Stir in the flaked almonds and microwave on High for 2-3 minutes or until lightly browned. Stir occasionally.

Remove the almonds and set aside.

Arrange the fish in a single layer, either overlapping the tails or pointing them towards the centre of the dish.

Baste the fish with the butter, season with salt and pepper and sprinkle with the lemon juice.

Cover with greaseproof paper.

Microwave on High for 5-7 minutes, giving the dish a quarter-turn 3 times during cooking.

Test the fish through the thickest part with the point of a knife – the flesh should flake easily.

Spoon the almonds over the fish and pour the cream round the sides.

Without covering, microwave on Low for 1-1½ minutes until the sauce is warm.

Be careful not to over-cook or the cream will curdle.
Serves 4

Variations
Omit the almonds and the lemon juice. Cook the trout in
the melted butter, allowing 4-5 minutes to every 450 g (1 lb).
Transfer the fish to a warm serving dish and remove the
upper skin.
Garnish with cucumber slices and serve a cucumber and
dill sauce separately.
Use some of the melted butter in this sauce.

4

Eggs and Cheese

Eggs and cheese are practically always microwaved on a Low setting. These ingredients are the most critical whether cooked by conventional or microwave methods. Both are high protein foods and if over-cooked will toughen and separate, spoiling your favourite dishes.

The egg is a basic food which can be cooked in a variety of ways to be eaten on its own or mixed with other ingredients. The amount of care taken depends upon these other ingredients. An egg and milk mixture, such as in custards, needs special attention, but an egg and flour mixture, such as in cakes, is less important.

When cooking conventionally the whites start to cook before the yolks. In the microwave the yolks cook first because the fatty substance in the yolk attracts the most attention from the microwaves.

Do not attempt to cook eggs in their shells. After a short time in the microwave oven tremendous heat builds up in the yolk so that it bursts through the white and shell to spatter everywhere. When eggs are shelled for cooking by microwave it is desirable to prick the yolks through the outer membrane for similar reasons. There is considerable carry-over cooking when dealing with an egg on its own and an over-heated yolk will explode, especially if it has been cooked covered without other ingredients present.

The easiest method of cooking eggs is scrambling, the whites and yolks being first blended so that cooking pressures are the same throughout. Poached eggs can be cooked in the poacher or water, and fried eggs on a plate or in the browning dish. You can even make an omelette.

Soft-boiled eggs for obvious reasons are excluded, but coddled eggs, which are almost as good, are immersed in a glass of boiling microwaved water. There is a way of cooking hard-boiled eggs too when you want them for chopping (see page 121). Eggs crackle when being cooked, particularly when fried, due to the water in the egg whites.

Eggs in custards, cakes and sauces and egg and cheese combination dishes are dealt with in various parts of the book. Only basic egg cookery is included in this section.

Whenever you can, grate cheese before microwaving and it will cook more evenly. Slices may frizzle on the edges but I often use a processed slice when I am in a hurry, after all, why make a fuss over a quick snack? Processed cheese seems to be more even-natured in the microwave oven, but as a general rule the lower the fat content the better the result. Cheese cooks better on Medium or Medium High and behaves remarkably well when sandwiched between other ingredients, e.g. a melted cheese roll. You can also use it to make excellent fondues and creditable soufflés. Curd and cottage cheeses are used in slimming diets and cheesecakes, and in combination with eggs and milk in quiches.

Whenever cooking either cheese or egg dishes be sure to stir and rotate as directed and treat the cooking times as approximate. Reheat carefully as 'cooking' starts immediately. You may even prefer to under-cook any critical ingredient foods that will be warmed up later.

It is important that you do not alter the quantities in these recipes as the cooking times cannot be easily adjusted to the change in the amount of food.

SOUFFLÉS

An acceptable hot soufflé can only be made in microwave ovens which have a low continuous power. Low power operating on the On-Off pulsing system does not produce good results, because the mixture is constantly rising and falling. Follow your favourite recipe and remember to use a dish large enough to contain the risen soufflé without any overspill. Turn the dish only once during the first half of the cooking time to give the soufflé a good chance to start rising. During the second cooking period you can give the dish a quarter-turn three times. Ovens fitted with turntables have a far greater chance of success since no draught can enters the cavity while the dish is being turned.

A six-egg soufflé will take 30-35 minutes on continuous Low, but alternatively, as a rough guide, you could microwave on Low for 30 minutes, then on Medium for 14-15 minutes. A two-egg soufflé should be cooked entirely on Low for 13-16 minutes.

Soufflés are based on a thick white sauce which should always be prepared by microwave.

Fried Egg

For a crispy fried egg use the browning dish.
Pre-heat the browning dish for 3-4 minutes, adding the butter during the last ½ minute.
Break in the egg(s). If using more than one, break them into opposite corners of the dish. Prick the yolks with a fork, then cover and microwave on High until the egg is cooked to your satisfaction.

Eggs	1	2	3	4
Salted butter	7 g (¼ oz)	15 g (½ oz)	20 g (¾ oz)	25 g (1 oz)
Prick, cover and micro-wave on High	½-1 min	1½-2 mins	2-2½ mins	2½-3 mins

Remove with a fish slice and leave for ½ minute for the heat to equalize before serving.

To cook a crisp-bottomed yet lightly cooked egg, break the egg(s) on to a pre-heated and well buttered browning dish, when the egg will cook without further microwaving.

Hard-cooked Eggs

Eggs cannot be hard-boiled in the microwave oven because they will explode and cover the oven in tiny yellow and white particles. You can, however, hard cook whites and yolks separately and chop them for sandwiches or use them separately in garnishing.

It is easiest to hard-cook six at a time, making the microwave distribution more gentle.

Grease two bowls.

Separate the six eggs.

Put the whites in one bowl and the yolks in the other.

Lightly stir the yolks.

Cover the bowls in cling film.

Cook the whites first by microwaving on Low for 5-6 minutes, stirring twice during cooking, drawing the cooked parts towards the middle, leaving them still slightly soft.

Remove from the oven and leave to stand while cooking the yolks.

Without stirring the yolks, microwave on Low for 2-3 minutes until nearly opaque.

Leave covered for 5 minutes while chopping the whites.

Chop or sieve the yolks.

Reduce cooking time for four eggs but more care must be taken not to overcook.

Partially cooked cooled egg yolks added to raw yolks help to stabilize mayonnaise.

Omelette

Prepare on a round lipped plate or in a round browning dish, if you can obtain one.

15 g (½ oz) butter
2 eggs
2 tablespoons water
Salt
Pepper

Put the butter on a shallow dish or a curved edged plate, 23 cm (9 in). A small undecorated dinner plate is usually the right size. Microwave on High for 30-45 seconds until the butter is just melted. Spread over the entire surface of the plate.

Beat the eggs and water together and season with salt and pepper.

Pour on to the dish. Cover tightly with cling film and microwave on High for 1½-2½ minutes, giving the dish a quarter-turn every minute.

The omelette is ready when it is just set and still slightly runny in the centre. Leave for 30 seconds until set, then carefully remove the cling film, fold the omelette and serve on the dish or transfer to a clean heated dish or plate.

Brown under a pre-heated grill if desired.

Serves 1

To cook in the browning dish, pre-heat for 2 minutes only, then add the butter and swirl over the surface. Pour in the beaten egg mixture and cover. Microwave on High for 1½-2½ minutes, giving the dish a quarter-turn every 30 seconds.

Should you wish to cook a second omelette wipe out the browning dish quickly with kitchen paper, pre-heat for 30 seconds and add a knob of butter before the egg mixture is poured in.

Poached Eggs

The best poached eggs are those cooked in water, the whites are far less rubbery. Cook poached eggs on Medium power so that the yolk and white can coagulate at the same time.

Combine the water, vinegar and salt in the cooking container and microwave on High until boiling rapidly.

Break in the eggs, spacing them out if more than one is being cooked.

Cover with cling film and microwave on Medium until the yolk begins to change colour.

After cooking allow a short standing time before serving. The eggs may cook further during this time, so under rather than overcook.

Eggs	1	2	4
Container	Cereal bowl	Deep dish	Large deep dish
Water	5 tbsp	450 ml (¼ pt)	600 ml (1 pt)
White vinegar or lemon juice	¼ tsp	½ tsp	1 tbsp
Salt	Pinch	½ tsp	1 tsp
Time on High to boil hot water	30 secs	1-1½ mins	3-4½ mins
Cooking time on Medium	15-30 secs	1-1½ mins	2½-3 mins

Baked Eggs

If you are accustomed to cooking eggs in a poacher rather

than directly in the water, use a ramekin dish or special plastic poaching mould.

Lightly grease each dish and break in an egg.

Puncture the yolks lightly with a fork through the outer membrane but do not plunge the prongs in deeply.

Cover with cling film.

Place on the oven shelf and microwave on Medium for 30 seconds to 1 minute per egg depending on how you like your eggs cooked.

Give the dishes a half-turn halfway through cooking if your oven is not fitted with a turntable.

Remove the cling film and leave to stand for a few moments before serving.

Scrambled Eggs

Since microwaves cook more round the edges than in the middle, better results will be obtained if scrambled eggs are cooked in a narrow-diameter container. Milk produces a creamier texture while water gives increased volume.

Put the butter in a bowl or jug. Microwave on High for 10-30 seconds until the butter is melted.

Add the remaining ingredients and beat lightly.

Microwave on High, stirring every 30 seconds, drawing the edges to the middle.

Cook until the eggs are only just set with some liquid showing because cooking continues after the eggs are taken from the microwave oven. Leave to stand for 1-2 minutes before eating.

Variations

Add chopped chives, chopped parsley, red or green peppers, cooked peas or chopped French beans, sweetcorn kernels, chopped anchovies, chopped ham, grated cheese to the scrambled egg mixture before cooking.

Eggs	2	4	6	8
Milk, water or milk and water mixed	2 tbsp	4 tbs	6 tbsp	8 tbs
Salt	Pinch	2 pinches	¼ tsp	½ tsp
Pepper	Shake	Shake	Generous shake	¼ tsp
Butter	7 g (¼ oz)	15 g (½ oz)	15 g (½ oz)	20 g (¾ oz)
Cooking time (mins)	1½-2	2½-3½	3½-4½	4-5

Welsh Rarebit

Do not leave the Welsh rarebit for too long under the grill or it will spill over. To serve 1 or 2 reduce both the quantities and the cooking times.

250 g (10 oz) grated Cheddar cheese
½ level teaspoon dry mustard powder
Pepper
4 tablespoons milk
1 egg yolk
¼ level teaspoon cornflour
Salt
4 slices hot buttered toast

Blend all the ingredients together in a bowl only seasoning with salt if necessary. Microwave on Low for 2½-3 minutes until only just melted. Stir occasionally to blend. Meanwhile make 4 slices of buttered toast and leave the grill switched on.

Spoon the mixture on to the toast and brown quickly.
Serves 4

Variations

Thinly slice 100 g (4 oz) button mushrooms and, without covering, microwave on High for 2 minutes. Drain and serve on top of the Welsh rarebit. Thickly slice 4 tomatoes and, without covering, microwave on High for 1 minute and serve on top of the Welsh rarebit.

5

Soups and Pulses

Soups cooked by microwave can be prepared and served in the same tureen thereby saving time and washing up.

Creamed, puréed and thick chunky soups can all be cooked very successfully in the microwave. For best results cook soups 24 hours in advance and store in the refrigerator so that a good flavour can develop. Reheat thoroughly, particularly if there is a meat content.

CREAMED SOUPS

Creamed soups are based on a white sauce made from cooking a combination of butter and flour (roux) with milk or stock. If you are in doubt, always err on the side of too much fat rather than flour. When the sauce is cooked (this may be thick or thin depending on the other items to be added) stir in the remaining soup ingredients and continue microwaving until cooked and the flavours well blended. Purée in the liquidizer if necessary.

Often a recipe will tell you to add fresh or soured cream. When using fresh double cream there should be no problems with curdling, unless the soup contains acid ingredients such as wine or lemon juice. If the soup *does* boil and curdling occurs, all you can do is carry it off with aplomb, saying it's meant to be like that. It will only affect the appearance, not the taste, so no harm is really done.

If you are cooking the soup entirely with milk make sure the bowl is deep and stir frequently as, when it is microwaved on High, it will boil over since the caseine in milk forms a skin which acts as a lid, preventing the steam from escaping.

PURÉED SOUPS

These are generally prepared from vegetables cooked in either water or stock and either processed in a liquidizer or passed through a sieve.

For a really good flavour it is best to sauté the vegetables in a little butter before adding the liquid.

For speedy results cook the vegetables in a minimum of liquid and add the remaining stock after puréeing. If you decide to thin the soup with milk, remember to bring the soup back to the boil to ensure you get the necessary lactic flavour that occurs when the sugars in the milk caramelize.

These soups can be further thickened with a blend of cornflour and cold water or beurre manié (tiny balls of butter and flour paste) whisked into the boiling soup, whereupon it will thicken immediately, or into the cold soup, when it will thicken on reheating.

FISH SOUPS

Fish soups can be cooked in water although I think it is better to use fish stock. It is the skin and bones that produce that gelatinous texture which is typical of a well-prepared fish soup. Sauté flavouring vegetables such as onion and leek in vegetable oil or butter in a large bowl on High before adding the pieces of fish. Be extra careful when stirring soups heavily laden with fish pieces – white fish flakes very easily and crabmeat disperses, but lobster is firm and prawns hold their shape.

THICK MEATY SOUPS

These soups must be based on a good, rich stock and unless you have a very low setting on your oven, the meat pieces will not cook properly so, regrettably, I recommend the use of a pressure cooker, slow cooker or saucepan over a thread of heat. However, an excellent goulash soup can be prepared in the microwave oven using mince.

PULSE AND BEAN SOUPS

Apart from lentils and possibly split peas don't attempt to use the microwave oven for making soups with pulses. However, you *can* use canned beans.

Pearl barley takes an age to cook but do not rule out its use in microwave soups after it has been softened conventionally.

CLEAR SOUPS AND CONSOMMÉS

These cannot be cooked very successfully in the microwave oven. They are basically stocks which require long, slow cooking, producing considerable amounts of steam which form condensation on contact with the cool oven lining. You may therefore find you have to mop up large pools of water from the base of the oven.

Make beef, chicken and vegetable stocks conventionally and remember to boil them up thoroughly before using if they have been stored for more than 24 hours. This can be carried out separately in a large jug in the microwave oven.

FISH STOCKS AND COURT BOUILLON

These are extremely successful when cooked by microwave. Use as large a bowl or jug as you can and reduce the setting to Medium or Low as soon as boiling point is reached.

CANNED SOUPS

Cans should be emptied either in to a tureen or individual

bowls. If of the condensed variety stir in an equal quantity of water. Three-quarters cover with cling film. Microwave on High, stirring once during and once after reheating. The contents of a 295 g (10.4 fl oz) can take 2-3 minutes.

PACKET SOUPS

These soups should be reconstituted according to the manufacturers' instructions. Microwave on High for 5-7 minutes until boiling.

If you have a clearish soup containing flecks of vegetables or meat allow at least 10 minutes, otherwise you will find that you have a hot soup with hard or chewy pieces of dry ingredients.

GARNISHES

Garnishes should be added to soups to improve the appearance, taste and texture. This is especially important if you are entertaining. Here are just a few speedy ideas.

Cut matchstick lengths of carrots or celery. Put in a small dish with a little water, cover and microwave for 1-2 minutes until just tender.

Save some mince mixture when making another dish, season well and make into pea-sized balls. Space out well on a covered plate and microwave on High for 30 seconds to 1 minute. Drain before adding to the soup.

To make croûtons quickly in the microwave oven, remove crusts and dice slices of bread. Melt butter in a dish – using more than you think necessary. Stir in the bread cubes and without covering, microwave for 2-3 minutes on High, stirring once or twice during cooking. Drain on kitchen paper and sprinkle on the soup.

To make puff balls, pipe tiny dots of choux paste on to a double sheet of non-stick paper and microwave on High until they are risen and set hard. Rotate the paper every minute. A 40 g (1½ oz) flour quantity makes 50 and takes 6-7 minutes on High.

Brown sliced apple in butter in the browning dish and use as a garnish for celery soup.

Thick fish soups look appetizing when decorated with whole prawns, and thin chicken broth is enhanced with thin strips of pancake. Pour lightly frothed egg through a sieve on to boiling beef broth and it will set in white spaghetti-like strands. If you are in a hurry, garnish soups with salted potato straws ('chipples'), watercress leaves or good old parsley which adds vitamins.

FREEZING AND REHEATING

Most soups will freeze successfully. Freeze without garnishes, adding these when reheating or serving. If you decide to freeze in the serving bowls only two-thirds fill them, as otherwise the soup will boil over during reheating.

Soups are slow to reheat so for maximum speed three-quarters cover with cling film, leaving a 2.5 cm (1 in) or so gap for stirring. Do not be misled when boiling begins around the edges as the centre may still be cool. Stir to equalize the heat before testing, when the underside of the bowl should feel very hot. Always microwave on High unless the soup is very thick. A single serving will take 2-3 minutes and a 4-portion quantity 4-6 minutes. Very thick soups should be heated on Low for about 10-12 minutes for a 4-portion quantity as these tend to form large bubbles which burst and splatter.

To speed thawing, remove frozen blocks of soup from the freezer a few hours in advance of serving. Stir before reheating to avoid spurting.

PULSES

Pulses include broad beans, kidney beans, chick peas, split peas and lentils among others. Because these beans are dry they require plenty of water to soften them. Cooking is slow and it is important that pulses are cooked thoroughly. Kidney beans in particular can be poisonous if under-cooked and require intense heat as well as long slow cooking.

Split peas and lentils can be cooked in the microwave oven and are better if they have been previously soaked. Pre-soaking will reduce the cooking time by half.

The larger the bean the longer will be the cooking period – perhaps 35-45 minutes – and the container must be deep enough to allow for boiling over. To lessen this risk you can start to microwave on High, reducing to Low halfway through cooking, stirring frequently.

Lentils are the only pulse that can be cooked in the microwave oven without pre-soaking. After rinsing, stir in plenty of hot water and microwave uncovered for 20 minutes on High or 10 minutes on High, followed by 25 minutes on Low.

Cream of Avocado Soup

A special soup to serve to dinner guests. For extra smoothness whirl the finished soup in the liquidizer and reheat gently on Low for a minute or two.

    2 large ripe avocados
    2 teaspoons lemon juice
    25 g (1 oz) unsalted butter
    1 small onion, grated
    25 g (1 oz) flour
    900 ml (1½ pints) chicken stock
    ¼ teaspoon celery salt

Pepper
1 egg yolk
3 tablespoons double cream

Halve the avocados, remove the stones, scoop out the flesh
with a teaspoon and mash with the lemon juice.

Put the butter in a large ovenglass dish and microwave on
High for 30-60 seconds until melted.

Stir in the onion and microwave on High for 1-2 minutes
until soft but not coloured.

Mix in the flour and microwave on High for 30 seconds.

Gradually blend in the stock and microwave on High for
4-5 minutes, whisking frequently until the sauce thickens
slightly and is smooth and silky-looking.

Add the well-mashed avocados, season with celery salt and
pepper and microwave on High for 2-3 minutes, whisking
from time to time.

Blend the egg yolk and cream thoroughly in a medium
bowl.

Stir in one ladleful of the soup.

Pour the mixture back into the soup and microwave on
Low for 2-3 minutes, but do not allow to boil.

Serves 4

Variations

For asparagus soup, liquidize a can of undrained
asparagus tips and substitute for the avocados and lemon
juice. Reduce the stock by 150 ml (¼ pint). For cucumber
soup, omit the lemon juice and substitute a peeled, sliced
and liquidized cucumber for the avocados.

Cream of Mushroom Soup

Blend in the liquidizer after cooking if you prefer a creamy
soup.

25 g (1 oz) butter
25 g (1 oz) flour
600 ml (1 pint) chicken stock
300 ml (½ pint) milk
Salt
Pepper
100 g (4 oz) mushrooms, finely sliced
2 tablespoons freshly chopped parsley
1 tablespoon fresh lemon juice

Put the butter in a large ovenglass bowl and microwave on High for 40-60 seconds or until melted.

Stir in the flour and microwave on High for 30 seconds.

Stir in the stock and microwave on High for 3-3½ minutes until the sauce thickens.

After the first minute as soon as the stock is warm, the mixture should be whisked every ½ minute during cooking.

Stir in the milk and season to taste with salt and pepper.

Add the mushrooms and parsley.

Half cover with cling film and microwave on High for 5-6 minutes, stirring occasionally until the mushrooms are *al dente*.

Stir in the lemon juice just before serving.

Serves 4

Variations

Use 1 tablespoon of chopped chives instead of the parsley, omit the lemon juice and stir in 2 tablespoons of double cream just before serving.

French Onion Soup

450 g (1 lb) onions, thinly sliced or chopped.
50 g (2 oz) butter
7 g (¼ oz) flour

900 ml (1½ pints) beef stock
150 ml (¼ pint) red wine
1 teaspoon Worcestershire sauce
Salt
Pepper
4 slices French bread
750 g (3 oz) Cheddar cheese, grated

Put the onions and butter in a large ovenglass bowl and cook for 10-12 minutes, stirring occasionally until the onions begin to brown.

Stir in the flour, then add the stock, wine and Worcestershire sauce.

Season to taste with salt and pepper. Microwave on High for 10-15 minutes until the soup begins to thicken. Stir occasionally during cooking.

Towards the end of the cooking period prepare the bread.

Toast the bread on one side and sprinkle the untoasted side with cheese. Cook under the grill until melted. Float a slice of cheesy toast on each portion of soup and sprinkle with a little extra cheese if you have it to hand.

French onion soup greatly improves if stored in the refrigerator for 24 hours before reheating. The toast must be made at the last minute. If you like a thicker soup increase the flour to 15 g (½ oz) and, for those who like a darker soup, enrich the stock with a crumbled Oxo cube.

Serves 4

Lentil Soup

Lentils are the best pulses to choose for microwave cooking because they can be cooked without prior soaking. Split peas are an alternative but need a minimum soak of 2 hours. Larger whole pulses must be soaked for at least 12 hours. When lentils have had no pre-soaking it is best to cook on Low. Lentil soup thickens on standing so more stock or water must be added when reheating.

100 g (4 oz) lentils, unsoaked but washed and drained
1 small onion, finely chopped
1 celery stalk, finely chopped
2 rashers lean bacon, derinded and chopped
20 g (¾ oz) butter
750 ml (1¼ pints) water or ham stock
1 tomato, chopped
1 teaspoon mixed dried herbs
Piece ham bone (optional)
Salt
Pepper

Combine the lentils, onion, celery, bacon and butter in a large ovenglass bowl. Microwave on High for 4-5 minutes, stirring occasionally. The lentils will still be crispy but the onions and celery will be soft.

Stir in the water or stock, tomato and mixed herbs, and add a piece of ham bone if you have it.

Microwave on High for 5-10 minutes until boiling rapidly.

Cover almost completely with cling film, leaving just a tiny gap for excessive steam to escape and microwave on Low for 45-50 minutes or until the lentils are tender.

Stir after the lentils have been cooking for 30 minutes, adding more boiling water if necessary.

Leave to stand for 10 minutes before removing the cling film and ham bone.

Purée the soup in the liquidizer or mash with a potato masher for a more textured soup.

Season to taste with salt (sparingly) and pepper.

Serves 4

Variations
Omit the bacon and ham for vegetarians and stir in 1 teaspoon yeast extract.

Garnish with croûtons (see page 142) or chopped salted peanuts.

Moorland Leek Soup

A chunky warming soup to serve piping hot on a wintry evening with chunks of wholemeal bread. The soup will be even better if refrigerated for 24 hours before reheating. You may find that it thickens during this standing time, so keep some extra stock to thin it if necessary.

20 g (¾ oz) butter
1 medium onion, chopped
350 g (¾ lb) leeks washed and thinly sliced
600 ml (1 pint) hot chicken stock
4 bay leaves
Salt
Pepper
1 level tablespoon flour
Croûtons (see page 142) for garnish

Put the butter in a large bowl and microwave on High for 30 seconds or until melted.

Stir in the onion and microwave on High for 2½-3½ minutes until soft but not brown.

Mix in the leeks and microwave on High for 5 minutes, stirring once or twice.

Add the stock, bay leaves, and salt and pepper to taste (use salt sparingly if the stock is made with a cube). Microwave on High for 10 minutes, stirring 2 or 3 times during cooking.

Blend the flour with 3 tablespoons of cold water, stir into the soup and microwave on High for 5-6 minutes, stirring occasionally until the leeks are tender.

Just before serving remove the bay leaves and adjust the seasoning.

Garnish with croûtons.
Serves 4-6

Variations
Season with celery salt and sprinkle cheese over the soup
when serving.

Shrimp and Corn Chowder

A substantial soup that is a meal on its own when served
with chunky rye bread or garnished with croûtons (see
page 142).

> 4 rashers unsmoked back bacon, derinded
> 1 small onion, very finely chopped
> 600 ml (1 pint) milk
> 1 × 295 g (10.4 oz) can creamed sweetcorn
> ½ teaspoon salt
> ¼ teaspoon pepper
> ¼ teaspoon paprika
> 100 g (4 oz) small peeled shrimps

Cut off the surplus bacon fat in strips. Chop the lean
bacon finely and mix with the onion.
Put the bacon fat in a shallow dish and microwave on High
for one minute or until sizzling.
Stir the bacon and onion and microwave on High for 2½-
3½ minutes until the bacon is tender and the onion soft.
Remove the strips of solid bacon fat and drain away all the
melted fat, leaving only the chopped mixture in the dish.
Stir in the milk, creamed corn and seasonings.
Microwave on High for 6-8 minutes until the soup is very
hot but not boiling.
Stir in the shrimps, then cover and leave for 3-4 minutes
before serving.
Serves 4

Variations

Add or substitute any cooked fish or shellfish and use half milk and half fish stock.

Spinach and Lemon Soup

Buy fresh spinach and cook it effortlessly in the microwave oven. Frozen spinach should be thawed before use in this recipe. You will require 225 g (8 oz).

    450 g (1 lb) fresh spinach or 225 g (8 oz) frozen spinach,
        thawed
    2 chicken stock cubes (omit if you are using fresh
        chicken stock)
    Boiling water or home-made chicken stock
    ¼ teaspoon freshly grated nutmeg
    25 g (1 oz) butter
    1 small onion, finely chopped
    20 g (¾ oz) flour
    600 ml (1 pint) milk
    Salt
    Pepper
    1 lemon, thinly sliced

Trim the stems from the washed leaves (if you use fresh spinach), put them in a large roasting bag and fold the top of the bag over or lightly tie with a piece of string, leaving a hole for steam to escape. Microwave on High for 5 minutes.

Strain the spinach liquid into a measuring jug and crumble in the stock cubes. Stir until dissolved.

Add boiling water or stock to make up to 600 ml (1 pint).

Put the butter in a large bowl and microwave on High for 30-60 seconds until melted.

Stir in the onion and microwave on High for 2-3 minutes until the onion browns slightly.

Stir in the flour, then mix in the milk. Microwave on High for 3 minutes, stirring occasionally.

Chop the spinach finely.

Add the stock and spinach to the milk mixture and stir briskly so that any flour remaining in the bottom of the bowl is mixed in.

Microwave on High for 4-5 minutes or until the soup boils. Beat thoroughly. Add the nutmeg and salt and pepper to taste and microwave on Medium for 10 minutes or on Low for 15 minutes, stirring frequently. Remove from the oven.

Slice the lemon thinly, discarding the top and bottom.

Spread the slices over a large plate, cover with cling film and microwave on High for 1-1½ minutes or until the juice runs out.

Carefully remove the cling film, mix the juice into the soup and float the lemon slices on top.

Makes 1.2 litres (2 pints)

Tomato Soup

A pleasant tomato soup can be made using a thick white sauce (see page 184) to which has been added a large can of tomatoes and a teaspoon of basil and a beef stock cube. For the finest flavour, it is best to sauté the onions before adding the tomatoes. Ripe fresh tomatoes have quite a different flavour from the canned variety.

    50 g (2 oz) butter
    2 medium onions, finely chopped
    50 g (2 oz) flour
    900 ml – 1 litre (1 × 1½-1¾ pints) hot chicken stock
    1 kg (2 lb) tomatoes
    2 tablespoons tomato purée
    1 teaspoon Worcestershire sauce
    2 thin strips lemon rind

2 or 3 sprigs parsley
¼ teaspoon bay leaf powder
½ teaspoon sugar
Salt
Pepper
4-6 tablespoons double cream

Combine the butter and onions in a large ovenglass bowl and microwave on High for 4-7 minutes or until the onions are just beginning to brown. Stir occasionally during cooking to be sure of even colouring.

Stir in the flour and microwave on High for 1 minute.

Carefully stir in 600 ml (1 pint) of the stock and microwave on High for 3-6 minutes, depending on the starting temperature of the stock, until a thickish sauce is formed. Whisk frequently to prevent floury lumps forming.

Add the tomatoes, tomato purée, Worcestershire sauce, lemon rind, parsley, bay leaf powder, and sugar and salt and pepper to taste.

Three-quarters cover and microwave on High for 10-12 minutes, stirring occasionally until the tomatoes are soft and the soup flavours well blended.

Purée in the liquidizer (you may have to do this in two or three batches) and press through a sieve if you object to the skin and pips.

Pour back into the cooking bowl and add as much stock as is necessary to thin the soup. Microwave on High for 3-4 minutes or until boiling. Stir occasionally to equalize the heat.

Adjust the seasoning and stir a spoonful of cream into each bowl.

Serves 4 to 6

Variations
Add crushed garlic to the onions.

Substitute 150 ml (¼ pint) red wine for an equal measure of stock.
Add the juice of one orange.
Stir in 2 tablespoons cooked rice.

Croûtons

Microwaved croûtons keep very well either in a plastic box in the refrigerator or in the freezer. Preferably use olive oil which is denser and heavier rather than corn or sunflower oil.

   3 slices thin-cut bread
   5 tablespoons olive oil
   1 generous teaspoon sweet paprika

Remove the crusts and cut each slice of bread into 16 squares.
Blend the oil and paprika in a shallow dish and microwave on High for 2 minutes to warm the oil.
Add the bread and toss with a fish slice to coat both sides.
Microwave on High for 3-4 minutes, stirring frequently until the croûtons are golden brown.
Makes 48 croûtons

Variations

Use wholemeal or rye bread but do not over-cook as it is difficult to judge the change of colour.
Add onion salt or lazy garlic powder to the oil.

6
Vegetables

Bright, no-fade vegetables are yours when you cook them by microwave. They have crisp textures, more vitamins, a better taste and a brighter colour. Microwaved vegetables are so good that they can even be reheated without deteriorating provided that they were in prime condition in the first place.

BUYING

When buying fresh vegetables look for bright clear colour and crispness. Don't buy green-leafed vegetables which have floppy brown edges, or courgettes that have soft patches for they will be bitter. Green-tinged potatoes are not good for the stomach and soft ones are unpleasantly squidgy when cooked. Carrots should snap, not bend, and parsnips, which are a superb micro-vegetable, should be white with a firm, non-puffy skin. Cucumbers are tastiest when narrow-ridged and hard, but if only needed for soups, any are acceptable provided you cut out the bad parts. Shiny-skinned vegetables, such as aubergines and green and red peppers, are not worth having if they are wrinkled, and if you detect any small black hole these indicate that the inside could be even blacker and be going off. Examine the stalks of onions and squeeze a radish or two before purchasing large ones – neither should be soft. Tomatoes are often sold in boxes in a mixture of shades. This is to enable you to use the ripe red ones first, leaving those with green tinges near the kitchen window to finish ripening. Soft tomatoes are better for cooking, unless they have white mouldy spots, and it is silly to buy fresh firm tomatoes for soups and stews, but very important if you are going to stuff them.

Frozen vegetables cook very well except cauliflower florets (unless you want them for soups, purées, curries or to be heavily coated in sauce) as they are a little tasteless and soft when cooked by microwave.

BLANCHING

Blanching vegetables prior to freezing is very successfully carried out in small quantities in the microwave oven. Put a maximum of 450 g (1 lb) prepared vegetables in a covered casserole with 4-5 tablespoons of water. You may find that there is enough left in the vegetables after rinsing. Do not add salt. Microwave on High for 2 minutes, stir and continue to microwave on High for 1-2 more minutes until the vegetables are hot throughout but not cooked. Immediately drain and plunge into ice-cold water (put in a few ice cubes) to prevent any further cooking and drain thoroughly before packing.

COOKING FROZEN VEGETABLES

All frozen vegetables should be cooked on High.

Peas, green beans and corn kernels: These and similarly sized vegetables are cooked in much the same way. Put them into a dish and add sufficient water to make the bottom layers swim. Make a well and add half a teaspoon of salt and stir into the surrounding water. Cover the dish loosely with cling film and microwave on High for 5-7 minutes. Leave for a minute or two before carefully peeling away the cling film, then drain.

Mushrooms: These contain a very high proportion of water. If you require a complete frozen pack for frying conventionally, slit the packet on the top surface and microwave on High for 3-4 minutes to take off the chill, then there will be less spluttering. If just a few are required, put them on a plate lined with kitchen paper and microwave for about one minute. For use in microwave cookery use straight from the packet. Frozen mushrooms create a considerable amount of liquid, so for omelettes, microwaved or otherwise, put the mushrooms in a dish, cover loosely with cling film and microwave for 2-3 minutes until soft. Strain the liquid and reserve for use in sauces.

Whole frozen corn on the cob: Put them in a dish in a single layer and dot with butter. Cover with greaseproof paper and microwave on High, turning over the cobs and repositioning halfway through the cooking.

> 1 ear takes   4-6 minutes
> 2 ears take   6-8 minutes
> 3 ears take 8-10 minutes
> 4 ears take 10-12 minutes

Brussels sprouts, shredded cabbage and baby carrots; Put into a deepish dish with half a cup of salted water. Cover with a lid or greaseproof paper and stir twice during cooking. Allow 13-15 minutes per 450 g (1 lb).

Broccoli spears and asparagus tips: Arrange in a shallow dish with the stems towards the outside. Add about one-third of a cup of salted water and cover with greaseproof paper. Turn the dish halfway through cooking and check to make sure that the tips and flowers are not too soft. Uncover and drain immediately. Allow 12-14 minutes per 450 g (1 lb).

Frozen spinach: Spinach may be leaf, chopped or in pellets. Frozen blocks should be placed ice-side up in the dish so that this part receives the full force of the microwaves. Ice is very microwave resistant so the heat generated inside will rise to assist thawing. Break up the block two or three times during cooking. Do not add water. Salt afterwards. Spinach pellets should be covered with cling film and the dish shaken occasionally. Allow about 12 minutes per 450 g (1 lb).

Small quantities of frozen vegetables can be left in their packets. Split the top and put the bag on a piece of kitchen paper to prevent the print from staining the oven shelf. Large quantities, however, should *not* be cooked in the pack as the centre will still be cold while the outside portions are over-cooked. It is virtually impossible to shake a limp hot bag.

COOKING FRESH VEGETABLES

Prepare fresh vegetables in the usual way. Cooking by microwave requires very little extra attention. With the exception of boiled potatoes and carrots cook fresh vegetables securely covered, so that trapped steam will hasten cooking and add only as much liquid as is essential. Valuable vitamins seep into the cooking water but there will be less loss because of the speed of cooking. Save what little liquid is left and use for sauces or soups. This must be kept under refrigeration and boiled up again before using.

Vegetables with skins: Vegetables enclosed in their skins, such as large potatoes, tomatoes etc., must be thoroughly pricked or the enormous steam built up inside will burst the vegetables and you will find particles splattered all over the oven. Peppers are usually sliced or cored and stuffed, so pricking will not often be necessary.

Root vegetables: Root vegetables are best when the pieces are of uniform size, as larger pieces mixed with the small will cook more slowly. Three-quarters cover with cling film or use a loose fitting lid.

A food processor produces beautifully even slices and it is evenness and not size that matters most.

Stalked vegetables: Arrange stalked vegetables, such as broccoli and asparagus, so that the stalks are towards the outside of the dish. Cauliflower, when cooked whole, must be turned upside down halfway through the cooking period.

Dishes should be rotated and vegetable pieces turned or stirred for best results, but I must admit that I do not always bother.

There is a carry-over when cooking vegetables so please remember to slightly under-cook, or cool under cold running water, then drain before returning to the dish to await reheating.

Asparagus: Remove the thick white stalk and scrape thicker stems. Place in two layers, each facing the opposite way in an oval dish. Add quarter of a cup of water. Cover and microwave on High for 8 minutes per 450 g (1 lb), rotating the dish four times during cooking.

Globe artichokes: Globe artichokes should be washed and trimmed in the usual way. Arrange in a dish containing half a cup of salted water. Cover loosely with cling film and microwave on High. Reverse to drain before serving.

> 1 artichoke takes 5-6 minutes
> 2 artichokes take 7-8 minutes
> 4 artichokes take 14-15 minutes

Green beans, celery and beetroot: Green beans and celery (both cut or whole) and unskinned beetroot should be put in a dish with half a cup of salted water. Cover with a lid and microwave on High for 14-16 minutes per 450 g (1 lb), stirring occasionally.

Parsnips: Put in a dish with a cup of salted water. Add a knob of butter and a tablespoon of lemon juice. Cover loosely with a lid or three-quarters cover with cling film, microwave on High for 12-16 minutes per 450 g (1 lb), stirring occasionally.

Broccoli, cabbage, carrots, cauliflower florets (cut or whole) and peas: Put in a dish with half a cup of salted water. Cover completely and microwave on High for 10-12 minutes per 450 g (1 lb), stirring occasionally.

Onions and leeks (sliced): Put in a dish with quarter of a cup of salted water. Cover and microwave on High for 10-12 minutes per 450 g (1 lb), stirring once.

Chicory and corn cobs: Place in a shallow dish with quarter of a cup of water (unsalted) and microwave on High for 5-8 minutes for 4 pieces of chicory or 2 corn cobs.

Aubergines (halved, sliced or cubed): Sprinkle liberally with salt (dégorgé). Leave for at least half an hour and you will find that they weep large brown tears so removing the bitterness. Rinse well and pack tightly into a well-fitting shallow dish. Add 2 tablespoons water, cover tightly and microwave on High for 7-9 minutes per 450 g (1 lb) (2 medium aubergines). Stir or turn the dish once during the cooking period. Aubergines may also be cooked in a pre-heated browning dish in melted butter. Start with the cut side down and microwave on High for 3-4 minutes before reversing. Cover with a lid for the remaining time.

Courgettes and marrow: The former can be cooked whole but marrow is better sliced.

In fact, whole small courgettes look so much more attractive on the dinner plate than when sliced and only the microwave can cook them this way without them shrivelling.

Top and tail the courgettes and score twice along the skin with a sharp knife. Arrange in a dish with the larger vegetables outside. Season with grated nutmeg (optional). Cover loosely with cling film and microwave on High for 20 seconds per courgette. Carefully peel back the cling film and reposition the courgettes so that the smaller ones are on the outside.

Without covering, microwave on High for a further 20 seconds per courgette. Press the skins lightly to test, the courgettes being ready to serve when there is still slight resistance. Cooking continues for 3-4 minutes after removal from the oven and soft courgettes are less pleasant. There is little point in reheating courgettes since they cook so quickly. Large courgettes make an appetizing buffet item or dressed vegetable or vegetarian meal.

Dot sliced marrow with butter, cover with cling film and microwave on High for 7-10 minutes per 450 g (1 lb).

Tomatoes: Take care with tomatoes as they quickly collapse. It is best to halve firm tomatoes and microwave skin-side down on Low. Watch very carefully if on High and reposition the tomatoes or rotate the dish frequently.

Potatoes: To boil, add plenty of salted water – almost as much as you would in a saucepan – and partially cover. Potato water froths up and forces itself out of the dish. It is only worthwhile boiling small quantities in the microwave oven as larger amounts will be just as quickly cooked in a saucepan.

Par-boiling by microwave is a good method of pre-cooking before transferring to the conventional oven or frying pan. Peel, cut up and cook in a roasting bag, folding the top of the bag loosely underneath. Do not bother with a dish as leakage will be minimal. Allow about 4 minutes for 450 g (1 lb) potatoes but test with a fork.

If you want to bake potatoes in their jackets, choose large, evenly shaped potatoes. Prick thoroughly and cook on a double sheet of kitchen paper directly on the oven shelf. Turn the potatoes over once during cooking and rotate or reposition four times. You may find it more convenient to use a roasting rack instead of paper if several potatoes are cooked simultaneously as then rotating will be easier. Potatoes are ready when there is some 'give' but do not microwave until completely soft as, during the carry-over or standing time, the potatoes will over-cook and become dry and spongy inside.

> 2 potatoes on High will take   6-8 minutes
> 3 potatoes on High will take   9-10 minutes
> 4 potatoes on High will take 11-12 minutes
> 5 potatoes on High will take 13-14 minutes
> 6 potatoes on High will take 15-16 minutes
> 8 potatoes on High will take 21-23 minutes

Eight is the maximum that you will be able to get in the oven at any one time.

Do not wrap in foil to keep in the heat as condensation will soften the skins. For added crispness, brown the potatoes under the grill.

If you are cooking several potatoes or batch-baking for a party, heat the conventional oven to 220°C (425°F/Gas 7). Half microwave the potatoes (see chart) and finish in a hot oven as each batch is ready. It is difficult to recommend a cooking time but one average 200 g (7 oz) potato will bake in about 4 minutes on High.

Green, yellow or red peppers: Peppers are usually stuffed and if a ready-cooked filling is to be used, and the peppers eaten cold, the peppers should first be blanched. Blanching is not necessary if the filling and peppers are to be cooked or reheated together. After coring and deseeding, arrange the peppers in a dish containing a tablespoon of water. Cover and microwave on High for 2-3 minutes re-positioning twice during cooking.

Spinach: Spinach has a very high water content so that it needs no additional liquid in cooking. Trim away the coarse fibrous stems and pack the spinach into a roasting bag. Fold the open end loosely underneath and cook directly on a lipped shelf or otherwise in a dish – as there may be some seepage. Microwave on High for 3-4 minutes by which time the spinach will have reduced to a small bundle about one-eighth the original volume. Very carefully drain through a corner of the bag (you can snip a hole in the bottom and let the water drain through), then turn out, chop and season.

Swedes and turnips: These are most unpredictable vegetables and so I can only give guide-lines for cooking times. Cut into even sized pieces and stir two or three times during cooking. Cover as tightly as you can. Cling film is not suitable as the liquid may boil over, forcing the film to balloon and burst. Cook in about a teacup of salted water to which you have added a teaspoon of lemon juice and microwave on High for 10-15 minutes depending on the quantity, type and age of the vegetable.

Onions: Onions require only 4 tablespoons of salted water, and juicy Spanish onions can be cooked without any at all. Cover loosely with cling film, turn over halfway through cooking and finish without covering. Four medium onions will take 10-12 minutes on High. Small onions do not need to be turned over and should be cooked covered, allowing about 1½ minutes per onion.

CANNED VEGETABLES

Generally these require reheating only. Drain well so that unnecessary time is not wasted in heating up the liquid. Put into a serving dish, cover, and stir or shake four times during reheating. An average canful takes 2-3 minutes. The ever popular baked beans will pop because of heat build-up in their skins and any sauce spreading to the edges of the plate will dry up. It is, therefore, important to cover them when reheating and also to stir frequently. An upturned lipped cereal bowl, or better still, a large undecorated cup is convenient as it is easier to grasp a handle than a plain round bowl.

Bacon-flavoured Fresh Spinach

> 2-3 rashers bacon
> 0.5-0.75 kg (1-1½ lb) fresh spinach
> Knob butter
> Salt
> Freshly ground black pepper

Put the bacon on a plate, cover with kitchen paper and microwave on High for 1 minute or until just cooked. Do not overcook the bacon or it will become tinny.
Remove the rind and any bone and chop the bacon.
Wash the spinach, shake off surplus water and trim away the fibrous stems.
Put the spinach and bacon in a roaster bag, fold the top loosely underneath and microwave on High for 7 minutes until the volume is reduced and the spinach is tender. If your oven is not fitted with a lipped shelf put the roaster bag on a plate – this will slow cooking by about 45 seconds. Remove the bag carefully so that the cooking juices do not pour out into the oven.
Drain. To drain, tip through a colander or, protecting

your hands with an oven glove, make a slit in the bottom
of the bag.
Chop up the spinach if desired and mix in the butter, salt
and pepper to taste.
Serves 4

Variations
Microwave a tablespoon of chopped onions in a little
butter and add to the spinach. Mix in chopped hard-
cooked egg just before serving. Put the cooked spinach in a
shallow dish, make two wells and break an egg into the
middle, cover with cling film, and microwave on High for
1-2 minutes until the eggs are set. *Voilà* – Oeufs Florentine.

Carmel Aubergine Supper

The joy of the microwave oven is that aubergines do not
always have to be 'dégorgé' (pre-salted and left for the
bitter juices to drain away).

    2 × 250 g (10 oz) aubergines
    15 g (½ oz) butter
    1 medium onion, finely chopped
    1 clove garlic, crushed
    1 tablespoon freshly chopped parsley
    ½ level teaspoon marjoram leaves
    450 g (1 lb) ripe tomatoes, skinned and chopped
    1 tablespoon tomato purée
    Salt
    Pepper
    100 g (4 oz) Cheddar cheese, grated
    1 × 198 g (7 oz) can tuna fish, drained

Remove the stalks and cut the aubergines in half lengthwise.
Arrange cut-side up in a single layer in a flame-proof
shallow dish that fits snugly.

Add 2 tablespoons water. Cover with cling film and micro-wave on High for 7-9 minutes or until the flesh is tender.

Drain the aubergine, then, using a grapefruit knife scoop out the inside flesh leaving a 5 mm (¼ in) wall and the skin intact. It is better to do this in the dish as the skins are very soft.

Put the butter into a large dish. Add the onion, garlic, parsley and marjoram and microwave on High for 3-4 minutes until the onion is just beginning to brown.

Stir in the tomatoes and tomato purée, and season to taste with salt and pepper.

Chop and add the aubergine flesh and add the mixture with one-quarter of the cheese. Microwave on High for 5-7 minutes, stirring occasionally until cooked.

Mix in the flaked tuna fish.

Pile the mixture into the aubergine skins and microwave on High for 2 minutes to reheat.

Sprinkle with the remaining cheese and brown under the grill.

Serves 4

Variations

Add browned minced beef instead of the tuna. Omit the garlic. Add breadcrumbs if you prefer a sturdier stuffing. Omit the cheese and top with finely chopped hard-boiled egg. Top with scrambled egg and do not brown. To prepare aubergines for conventional fritters simply slice thickly and cut into quarters. Put into a dish and, without covering, microwave on High for 3-4 minutes by which time the flesh will be soft and the juices can be poured away. Dip the pieces in a thick seasoned paste of Indian gram flour and deep fry.

Carrot Barrels

For special occasion dinner party garnish buy large

carrots, cut off the top and sides and make an oblong, cut each oblong into 4, then shape like little barrels using a sharp knife.

450 g (1 lb) firm even-shaped carrots
Salt
1 teaspoon sugar
Knob butter
1 orange, segmented
Orange slices for garnish

Put the carrots into a deep casserole dish containing sufficient salted water to cover.
Add the sugar, butter and orange segments.
Cover loosely with cling film and microwave on High for 10-12 minutes or until nearly cooked, stirring halfway through cooking.
Replace the cling film with a lid and leave to stand for 5 minutes to finish cooking. Drain and serve garnished with the remaining orange slices.
Serves 4

Denali Carrot Salad

450 g (1 lb) carrots
½ teaspoon salt
1 clove garlic
¼ teaspoon paprika
¼ teaspoon ground cumin
¼ teaspoon ground coriander
⅛ teaspoon Cayenne pepper
2 tablespoons freshly chopped parsley
1 teaspoon vegetable oil
2-3 tablespoons fresh lemon juice

Peel the carrots and cut into long strips about the diameter of a child's paintbrush. Put into a deep dish and add 8 to 10 tablespoons water, salt and the garlic clove, whole.

Cover with cling film and microwave on High for 6-8 minutes until only just cooked.

Pour into a colander and rinse in cold running water. Drain well.

Remove the garlic clove.

Mix the remaining ingredients together. Pour over the carrots and toss well.

Chill for at least one hour before serving.

Serves 4

Corn and Ham Courgettes

2 large courgettes
20 g (¾ oz) cornflour
150 ml (¼ pint) milk
1 × 150 g (5 oz) can sweetcorn kernels, drained
50 g (2 oz) ham, chopped
Salt
Pepper
25 g (1 oz) Cheddar cheese, grated

Halve two large courgettes and carefully scoop out the flesh, leaving the skin intact. Chop the flesh finely.

In a medium bowl mix the cornflour with a little of the milk, then add in the remainder, stirring so that no deposit remains on the bottom of the bowl.

Microwave on High for 1-1½ minutes or until thickened, beating every 30 seconds.

Mix the sweetcorn, ham and courgette pulp into the thickened milk and season with salt and pepper to taste.

Fill the courgette cases with the mixture and cover with grated cheese.

Microwave on High for 3 minutes, giving the dish a half-turn after 1½ minutes.

Transfer to a flameproof serving dish and brown under the grill.

Serves 2 as a starter or 4 as a main vegetable.

Variations

For vegetarians omit the ham. Add chopped pimiento.

Lyonnaise Potatoes

1 medium onion, finely chopped
20 g (¾ oz) butter
4 tablespoons double cream
450 g (1 lb) potatoes, peeled and sliced 5 mm (¼ in) thick
Salt
Pepper

Combine the onion and butter in a large shallow dish and microwave on High for 2½-3 minutes until the onion is soft.

Stir in the cream and add the potatoes, seasoning well, then toss so that all the slices are coated with the buttery mixture.

Cover with cling film and microwave on High for 10-12 minutes until the potatoes are tender. Give the dish a quarter-turn every 3 minutes during the cooking period.

Test the potatoes by pressing through the cling film cover and if they are not quite ready, leave to stand before removing the cover.

Remove the cling film and brown the potatoes under the grill.

Serves 3 to 4

Pommes Parisiennes

I only make these for special occasions because it takes so long to carve out the balls. Once you are ready to cook the microwave oven will do the rest. Use up the potato scraps in Lyonnaise potatoes (see page 157). Pommes Parisiennes are generally used as a garnish for meat, poultry or fish dishes, but are equally appetizing served as a main vegetable.

> 450 g (1 lb) large potatoes, peeled
> 1 tablespoon flour
> 1 teaspoon salt
> 1 teaspoon paprika
> 50 g (2 oz) butter

Cut out as many even-shaped marble-sized pieces of potato as you can, preferably using a potato baller, but a teaspoon will do. Shake in a clean tea-cloth to remove excess moisture, then toss the potato balls in the mixture of the flour, salt and paprika.

Pre-heat a large browning dish to maximum, adding the butter during the last minute. Quickly toss in the potatoes, stir once to coat evenly with the browning butter and microwave on High for 4-6 minutes until the potatoes are tender. Stir the potatoes sides to middle halfway through.

The dish may be covered to speed the cooking after 2 minutes, but the potatoes will not then be crisp.

Remove with a slotted spoon.

Serves 4

Stir-fried Vegetables

Use an ordinary dish or pre-heated browning dish – both are good for stir-fried vegetables. Microwave on High and allow 6-7 minutes for 450 g (1 lb) vegetables.

25 g (1 oz) butter
1 small onion, chopped
2 medium green peppers, thinly sliced
2 medium red peppers, thinly sliced
1 tablespoon soy sauce
1 tablespoon sherry
½ teaspoon cornflour
¼ teaspoon ground ginger
Salt
Pepper

Put the butter in a large shallow dish and microwave on High for 1-1½ minutes until well and truly melted and just sizzling.
Stir in the onion and microwave on High for 1-2 minutes.
Stir in the peppers and microwave on High for 4-5 minutes, stirring occasionally.
Blend the soy sauce, sherry, cornflour and ground ginger together, adding a shake of salt and pepper.
Stir into the vegetables and microwave on High for 1½-2½ minutes, stirring once during cooking.
Serve as a vegetable or on a bed of rice for a main course.
Serves 3 to 4

Variations

Substitute or add cauliflower florets, firm quartered tomatoes, cut green beans, whole button mushrooms, bean sprouts, canned bamboo shoots, halved walnuts, cashew nuts, sliced courgettes, aubergines or young leeks.

Stuffed Peppers

Red, green and yellow peppers are often available in the shops at the same time so that you can easily produce a platter of multi-coloured stuffed peppers. Use a sweet stuffing with the red or yellow and a savoury with the green or yellow. Short, fat, flat-bottomed peppers are best for stuffing. I prefer to use a rice stuffing but substitute breadcrumbs for the rice if you wish.

Red, green or yellow peppers
25 g (1 oz) savoury or fruity rice stuffing per pepper
  (see pages 175-6)

Remove the tops from the peppers and set aside for garnish. Scoop out the seeds and pith to leave a clear cavity. Pile the stuffing into the peppers but do not press down too firmly. Arrange the stuffed peppers in a circle in a shallow dish and pile the reserved tops in the centre.

Pour about 150 ml (¼ pint) warm water into the dish which should be just enough to create the steam needed to soften the peppers (the stuffing only requires reheating).

Cover with cling film and microwave on High for 2½-4 minutes per pepper. About three-quarters through the cooking period remove the cling film, give each pepper a half-turn and remove and drain the pepper lids which will be cooked sufficiently by this time.

Drain the peppers on kitchen paper, cover with their lids and serve hot.

Serve with a sauce if desired, choosing a suitable blend such as brown or tomato sauce with the savoury and a lemon sauce with the sweet peppers.

7

Pasta

Pasta is a cereal produced from wheat which is mixed into a paste – hence the name – with water. The paste is then rolled out and cut to a variety of shapes. The protein content is in fact higher than in potatoes or ordinary bread and it forms the basis of many a cheap nutritious meal.

There are at least three dozen different shapes but the most common are:-

Vermicelli – long thin and round, often dropped into soup.
Macaroni or *elbow macaroni* – tubular and broken into small pieces.
Spaghetti – the favourite – long, thin and solid.
Cannelloni – comes in flat squares that you can stuff for yourself or tubes of 2½ cm (1 in) diameter.
Tagliatelle – flat or ribbon-shaped noodles.
Ravioli – small stuffed squares.
Lasagne – flat sheets sometimes plain and sometimes coloured with spinach (there is a partially cooked lasagne closely resembling the regular kind which requires no boiling at all).

Home-made pasta is softer than the packet kind and, if you do make it yourself, cut down the cooking times. Commercial pasta, regardless of type and variety, cooks at much the same speed in the microwave oven.

Half fill a large casserole with fast boiling water. Add a level teaspoon of salt and a teaspoon of vegetable oil. Microwave on High for a minute or two to bring the water back to a full rolling boil. You can either boil the water in the microwave oven (6-8 minutes on High) or use a kettle. I like to cook pasta in a deep 2.25 litre (4 pint) size dish when using the maximum quantity (225 g [8 oz]). On average, 100 g (4 oz) will require 600 ml (1 pint) water and 225 g (8 oz) 1 litre (1¾ pints). Add the pasta, broken into suitable lengths, if necessary. The pasta must be fully covered so have extra boiling water ready.

When cooking larger amounts stir in only half the pasta, then microwave on High for 1-1¼ minutes until the water comes back to the boil. Quickly add the remaining pasta and without covering microwave on High for 5-6 minutes stirring once during cooking. Cover tightly and leave to stand for 8-10 minutes to complete cooking. Drain.

It is particularly important when cooking spaghetti to discourage the strands from sticking together. Sheets of lasagne should be added to the casserole in two stages. Lower two or three pieces into the boiling water, microwave on High for 2 minutes to bring the water back to the boil, then add the remaining lasagne.

After this cooking time the pasta will still be on the hard side so cover with a lid and leave to stand for 10 minutes before draining.

Pasta may be par-cooked in advance if you wish. To be sure of well separated strands drain the cooked pasta in a colander and refresh under the cold tap. Replace in the rinsed container and just cover with cold water. When required, drain and reheat by microwave on High for 2-3 minutes, stirring once or twice.

Pasta can be quickly reheated from cold but will take almost as long to thaw as it would to cook fresh in the microwave oven. If you do freeze left-over pasta in a sauce and wish to reheat by microwave, it must be covered tightly and frequently stirred. I would suggest that you cook largish quantities of sauce in your microwave oven, which you can divide up and freeze separately. Thaw the sauce during the carry-over 10 minutes after the pasta is removed from the microwave oven. When freezing pasta make a well in the centre, so that it will thaw out evenly.

225 g (8 oz) is the maximum quantity of pasta that you can cook in the microwave oven at one time, so if you wish to cook a double quantity, start the second half during the carry-over cooking time. This can be a great advantage as your 'seconds' will be fresh, hot and uncongealed.

Spaghetti Bolognese

In this recipe the sauce is cooked in a browning dish. A simpler version can be found in the sauce chapter.

225 g (8 oz) spaghetti

Sauce
2 rashers streaky bacon, chopped
225 g (8 oz) lean minced beef
1 medium onion, finely chopped
1 clove garlic, crushed
450 ml (¾ pint) hot beef stock (an Oxo cube deepens the
    colour)
4 tablespoons tomato purée
50 g (2 oz) mushrooms, chopped
1 teaspoon dried oregano or frozen marjoram leaves
Salt
Pepper
2 level teaspoons cornflour
2 tablespoons red wine
Parmesan cheese

Pre-heat the browning dish to maximum, adding the butter for the last 30 seconds.
Quickly stir in the bacon, beef, onion and garlic (it will be easier if you have previously mixed these together).
Microwave on High for 5-6 minutes, breaking up the lumps and stirring after 2 minutes.

Stir in the stock, tomato purée, mushrooms, oregano and salt and pepper to taste.

Cover with the lid and microwave on High for 10-12 minutes, stirring occasionally. Taste and adjust the seasoning if necessary.

Blend the cornflour with the wine and stir into the sauce. Without covering microwave on High for 2 minutes, stirring once during cooking.

Cover and remove from the oven while cooking the spaghetti (see page 162).

If necessary reheat the sauce on High for a minute or two and stir before pouring over the hot spaghetti.

Sprinkle with grated Parmesan cheese and serve extra cheese separately.

Serves 3 to 4

Variations

Add chopped tomatoes, substitute diced green peppers sautéing them with meat in place of mushrooms. Use lamb or veal. Use tagliatelle or macaroni or thick ribbon noodles.

LASAGNE

Look closely at the packets, as there are now two types available – the regular and a pre-cooked kind. To cook the regular kind, use the usual pasta method but after adding each two leaves, pop the dish back into the oven and microwave on High until the water comes back to the boil, otherwise you may finish up with a solid pasta pudding. When using the pre-cooked lasagne add more liquid to your recipe.

Lasagne al Forno

The traditional recipe is a combination of a meat sauce, a

white sauce, lasagne (either green or white) and grated cheese. The dish is baked mainly for reheating reasons and to brown the top. When microwaving, reheating is a matter of seconds before adding a topping of grated cheese and browning under the grill.

175 g (6 oz) (8 leaves) green or white lasagne, cooked, drained and separated

Sauces
600 ml (1 pint) Béchamel sauce using 35 g (1¼ oz) butter, 35 g (1¼ oz) flour and 600 ml (1 pint) milk (see page 186)
450 ml (¾ pint) Bolognese sauce (see page 192)
100 g (4 oz) grated Cheddar or Parmesan cheese
2.25 litre (4 pint) greased oblong shallow fireproof dish, greased

First make the sauces and, if you are doing this ahead of time, add slightly more liquid as sauces thicken during storage.

Mix three-quarters of the cheese into the white sauce.

Cook the lasagne, putting an extra teaspoon of oil in the cooking water. Turn the pasta into a colander and pass under cold running water to separate the leaves.

To assemble, spread a layer of meat sauce in the base of the dish and cover with a single layer of pasta. Pour over a layer of white sauce and continue layering, finishing with the white sauce. Make sure that the pasta leaves are well inside the dish as any that protrude will overcook and become crispy.

To reheat, microwave on Medium for 8-10 minutes. If using a narrower dish with deeper layers of lasagne mixture, microwave on High for 5 minutes.

Cover with the remaining cheese and brown under the grill.

Serves 4

Variations

Use a tomato sauce and add chopped Mortadella sausage
or cooked fish, flaked.

For vegetarians, sauté chopped onion and celery in butter
and add well-drained cooked chopped spinach and 25 g
(1 oz) chopped cashew nuts to a little tomato sauce.

Macaroni Cheese

This very popular and cheap dish can be raised into the
'Fromage au Macaroni' class by adding extra ingredients.
Cut down the cooking time for easy-cook macaroni.

   100 g (4 oz) macaroni

Sauce

   40 g (1½ oz) butter

   25 g (1 oz) flour

   600 ml (1 pint) milk, or milk and macaroni water equally
     mixed

   ½ level teaspoon mustard powder

   175 g (6 oz) grated cheese – Cheddar or Cheddar and
     Parmesan mixed

   Salt

   Pepper

Cook the macaroni in the usual way (page 161) in lots of
boiling, salted and slightly oiled water, covering after
microwaving finishes.

Make a white sauce (page 179), mixing in the mustard
when adding the flour.

Mix the drained cooked pasta, sauce and two-thirds of the
cheese together with salt and pepper and any ingredients of
your choice.

Sprinkle the remaining cheese on top and brown under the
grill.

Garnish with parsley.

Serves 4

Variations

Substitute any fairly solid pasta, a Béchamel or tomato sauce. Add canned oysters, prawns, shrimps, chopped ham or cooked chicken, grated onion, or crushed garlic with chopped pimientos. Garnish with sliced tomatoes put on before browning, or croûtons (page 142) or pineapple rings.

Devilled Pasta Salad

There is no point in freezing the pasta for this dish. No microwave minutes will be lost as you can make the mayonnaise and mix the salad while the pasta finishes cooking. Choose small-sized pasta as it grows during cooking.

Salt
1 teaspoon vegetable oil
50 g (2 oz) small bow pasta or pasta shells

Sauce

2 tablespoons mango chutney
4 tablespoons mayonnaise
1 tablespoon sultanas
2 tablespoons single cream
1 stick celery, finely sliced
Small piece green pepper, diced
50 g (2 oz) button mushrooms, sliced

Half-fill a large casserole with boiling water, add salt and vegetable oil. Microwave on High for 30 seconds until the water is again rapidly boiling. Immediately stir in the pasta and, without covering, microwave on High for 5 minutes.
Remove from the oven, cover with a lid and set aside for 8-10 minutes until tender.
Turn into a colander and pass under running water until cold. Drain thoroughly.

While the pasta is cooking, mix remaining ingredients in a salad bowl.
Add the drained pasta and toss thoroughly.
Serves 2 to 3

Variations
Use wholemeal pasta and cook for 2 more minutes.
Add skinned and depipped small green grapes.
For less sweet palates, substitute Pan Yan or Branston pickle for the mango chutney.

8

Rice

Rice cooks, reheats and thaws perfectly in a microwave oven. There are no problems of boiling over, boiling dry or getting a crispy top during reheating. Nowadays more and more varieties are available, making it difficult to advise any one cooking method.

Long-grain rice includes the American type, which does not need rinsing before cooking, because it is grown in hygienic conditions with less risk of contamination. The rice from the paddy fields in the east may have the odd spot of grit and dirt and so needs rinsing thoroughly, but the slender grains remain well-separated long after cooking. Many varieties are partially treated so requiring less cooking, and there is also brown rice which, though darker than bleached rice, is not in fact brown, and wild rice which takes too long to cook in the microwave oven. Short-grain (Carolina) rice is usually used in stuffings and puddings.

Rice absorbs a large quantity of water and the amount is determined by the type and treatment of the grain. Amounts are indicated on the packet when the 1.2.1 or all-in-one method, in which the rice is ready when all the water is absorbed, is recommended. When using these proportions in the microwave oven it will probably be necessary to add a few extra tablespoons of water.

Long-grain rice: Put the rice in a large casserole, stir in the salt and water, cover with the lid and stir once during cooking. Inspect at the end of the cooking time and if the rice is swimming in water, spoon this away. For correct cooking, there should be a minimal amount of liquid. Replace the lid and leave to stand for 5 minutes before serving, when all the water is absorbed and the rice tender.

For every 25 g (1 oz) long-grain rice you will need approximately 75 ml ($\frac{1}{8}$ pint) hot water and ¼ teaspoon salt. The timings will depend more on how long the water takes to boil than on the quantity of rice involved.

50 g (2 oz) rice will take   6-8 minutes) plus
100 g (4 oz) rice will take 10-12 minutes } 5-8 minutes
225 g (8 oz) rice will take 15-18 minutes) standing time

Prefluffed rice, being partially cooked, will be even quicker.

I prefer to cook rice in the old-fashioned way (still using the microwave) in lots and lots of boiling salted water without covering. Microwave on High until tender, then pour through a colander (no, the grains won't all run away) and cool under cold running water. Stand the colander on the draining board or over a bowl and, using the handle of a wooden spoon, make several wells in the rice. Leave to drain thoroughly. Place as much as you need in a dish and reheat in the microwave on High for 2-3 minutes uncovered.

For every 25 g (1 oz) rice you will need approximately 150 ml (¼ pint) water and ½ teaspoon salt, but measuring is quite unnecessary. Use a large bowl or casserole and add water until you can no longer see the rice underneath. The rice will swell to three times its dry volume when cooked.

50 g (2 oz) rice will take   8-10 minutes) Rinse and
100 g (4 oz) rice will take 10-12 minutes } cool
225 g (8 oz) rice will take 12-14 minutes) immediately

Brown rice: Nutty brown rice is filling and nutritious. It has a distinctive flavour and texture and is actually a creamy rather than a brown colour. It absorbs twice as much water as polished white rice and should be cooked by the all-in-one method so that all its precious goodness is maintained. To 100 g (4 oz) brown rice add 450 ml (¾ pint) hot water and ½ teaspoon salt. Cover with a lid and microwave on High for 20-25 minutes, stirring once during cooking. Stir once again and leave to stand covered for 5 minutes to allow the rice to finish cooking.

225 g (8 oz) is the maximum weight of rice recommended for microwave cooking. This quantity is sufficient for 4 servings.

Try sautéing cooked rice in a pre-heated browning dish. Add 25 g (1 oz) unsalted butter, and the rice when the dish is fully heated. Stir briefly and microwave on High for 30-60 seconds until the rice is hot. Also try cooking raw rice in melted butter in an ordinary dish before adding other ingredients for pilau or risottos. The rice starts to colour first around the edges of the dish so should be stirred for even browning. When light brown the rice will become crisp and lumpy. Break up the lumps when adding liquid. Onions can also be browned before the rice is added.

Rice is really special when cooked in stock or wine rather than water alone and any left-overs may be dropped into soup as a garnish.

Rice puddings are easy to cook by microwave if your oven is fitted with a probe or sensor or if it has a very low minimum setting. When cooking on High it is desirable to cook in water, adding the milk when the grains are tender.

Chicken Fruit Risotto

The rice will cook more quickly if the stock is added when very hot or boiling, but if cold water and a crumbled stock cube are used, stir once as soon as the liquid is hot in order to blend in the cube.

25 g (1 oz) butter
1 medium onion, finely chopped
25 g (1 oz) walnuts, chopped
100 g (4 oz) long-grain rice
300 ml (½ pint) hot chicken stock
½ teaspoon ground nutmeg
225 g (8 oz) cooked chicken
3 fresh peaches, peeled
1 orange, peeled and segmented
10-12 cherries, stoned
1 hard-boiled egg
175 ml (6 fl oz) single cream
3 or 4 pairs of cherries for garnish

Put the butter in a large casserole and microwave on High for 30-60 seconds until melted. Stir in the onion and microwave on High for 2-3 minutes until the onion is soft and just beginning to brown.

Add the walnuts and microwave on High for 1 minute.

Stir in the rice and stock, or water and stock cube, and flavour with nutmeg. Cover with a lid or greaseproof paper and microwave on High for 10-12 minutes or until the rice is tender and the stock almost absorbed.

While the rice is cooking, cut the chicken into bite-sized pieces and roughly chop the fruit and the egg.

Mix the fruit into the rice, then cover tightly for 5-8 minutes until all the stock is absorbed and the chicken hot.

Stir in the cream and turn the mixture on to a serving dish.

Garnish with pairs of red cherries.

Serve hot with a green salad.

Serves 4 to 6

Variations
Substitute turkey, ham, or a mixture, for the chicken, grapes, apricots or plums for the fruit.

Hot Seafood Cocktail

Frozen seafood may be used but should be defrosted on Low for a few moments in advance. The sauce can be cooked on High for 1-1½ minutes but must be stirred every 15 seconds to avoid curdling.

15 g (½ oz) butter
4 scallops, washed and cut into quarters
100 g (4 oz) peeled prawns
150 ml (¼ pint) double cream
2 teaspoons brandy
Salt
Pepper
1 level tablespoon tomato ketchup
1 egg yolk, beaten with 2 drops cold water
100-175 g (4-6 oz) cooked long-grain rice
4-6 lemon slices, slit from one edge to the centre for garnish

Put the butter in a shallow dish and microwave on High for 30-60 seconds or until melted.
Stir in the scallops, cover with greaseproof paper and microwave on High for 1½-2½ minutes or until the scallops are cooked. Stir once or twice during cooking.
Stir in the prawns, cream and brandy and microwave on High for 1 minute.
Season with salt and pepper.
Mix in the beaten egg yolk and, without covering, microwave on Low for 4-5 minutes, stirring every 30 seconds until the sauce thickens sufficiently to coat the back of a spoon. Stir in the tomato ketchup. Divide the rice between 4 or 6 ordinary wine glasses (not crystal).
Space out on the oven shelf and microwave on High for 30 seconds or until the rice is hot.

Top with the seafood mixture and garnish with a slice of lemon hooked over the edge of the glass.
Serves 4 to 6

Spanish Rice Salad

While stock has flavour there is no reason why the rice should not be cooked in water alone.

    100 g (4 oz) brown rice
    450 ml (¾ pint) hot chicken stock, well flavoured
    175 g (6 oz) salami, skinned and cubed
    4 artichoke hearts, canned or cooked
    6 black olives
    1 small firm raw courgette, topped, tailed and thinly
        sliced
    Small piece green pepper, chopped
    Small piece red pepper, chopped
    1 small onion, chopped
    6-8 tablespoons French salad dressing

Combine the rice and stock in a large, deep casserole dish and microwave on High for 20 minutes or until the rice is tender and most of the liquid has been absorbed. Stir occasionally during cooking to ensure that all the grains are equally soft. Drain if necessary. Fluff with a fork and leave to cool.
Combine the rice with the salami and vegetables, and mix in the French dressing.
Serves 4

Variations

Substitute white long-grain or organically grown rice and add spices or herbs to the cooking liquid. Use shrimps instead of salami. Use any combination of vegetables such as   cucumber,   chopped   tomato,   yellow   peppers, mushrooms, carrots, watercress, spring onions, grated red cabbage, salted peanuts or radishes, making sure there is a mixture of colour. Garnish with cress and chopped hard-boiled egg.

RICE STUFFING

Stuffings should neither be wet or sloppy nor packed in too tightly, otherwise they will tumble out while the dish is cooking. Use savoury rice stuffing for a crown roast, chicken or turkey, or in stuffed peppers or tomatoes.

Choose the sweeter fruity stuffing in red peppers, pork chops, gammon rolls or trout.

Allow approximately 25 g (1 oz) stuffing per portion.

Savoury Rice Stuffing

Use any herbs of your choice. You will find fresh or frozen herbs much more satisfactory than dried ones. Two sprigs of any fresh herb are equal to about one-eighth of a teaspoon of the dried version.

25 g (1 oz) butter
1 medium onion, finely chopped
100 g (4 oz) long-grain rice, washed and well-drained
300 ml (½ pint) hot beef or chicken stock
1 teaspoon freshly chopped herbs (rosemary, thyme, marjoram or sage)
Salt
Pepper

Put the butter in a deep casserole dish and microwave on High for 30-60 seconds until melted.
Stir in the onion and microwave on High for 2-3 minutes until soft but not coloured. Stir occasionally during cooking.

Mix in the rice and microwave on High for 2-2½ minutes. The rice may pop and jump about and, if you are concerned about this, cover with greaseproof paper.

Pour the stock and add herbs and salt and pepper to taste. Microwave on High for 1-2 minutes until boiling, then stir and continue on High for 8-10 minutes until the rice has absorbed nearly all the liquid and is practically cooked. Cover with a lid and leave for 5 minutes, then fluff with a fork.

Makes 350-400 g (12-14 oz)

(You need 225 g (8 oz) stuffing for an average-sized chicken.)

Fruity Rice Stuffing

Boil the rice freshly or use cold cooked rice. Short-grain rice is my choice for this recipe. Don't use ancient walnuts that have been in the cupboard for ages. To refresh over-dry shelled walnuts, put them in a jug, cover with cold water and bring to the boil in the microwave oven. Repeat three times, then soak in cold water and refrigerate overnight.

    50 g (2 oz) short-grain rice, boiled (making 175 g (6 oz)
        when cooked)
    50 g (2 oz) seedless raisins
    1 thin slice fresh or frozen pineapple, chopped
    40 g (1½ oz) chopped walnuts
    1 level teaspoon freshly chopped parsley
    40 g (1½ oz) butter
    1 large egg, beaten
    1 level teaspoon grated nutmeg
    Salt

Mix all the stuffing ingredients together, adding salt to taste. The amount will depend on the saltiness of the rice.

Makes 350 g (12 oz)

Rice Pudding

  100 g (4 oz) round pudding rice
  ½ teaspoon ground nutmeg
  50 g (2 oz) sugar
  1 × 411 g (14.5 oz) can evaporated milk
  Walnut-sized knob of butter

Boil 1 litre (1 ½ pints) water either in the kettle or in a deep casserole dish in the microwave oven. Stir in the rice and nutmeg and microwave on High for 20 minutes until the rice swells.

Stir in the sugar and evaporated milk and microwave on Low for 25-30 minutes, stirring occasionally. Add extra water towards the end of the cooking time if the pudding is creamy yet the rice is under-cooked.

Add the butter, stir thoroughly, cover with a lid and leave to stand for 5 minutes before serving.

Serves 4

Variations

Use creamy milk, or half milk and half single cream. Stir in raisins or sultanas 5 minutes before the end of the cooking time. Mix in chopped poached pears and a few chopped glacé cherries (the colouring from the cherries turns the rice a pretty pale pink).

9

Sauces

Microwave sauces are lump-free, smooth, silky and shiny, which is what a perfect sauce should be. The heat is generated within the mixture and distributed evenly by frequent whisking, so that when 'thickening' point is reached, the sauce is of a uniform consistency.

The reason why sauces frequently fail when cooked conventionally is because of the intense heat generated from direct contact of the base with the hob. In 'roux'-based sauces the flour remains at the bottom of the saucepan and, combining with a thin layer of rapidly heated liquid, the starch grains in the flour burst and form gelatinous lumps which are hard to eliminate. This often results in thin sauce, full of doughy lumps. Only constant stirring over low heat prevents this and even then it is not easy to reach all the corners of a flat-based pan – and it takes a long time.

Sauces thickened with eggs have a similar fate because of their rapid coagulation in hot liquid. These sauces are the very devil to cook successfully conventionally. The only sure way is to use a double saucepan but even this is a long exacting process.

Whichever sauce you choose to make will be a success every time in the microwave oven. The use of a bowl with a curved base removes the 'can't reach the corner' hazard. Frequent rather than constant whisking is less tedious, the sauces are ready in a few minutes and there is no sticky saucepan to scour. In microwave sauce-making there are very definite stages of cooking which are easy to recognize and you can learn these in one easy lesson. If you are not fussy about sauces tasting 'floury' put all the ingredients in the bowl and microwave on High together, starting the beating process after 30 seconds. To prevent sauces forming a skin, place a damp piece of greaseproof paper wet-side down on the surface of the sauce. Beat thoroughly with a whisk before reheating to avoid lumpiness.

WHITE SAUCES

Use a bowl that has at least twice the capacity of the ingredients. I use a 1.2 litre (2 pint) glass pudding basin for 300 ml (½ pint) sauce and a 2 litre (3½ pint) mixing bowl for 0.6-1.2 litres (1-2 pint) sauce.

Best of all use a mix'n'measure bowl which has a pouring lip.

It is always better to have a larger ratio of butter to flour – never the other way round. Melt the butter, then stir in the flour exactly as you would in a saucepan but there is no need to stir while the roux is cooking. When ready, the mixture resembles uncooked pastry with a bubbly crust which, when broken, reveals small spongy particles. Gradually stir in the liquid and then put the sauce in the microwave oven to start cooking. At this point, set aside the stirring spoon and change to a whisk. Nothing critical happens for the first third of the cooking time as the liquid is still only warm, so there is no need to stir, but after this stage is reached, you must beat every 30 seconds with the wire whisk. You will feel the resistance of a thin paste forming in the lower section of the sauce. This has to be combined with the thinner liquid floating on top before the liquid boils. As boiling occurs, you will see a thickening around the edge of the sauce and this is one indication that the sauce is nearly ready and time to give it another whisk. Beginners should use a glass bowl for cooking sauces because you can see as well as feel the cooking changes occurring.

BROWN SAUCES

Use the browning dish to start off brown sauces or prepare in an ordinary dish, adding dark-coloured ingredients for more depth of colour e.g. a brown stock cube, tomato purée, red wine. The usual method is to cook chopped onions in butter or oil until they brown, then add flour and cook for an extra minute so that this too will brown.

You can also make a good brown roux sauce which is excellent for slower-cooking stews and casseroles. A large quantity is easier to make than a small amount and can be stored for future use. Combine an equal 'volume' of flour and oil (50 g/2 oz flour to 6 tbsps oil, approx.) in a deep shatterproof casserole which must be absolutely heatproof and in perfect condition. Microwave on High until the roux is a deep fawn colour. Do not stir while this is happening unless absolutely necessary. The mixture round the edges can become very dark but this will lighten when all is mixed together. Add chopped onions or meat and continue cooking until these are brown, then add the remaining ingredients.

The stock should be hot which will lessen spattering, but do be careful not to stir beneath your face. Ovengloves are a must when making a sauce this way, and when removed from the oven the casserole must be put on a dry, heat-resistant surface so that the dish will not crack. Please don't be alarmed by these warnings because, if carefully carried out, you will have a superb sauce.

EGG AND MILK CUSTARD SAUCES

Custard sauces made with eggs and milk can be cooked in the microwave oven on Low without fear of curdling. Use 2 egg yolks to 300 ml (½ pint) milk but, for best results, make double the quantity (this is to do with 'diluting' the microwaves). If your oven only has a High setting, you must make the larger quantity and stand the bowl in a dish of hot water throughout the cooking period. 300 ml (½ pint) egg custard sauce takes about 5 minutes on Low and should be stirred frequently after the first 20 seconds. The custard is not meant to thicken beyond the consistency of single cream and prolonged cooking will only result in separation of the solid proteins, not in thickening. If by mischance the sauce begins to curdle, pour it immediately into a cold bowl and whisk furiously. If after all you feel particularly uncertain of your prowess at making egg custard, stir in ½ teaspoon of flour when initially blending.

EMULSIFIED SAUCES

These include mayonnaise, Hollandaise and Béarnaise and are thickened by the thorough blending of oil or butter and eggs. If you can spot curdling in time – the danger sign with Hollandaise sauce and Maltaise sauce is when you see particles of solids floating closely together in the sauce – quickly take the sauce out of the oven. For Hollandaise sauce, boil 2 tablespoons milk in a glass, which will take 20 seconds on High, pour in slowly, beating vigorously all the time with a hand whisk. For Maltaise sauce use 1 tablespoon boiling water.

Sauces are even easier to use with a blender. Use it for making mayonnaise, having made sure that the ingredients are not cold. To make butter-based sauces first blend all the ingredients except the butter and leave in the goblet. Melt the butter in the microwave oven until it is bubbling, switch on the blender and pour in the butter in a steady stream. The ingredients must be at room temperature. In mayonnaise making the oil can be warmed in the microwave oven for a few seconds and the chill taken off the egg in the same way. Mayonnaise is not 'cooked'.

The Hollandaise type sauces are blends of eggs and a large amount of butter and possibly cream, lemon juice or other liquids. After melting the butter, the other ingredients are added and the sauce is microwaved, preferably on Medium, but clever cooks will microwave on High. Whisk the sauce vigorously as soon as you see a thin curd rising and do not continue cooking unless you are sure that more time is required. Continue beating as the sauce cools. Only reheat the sauces very gently on the lowest setting.

Maltaise sauce, because it has a high proportion of orange juice, can be frozen and regenerated better than the others of this type.

CORNFLOUR SAUCES AND CUSTARDS

To make cornflour-thickened sauces, such as custard, first blend the cornflour with a little of the cold measured liquid. Stir or whisk frequently while microwaving on High. 300 ml (½ pint) takes about 2½ minutes to cook.

FRUIT SAUCES

Arrowroot is often used when a translucent sauce is required and these are usually sweet.

About 2 level teaspoons will thicken 300 ml (½ pint) liquid – normally a fruit juice or syrup. Sugar is added according to taste. Blend the arrowroot thoroughly with the cold liquid and bring to the boil in the microwave oven, stirring frequently. At first the sauce will appear cloudy but this clears as cooking continues. Add a few drops of suitable food colouring to improve the appearance. 300 ml (½ pint) takes about 3 minutes.

Basic Brown Sauce

Use this sauce for all meat dishes and make up a large quantity. Store surplus sauce in the refrigerator for a few days or in the freezer. Use a pre-heated browning dish for an even deeper colour. Use 1 × 285 ml (10 oz) can condensed consommé and make up to 600 ml (1 pint) with hot water.

25 g (1 oz) butter or margarine
1 rasher of bacon, derinded and finely chopped
1 small onion, finely chopped
25 g (1 oz) flour
1 carrot, grated
1 celery stalk, finely chopped
600 ml (1 pint) diluted condensed beef consommé, brown beef stock, or water plus 2 red Oxo cubes and ½ beef stock cube
1 tablespoon tomato purée
Salt
Pepper

Put the butter, bacon and onion in a large casserole dish and microwave on High for 1½-2½ minutes, stirring occasionally until the onion browns.
Stir in the flour, carrot and celery and microwave for 2 minutes.
Add the consommé or stock and tomato purée and without covering microwave on High for 10-15 minutes, stirring occasionally until the vegetables are soft and the flavours are blended.
Add salt and pepper to taste.
Leave to cool and store for several hours before reheating.
If the sauce is too thick add extra stock.
Strain before serving, discarding the vegetables and bacon.

Basic White Sauce

This is the most popular of the sauces and is worth perfecting as it has so many uses. It can be made in various consistencies and forms the basis of soufflés or soups as well as sweet or savoury sauces. Use the following quantities for plain white or Béchamel or velouté sauce.

	Butter/ margarine	Flour	Liquid
Thin pouring sauce	25 g (1 oz)	25 g (1 oz)	600 ml (1 pt)
Coating sauce (thick enough to coat the back of a spoon)	25 g (1 oz)	25 g (1 oz)	300 ml (½ pt)
Thick sauce (panada used in soufflés)	25 g (1 oz)	25 g (1 oz)	150 ml (¼ pt)

Put the butter in a large bowl and microwave on High until melted. Stir in the flour and continue on High until the mixture is spongy. Mix the milk with a wire whisk. Microwave on High for one-third of the total expected cooking time, then whisk thoroughly. Continue on High, whisking every 30 seconds until the sauce thickens.

Thicker sauces cook proportionately quicker than thin sauces after the liquid is added. No precise melting time can be given for butter and margarine owing to the differences in content and starting temperatures. As a guide use the following melting times.

Butter/margarine	Time on High
15 g (½ oz)	20-30 secs
25 g (1 oz)	½-1 min
50 g (2 oz)	1-1½ mins
75-100 g (3-4 oz)	1¼-1¾ mins

The approximate time taken for cooking after the flour is added is:

Flour	Time on High
25 g (1 oz)	½ min
50-100 g (2-4 oz)	1 min

After liquid is added the following times are relevant:-

Quantity	Time on High
300 ml (½ pt)	2-3½ mins
600 ml (1 pt)	4-5 mins
1.2 litre (2 pts)	5-6 mins

Béarnaise Sauce

This sauce is served with steaks, chops or vegetables. Because it requires chopped onion, the quickest method is to use a liquidizer or food processor, otherwise prepare as for Hollandaise sauce. The mixture will be thick.

1 small onion, quartered
4 egg yolks
1 tablespoon tarragon vinegar
100 g (4 oz) slightly salted butter
White pepper
Salt

Put the butter in a jug and microwave on High for 1¼-1¾ minutes until melted and clear.

With the motor running at high speed, blend the onion, egg yolks and vinegar together in the liquidizer until light and fluffy. Without switching off slowly pour in the butter, blending until a thick sauce is formed.

Makes 150 ml (¼ pint)

Béchamel Sauce

This roux-based sauce is superior to a basic white sauce and is used for savoury dishes. The proportions given here are for 300 ml (½ pint) of a coating sauce but you can vary the thickness by referring to the chart on white sauces. Vary the herbs to suit youself.

    300 ml (½ pint) milk
    1 bay leaf, crumbled
    1 sprig thyme
    1 sprig parsley, roughly chopped
    ¼ teaspoon grated nutmeg
    Small piece onion
    Small piece carrot or celery
    25 g (1 oz) butter
    25 g (1 oz) flour
    Salt
    Pepper

Put the milk in a jug with the herbs and vegetables and microwave on High for 1½-2 minutes until the milk steams but does not boil. Cover and leave to infuse for at least 15 minutes. Strain into another jug or lipped bowl.

Put the butter in a large bowl and microwave on High for 30-60 seconds until melted.

Stir in the flour and cook on High for 30 seconds.

Using a whisk, gradually add the strained milk (it is

difficult to strain the milk directly on to the roux and stir at the same time).

Microwave on High for 2-3 minutes, whisking every 30 seconds until the sauce thickens.

Season to taste with salt and pepper.

You must beat Béchamel sauce more frequently in the first stages of cooking if the milk was not completely cold. This also shortens the total cooking time.

600 ml (1 pint) milk takes 3-3½ minutes to reach steaming point.

Variations

To white or Béchamel sauce add: grated cheese and mustard; cooked chopped mushrooms; chopped onions; tomato ketchup; chopped shrimps; capers.

Velouté sauce

Substitute well-flavoured chicken stock for the milk and use in savoury meat or vegetable dishes.

Fish sauces

Substitute fish stock for half the milk.

Hollandaise Sauce

There are several Hollandaise sauce recipes. This one is a little cheaper to make than the luscious ones enriched with fresh cream. Serve warm or cold.

100 g (4 oz) unsalted butter
3 egg yolks
2 tablespoons lemon juice
¼ teaspoon salt
⅛ teaspoon white pepper

Put the butter in a large bowl and microwave on High for 1-1¾ minutes until just melted.

Beat the yolks and the lemon juice with the salt and pepper.

Stir into the melted butter.

Microwave on High for 45-60 seconds, beating vigorously every 15 seconds, or on Low for 2-2½ minutes, stirring every 30 seconds until the sauce thickens. Continue beating as the sauce is cooling when it will thicken further.

Makes just under 300 ml (½ pint)

Mayonnaise

Mayonnaise ingredients must all be at the same warm temperature, so that microwave-assisted mayonnaise is highly successful. Indeed, it will be infallible if you use 2 egg yolks which, because they are beaten to a greater volume of foam, emulsify more readily. Corn oil or sunflower oil produce a light sauce; olive oil has a more pronounced flavour and is more viscous. If you prefer a more acid tang use vinegar rather than lemon juice and make your choice from malt, wine, tarragon or garlic vinegar.

  300 ml (½ pint) vegetable oil
  2 egg yolks
  ¼ teaspoon salt
  ¼ teaspoon white pepper
  ¼ teaspoon sugar
  ¼ teaspoon dry mustard
  1-2 tablespoons lemon juice or vinegar

Pour the oil into a jug and microwave on High for 25-30 seconds until just warm to the touch.

Combine the egg yolks, salt, pepper, sugar and mustard together in a curved-based bowl.

Using a rotary or electric whisk, beat the egg mixture until it thickens and is foamy – don't on any account forget to put the mustard in, as this is an important stabilizer.

Slowly pour in the oil, drop by drop, beating continuously and vigorously until the mayonnaise begins to thicken. Add the lemon juice or vinegar to thin the mayonnaise and give it its flavour.

Add any remaining oil in a steady stream while still beating. Store in an airtight container in the refrigerator for not more than a few days. In the highly unlikely event of a curdle, mix a level teaspoon of made mustard with a teaspoon of the curdled mayonnaise in a 600 ml (1 pint) bowl. Microwave the mayonnaise on High for 4-5 seconds only, then beat in the curdled mixture, one spoonful at a time.

Makes 300 ml (½ pint)

Sauce Chasseur

This luxury sauce of red wine and mushrooms is gorgeous with all red meats. Substitute white wine for use with pork, veal and lamb. Cook the sauce in a large shallow dish and double the ingredients if you wish, increasing the cooking time by two-thirds. The sauce can be made in the browning dish but there is no appreciable difference in colour.

All sauces thicken during storage. To thin down, add wine and allow 2-3½ minutes for reheating the sauce, which should be covered with cling film.

20 g (¾ oz) salted butter
1 small onion, chopped
1 level tablespoon flour
100 g (4 oz) button mushrooms, chopped
6 tablespoons medium red wine
4 tablespoons canned condensed beef consommé
3 tablespoons water
½ teaspoon freshly chopped or frozen rosemary leaves

½ teaspoon salt
¼ teaspoon black pepper
½ teaspoon paprika
¼ teaspoon sugar
2 tablespoons double cream

Put the butter and onion in a large shallow dish and microwave on High for 3-4½ minutes, stirring occasionally until the onion browns.

Stir in the flour and microwave on High for 30 seconds. Add the mushrooms, mixing well. The flour may look gungy and sticky at this point but all will be well when the mushrooms are cooked.

Microwave on High for 2 minutes, stirring once during cooking. Add the wine, consommé, water, rosemary, salt, pepper, paprika and sugar.

Three-quarters cover with cling film and microwave on High for 5-6 minutes, stirring occasionally until a thick rich sauce is formed.

Mix in the cream and use as desired.

Makes just under 300 ml (½ pint)

Cucumber and Dill Sauce

This is an ideal sauce for serving with fish or egg dishes. Because it is an emulsified sauce including butter and eggs mixed with a high liquid content it is best cooked on Low. If your oven has no Low setting cook on High but whisk the sauce every 15 seconds and remove it from the microwave oven as soon as it begins to thicken.

100 g (4 oz) butter
3 large egg yolks
6 tablespoons double cream
Juice half lemon
Salt

Pepper
2 sprigs dill weed, chopped
1 sprig parsley, chopped
Half cucumber, peeled and finely chopped

Put the butter in a medium bowl and microwave on High for 1-1¾ minutes until melted.

Add all the ingredients, except the cucumber, and whisk until smooth. Microwave on Low for 2-3½ minutes or until the sauce thickens, beating vigorously every 30 seconds during cooking.

Fold in the cucumber.

Microwave on Low for 30 seconds.

Makes 300 ml (½ pint)

Sauce Maltaise

The orange flavour of this sauce enhances fish and delicate vegetables. It is one of the few sauces that freeze well, regenerating perfectly when thawed gently in the microwave oven. Thaw for only a few seconds on High or for 2 minutes on Low, beating frequently.

100 g (4 oz) unsalted butter
4 tablespoons double cream
3 egg yolks
Grated rind and juice of 1 medium orange
¼ teaspoon salt
¼ teaspoon pepper

Put the butter in a medium bowl and microwave on High for 1¼-1¾ minutes or until just melted.

Add all the remaining ingredients and whisk until smooth. Microwave on Low for 2½-3½ minutes, beating after 1 minute and then every ½ minute until the sauce thickens, or microwave on High for 45-90 seconds, beating briskly with a wire whisk every 15 seconds.

Continue beating as the sauce cools.
Makes 150 ml (¼ pint)

Simple Bolognese Sauce

15 g (½ oz) butter
1 small onion, chopped
15 g (½ oz) flour
1 × 397 g (14 oz) can tomatoes
1 red Oxo cube, crumbled
1 level teaspoon dried herbs
Squeeze garlic powder
Salt
Pepper
1 small can minced beef, corned beef or kidney beans, drained
Parmesan cheese (optional)

Put the butter and onion in a large casserole dish and microwave on High for 2-2½ minutes until the onion is soft.

Stir in the flour, blending thoroughly, then add the tomatoes and their juice, crumbled stock cube, herbs, garlic powder, salt and pepper to taste, and the canned meat or kidney beans. Lightly crush the tomatoes with a fork.

Cover and microwave on High for 6-10 minutes, stirring occasionally until thoroughly heated. Add cheese if desired.

Makes 450 ml (¾ pint)

Teriyaki Sauce

Use as a marinade for chicken pieces or duck or pork cubes and then cook the meat or poultry in the same sauce.

175 ml (6 fl oz) soy sauce
120 ml (4 fl oz) frozen concentrated orange juice (thawed)
1 teaspoon ground ginger
2 tablespoons sweet sherry
1 garlic clove, crushed
4 tablespoons vegetable oil

Combine the ingredients together, store in a screw-top jar and use as required.
Makes 300-450 ml (½ - ¾ pint)

Tomato Pimiento Sauce

1 tablespoon vegetable oil
1 large onion, finely chopped
1 clove garlic, crushed
1 × 184 g (6½ oz) can pimientos, drained
1 × 397 g (14 oz) can tomatoes
2 tablespoons tomato purée
½ teaspoon sugar
Salt
Pepper

Combine the oil, onion and garlic in a large shallow dish and microwave on High for 3-4 minutes or until the onion browns. Empty in the tomatoes and crush lightly with a fork. Add the pimientos, tomato purée and sugar.
Cover and microwave on High for 4-5 minutes or until boiling, then reduce the setting and microwave on Low for 12 minutes without stirring until the sauce is thick.
Alternatively, microwave on High for 5 minutes stirring occasionally, otherwise the boiling sauce will splutter.
Season to taste with salt and pepper.
Makes generous 300 ml (½ pint)

Gravy

2 tablespoons dripping, retained from draining the roasting dish after the joint has been removed
1 tablespoon flour or gravy powder
300 ml (½ pint) stock or water
Salt
Pepper
½ teaspoon liquid caramel

Stir the flour or gravy powder and stock into the dripping in the roasting dish.

Without covering, microwave on High for 3-4 minutes, stirring occasionally with a wire whisk until the sauce thickens.

Season with salt and pepper and add a little liquid caramel for extra colour.

Makes 300 ml (½ pint)

Liquid Caramel

It is going to be a long time before we accept that pale foods taste just as good as when they are brown. Make up a bottle of liquid caramel to use to deepen the colour of cakes, bread or casseroles. Mix this with herbs and spices for brushing over pale meat and poultry (see below).

4 tablespoons water
100 g (4 oz) granulated sugar
1 teaspoon vegetable oil

Put the water in a large glass measuring jug or lipped bowl and stir in the sugar until nearly dissolved.

Microwave on High for 5-6 minutes without stirring until the syrup is mid-brown.

Put 3 tablespoons cold water in an undecorated cup or glass and place on the oven shelf beside the jug of syrup.

Microwave on High for 1½-2 minutes until the water is boiling and the syrup in the jug becomes dark brown. Watch carefully that it does not burn.

Protecting your hands with oven gloves, add the water to the syrup, shaking the jug gently to mix, then stir in the oil. Leave to cool, then pour into a screw-top jar and store for up to 6 months.

Makes generous 200 ml (¼ pint)

Liquid Browner

Use for brushing over meat and poultry.

    4 tablespoons liquid caramel
    1 tablespoon Worcestershire sauce
    ½ teaspoon sweet paprika
    ¼ teaspoon ground turmeric
    ½ teaspoon salt
    ½ teaspoon black pepper
    1 level teaspoon mixed dried herbs or 1 tablespoon fresh
        chopped herbs
    1 teaspoon tomato purée

Combine all the ingredients in a jar and shake thoroughly. Use as required.

This browner will only keep satisfactorily for 1-2 weeks.

Stock Syrup

Use stock syrup whenever you require a sugar syrup. The consistency is just right for fruit salads, but you can cook for longer to use in confectionery. Stock syrup keeps very well in a covered container for a long time. It can be stored in the freezer for several months. Ignore any crystals that may form against the sides of the dish. The syrup can be poured out without incorporating them.

Make a double quantity if you wish, adding only a fraction more cooking time. Stock syrup should be viscous but of an easy pouring consistency, rather like undiluted orange squash. You need only boil for 1-2 minutes after boiling point is reached and a confectionery thermometer registers 105°C (215°F). Do not leave the thermometer in the microwave oven during cooking.

225 g (8 oz) granulated sugar
150 ml (¼ pint) cold water

Mix the sugar and water together in a very large jug or ovenproof bowl.
Microwave on High for 1-2 minutes until the water is hot.
Stir until the sugar is completely dissolved.
Microwave on High for 30-90 seconds until the syrup bubbles.
Without stirring, microwave on High for 1½-2 minutes or until an almost colourless syrup is formed.
Test after 1½ minutes as both your microwave oven and the container influence the cooking times required.
Makes 300 ml (½ pint)

Confectioner's Custard

Use as a pastry cream base in tarts or as a cake filling or fold into puréed fruit for a fruit fool. To produce delicious ice-cream mix with an equal quantity of freshly whipped or microwaved cream and freeze.

300 ml (½ pint) milk
50 g (2 oz) flour
50 g (2 oz) sugar
1 egg yolk, beaten
½ teaspoon vanilla essence
50 g (2 oz) unsalted butter
2 tablespoons whipped double cream

In a litre (2 pint) bowl blend 5 tablespoons of the milk with the flour, sugar, egg yolk and vanilla essence.

Put the remaining milk in a large jug, add the butter and microwave on High for 1½-2 minutes until the milk is warm and the butter melted.

Gradually pour into the flour mixture, beating with a wire whisk.

Put the bowl in the oven and microwave on High for 1-1½ minutes beating vigorously every 30 seconds until the custard thickens to a consistency of whipped cream.

Stir in the cream.

Damp a circle of greaseproof paper and put wet-side down against the surface of the custard to prevent a skin forming.

Leave to cool and use as required.

Makes generous 350 ml (½ pint)

10

Cakes and Puddings

Cakes and puddings are so simple to make in the microwave oven that you will be only too happy to sacrifice that traditional golden look. You can use most conventional cake recipes and these are improved by the addition of a tablespoon of milk or water. Commercial cake mixes are highly successful and can be dressed up to be very delicious indeed. Microwave cakes can be light and moist but do not always have the same texture as those conventionally baked – they may even be better. However, since I am asked more questions on this subject than any other form of microwave cooking, I feel I should explain the possible differences.

In a conventional oven, the dry hot air causes the cake mixture to rise and stay in position. This is because the fine layers are baked separately as each heats and cooks the next. The hot air in a conventional oven dries and sets and crisps the top of the cake at the same time browning the starch in the flour and caramelizing the sugar.

The microwave oven is not pre-heated, so everything starts from cold. There can be no whoosh of hot air to force liquid content into steam for, in the microwave oven, heat is generated from the friction of the food particles. Cakes will rise fantastically but if the mixture rises much above the baking container, it will spill over before setting.

CONTAINERS

These must of course be microwave suitable, having no metal content. They do not have to be suitable for the conventional oven so you can let your imagination roam, choosing all sorts of different shapes. Bake microwave cakes in a pudding basin to achieve an igloo shape, or in a clay flower pot for a conversation stopper. Chocolate boxes, provided they have no metal trim, are particularly useful for double-coloured mixtures like Battenburgs, for you can simultaneously cook the pink and the plain with a cardboard separation down the middle.

Before embarking on a shopping spree for new containers have a look in your cupboard and see what might be suitable. Make the usual test of putting the dish and a half glass of water in the oven cabinet and micro-wave on High for 1½ minutes, after which the water should be hot, but the dish still cool. Do not worry if the dish is slightly warm – all containers absorb some microwave energy but this slows down the cooking. If the cake if squiggy round the edges this could be because the dish is at fault – some cool more rapidly than others.

Highly glazed dishes are less efficient and finished cakes seem to stick round the side.

As microwaves bake best in a ring doughnut shape you are going to get more even cooking if you choose a savarin or ring mould. I unhesitatingly recommend the re-usable white plastic ones obtainable from shops selling microwave ware. Cakes turn out easily if you lift up one of the edges of the ring mould so the air can enter. If this action doesn't loosen the cake, then squeeze the upturned bottom of the mould between the thumb and fingers and the cake will come out without damage.

Lakeland and Microwave Ovenware both have these moulds in their range. Anchor Hocking produce a sturdier container that is also suitable for use in the conventional oven and so does Corning's Pyrex. Vitri Micro-dur casseroles are a range of rigid plastic containers and I find their round flat 1 litre (1¾ pint)/21 cm (8¼ in) size the best. While mentioning these brand names it does not mean that there are others not equally good.

Straight-sided dishes are better than curved and although loaf shapes are attractive you may find that the centre third cooks more slowly, so that you have to shield the ends with foil as soon as they are cooked. Select a 20 cm (8 in) square dish but try to find one with curved rather than sharp corners. Small cakes can be baked in a double paper case or in a 'muffin' container so that they will not become misshapen. Sandwich cake reusable plastic shapes are useful for layer cakes.

GREASING AND LINING

Brush ring shapes and plastic containers lightly with oil or melted butter, margarine or cooking fat, but not the 'slimming kinds'. Avoid spreading with hard fat as any small lumps that adhere will cause pitting.

Do not grease and flour as for many conventionally cooked cakes as trapped moisture will cause the flour to gunge. Straight-sided dishes are best if lightly greased and the bases lined with non-stick paper.

Cling film, if used, should be eased in loosely because it shrinks away from the corners during cooking and you could find your beautifully fitting cake has a flattened corner. However it does reduce the washing up. Normally, you will find you have very smooth sides and base which provide a surface suitable for icing, but on the other hand the cake does not have an open-looking texture. If you choose this method, turn the cooked cake out and remove the cling film immediately or the top layer of the mixture will peel off.

BAKING

Leave batters for a few moments in the dish before cooking so that the raising agents can start to work. Only half-fill the cake dish to allow for rising, and use any surplus for little cakes. Rotate the dish four times during cooking if your oven is not fitted with a turntable and, if you still have problems, try raising the dish nearer to the top of the oven. Stay in the kitchen and do other jobs during this time as it is quite important to inspect from time to time. Do not fear a draught when opening the oven door as microwave cakes don't mind at all. They *will* sink but will rise again with no adverse effect, provided half-cooked mixtures are not left to get cold while you have a long 'phone conversation. Cakes will rise unevenly at first and you will observe a wet mound appearing on one of the sides but this evens itself out. Except for 'ring' cakes, centres will be the last to cook, and this process will take place during the carry-over or standing time. Cakes are ready when they are just dry on top. Under-cooking is better than over-cooking. Leave cakes in the dish for 3-4 minutes before turning out, then remove the lining paper which will probably adhere to the base of the cake. If, after a few more minutes, the base of the cake is still under-cooked, put it, under-cooked side up, on a plate and microwave for a little longer. Sometimes you will see moist mixture around the sides but this will dry up as the cake cools. If you are willing to take a risk on sticking and grease rather than line the bases of see-through dishes, you will be able to see when the cake is cooked by looking through the base. Vitri Micro-dur ware allows you to do this easily. Cakes cooked in the bases of greased rigid Tupperware or Vitri require no lining paper, provided there is no jam or syrup underneath the mixture, e.g. pineapple upside-down cake.

Microwaves cook evenly for the first 5 cm (2 in) of cake mixture. As the heat is created inside, a thin outer layer remains tacky due to humidity created in the cavity, resting on the cake surface. When turning out the cake, this thin layer may stick to the cooling wire. If you first turn the cake out on to non-stick paper then immediately reverse it on to the wire, you will have more chance of retaining the top layer, although undecorated cakes often look nicer when this is scraped off. Alternatively you can serve the cake bottom-up. For sandwich cakes it is preferable to bake the two halves separately as splitting a microwave cake is more difficult.

Plain cake mixtures will turn out pale because the microwave oven doesn't brown. If you don't like its appearance, brown the cake under the grill either before or after turning out, depending on the material of the container, or decorate by pouring sugary icings over warm cakes or butter-ice or pipe with fresh cream after refrigerating.

Use brown instead of white sugar in plain mixtures and add a few drops of yellow food colouring to the uncooked mixture. Improve the flavour of plain cakes with a few drops of dairy butter flavouring.

Whisked sponge mixtures can be baked in the microwave oven and a 2 egg mixture, divided and baked in 2 'sandwich shapes' takes only 2 minutes. Provided it is not overcooked the cake will be 'acceptable' with a definite spongy texture, but I would only serve it to accustomed microwave-cake eaters.

Rich chocolate cakes have a really 'Viennese' texture and can also be served without decoration. Dust plainer circular cakes with icing sugar through a paper doily.

Fruit cakes will be darker if the ingredients are dark, so use the brownest possible sugar and add a teaspoon of gravy browning or black treacle. For light fruit cakes brush with microwave-melted apricot jam and sprinkle with nuts.

Plain cakes harden on the outside after standing for a few hours but this does not imply that they are stale. Brush with melted clear jam to keep them soft, wrap in cling film or foil and store. The reason that cakes appear to stale quickly is not the fault of the microwave oven but of the length of cooking time. You must remember that cakes continue cooking after being removed from the microwave oven and this is particularly relevant where high proportions of fat or sugar have been used. This especially applies to fruit cakes. Cooked properly, cakes should remain as moist as when conventionally baked.

When making microwaved or conventionally baked cakes the ingredients should be at room temperature. Hard butter will not cream easily and cold eggs curdle. Soften the butter for 20-30 seconds on High and put eggs straight from the refrigerator into the microwave oven, making sure that they are not rolling about, and microwave for 3-4 seconds *only*. This will just take the chill off. I cannot be responsible if you leave them in for longer. They will then start to cook and very soon burst.

Most cakes cook well uncovered at a high setting. If you are concerned about an uneven rise, cover the top of the dish with greaseproof paper (provided the dish is deep enough to prevent the risen mixture from touching the paper). To blend the ingredients better, cook on Medium for some of the time. The best way of approaching this is to divide the specified cooking time on High by half. Then cook on Medium for that amount of time plus half as much again. Finish cooking on High for the other half of the specified time. For example, if the recipe says microwave on High for 6 minutes, you should microwave on Medium for 4½ minutes, then continue on High for 3 minutes.

Fruit cakes will have more flavour when microwaved on Low, which will take 2½ times as long as cooking on High. If the recipe says microwave on High for 6 minutes, you should microwave on Low for 15 minutes.

FREEZING

Follow your usual methods for freezing but remember you

cannot thaw iced cakes by microwave. If you are making party specials, freeze the cake bases and icing separately. Cakes should be thawed slowly on Low or Defrost which will take 3-5 minutes, depending on the temperature of the freezer and the proportion of sugar in the cake. A tiny fairy cake will be soft in half a minute.

PUDDINGS

The most famous of all, the Christmas pudding, can be cooked in 10 minutes on High, but will be better if you cook it on Low for 25-30 minutes. Either way, it is considerably less time than boiling in a pudding basin in a pan of hot water which needs topping up at frequent intervals.

Suet puddings, sponge and all steamed puddings are excellent cooked by microwave and eaten hot. Prepare them in the usual way, adding an extra tablespoon of liquid. Only half-fill the pudding basin and cover loosely with cling film for a moist result but make sure it is very loosely applied. A pleat down the middle will allow the pudding to rise and yet be contained without spilling over. Although you can use any microwave suitable basin, if the base is to be covered with jam or syrup only oven glass or pottery are suitable. Hot syrups reach a temperature well above boiling point which is too great for even boilable plastics and scarring will occur. Take care when reheating these puddings – a Medium setting is advisable so that the jam will not burn before the pudding is hot.

Crumbles are ideal for microwave desserts and toppings for cakes and fruit. Make up a large quantity of basic mix and store in the freezer.

Milk puddings will not boil over if cooked on Low, or if you have an oven fitted with a probe or sensor. But since many people have high setting ovens only, their best method is to cook the grains in water and add milk as soon as they are tender. A mixture of milk and water in a pudding is naturally less rich so if you prefer creamier puddings, substitute evaporated milk for fresh.

Egg and milk custards such as crème caramel, baked custard and crème brûlée, should really be microwaved on Low, but this does not mean that these cannot be successfully cooked on High. The secret is to put a container of water or other slow-cooking food in the microwave oven simultaneously with the custards. Because the microwaves have to share themselves between these foods, the cooking process takes longer and is therefore more gentle.

Custards microwaved on High in small ramekins should be spaced out on the oven shelf and repositioned every 30 seconds. Place large dishes in a container three-quarters full of water and stir two or three times for the first 1½ minutes to draw the mixture away from the sides of the dish. Bread and butter puddings being set with custard, are best cooked on Low. When using a High setting, arrange a thinner bread layer in the centre or bake in a 'ring' mould.

Custards, creams and blancmanges thickened with cornflour must be stirred frequently. Blend the cornflour with a little cold milk or recommended liquid and make sure that the soaked cornflour does not form a gelatinous layer on the bottom of the bowl. These custards will be lump-free if they are frequently stirred, even when still unheated. Use a bowl with a curved base, so that the mixture cannot stick in the corners and a wire whisk for stirring. Cook in a large vessel to eliminate chances of boiling over.

Although pancakes will cook in a microwave oven it simply is not worth the bother and a batch takes as long as in the frying pan. Make pancakes conventionally at your leisure and store them. Then you can layer or stuff with a microwaved filling, and reheat. Pancakes retain their original texture when heated through by microwave.

A FEW SUGGESTIONS FOR CAKE DECORATIONS

Cover cake with a paper doily and shake sieved cocoa over a pale cake and icing sugar over a dark cake.

Brush with warmed apricot jam and sprinkle with toasted almonds, halved glacé cherries or walnut halves.

Cover with glacé icing.

Ice with fudge icing. (Microwave on High for 1½ minutes 50 g (2 oz) unsalted butter and a few drops flavouring or 1 tablespoon cream. Stir in 200 g (7 oz) sieved icing sugar and beat until smooth. Add food colouring.)

Pipe with rosettes of fresh cream.

Cover with almond paste and royal icing.

Pipe with butter cream.

Ice with melted chocolate and sprinkle with chocolate vermicelli.

Cover with crumbled or grated digestive sweetmeal or chocolate biscuits or toasted desiccated coconut.

Coat with coloured sugar frosting. (Add a drop of food colour to white sugar and mix in with a fork until the sugar takes on a pale hue. Leave uncovered for several hours to dry out. Granulated sugar adds a sparkle and should be sprinkled over the cake when cold. Thickly apply the caster sugar frosting which forms a crunchy crust when the cake is warm. The moisture from the cake will not discolour the topping.)

Alabama Tea Loaf

This is more a cake than a bread. It is mouth-watering when fresh and warm but will also taste good when stale, toasted and spread with butter and jam or honey. The cake has excellent keeping qualities.

225 g (8 oz) self-raising flour
1 teaspoon ground nutmeg
1 teaspoon mixed spice
100 g (4 oz) soft margarine
100 g (4 oz) soft dark brown sugar
50 g (2 oz) chopped walnuts and flaked almonds, mixed
½ teaspoon bicarbonate of soda
2 teaspoons milk
1 rounded tablespoon molasses (or black treacle)
2 large eggs, beaten
1 × 1 litre (4½ × 7 × 9in) or similar sized loaf shape, greased

Sift the flour, nutmeg and mixed spice in a mixing bowl and rub in the margarine.

Stir in the sugar and nuts.

Blend the bicarbonate of soda with the milk and add to the mixture with the molasses and eggs.

Beat thoroughly. The mixture is a dark brown heavy batter. Spoon evenly into the prepared dish and microwave on High for 6-8 minutes until the cake is just dry on top. Give the dish a quarter-turn every 2 minutes during cooking.

If the cake appears to be baked at either end, yet still have a moist dip in the centre, cover the cooked parts with foil and microwave on High for 1 more minute. The cake should now rise and cook in the middle section.

Leave for a few moments before turning on to a cooling wire.

Makes 1 kg (2 lb) loaf

Chocolate Cake

This is a light spongy cake which can be served as it is or

decorated with a soft or easy-pouring icing. The cake will crumble if you try to spread a sticky icing on top. I simply sprinkle the top with finely grated plain dessert chocolate.

150 g (5 oz) plain flour
1 rounded teaspoon bicarbonate of soda
1 rounded teaspoon baking powder
2 level tablespoons cocoa
100 g (4 oz) soft margarine
100 g (4 oz) caster sugar
¼ teaspoon dairy butter flavouring (optional)
¼ teaspoon vanilla essence
2 large eggs, beaten
2 level tablespoons golden syrup
5-6 tablespoons milk

Sift the flour, bicarbonate of soda, baking powder and cocoa together.

Beat the margarine, sugar and flavouring together until creamy.

Beat in 1 tablespoon of the flour mixture, then mix in alternate spoons of beaten egg and the flour.

Add the syrup and sufficient milk to mix to a creamy batter.

Turn into a 20 cm (8 in) deep greased cake dish and microwave on High for 5-5½ minutes until the cake is just dry on top and shrinks from the sides of the dish.

Give the dish a quarter-turn three times during the cooking period.

Turn out on to a sheet of non-stick paper, then reverse on to a cooling wire.

Decorate as desired.

Serves 8

Cherry Truffles

Make these fabulous little cakes all in one bowl. Chocolate continues melting after leaving the microwave oven. It is usually ready when moist on top.

10 pitted cherries or glacé cherries
2 tablespoons rum
50 g (2 oz) cooking chocolate
50 g (2 oz) granulated sugar
50 g (2 oz) butter at room temperature
1 large egg
½ teaspoon vanilla essence
½ teaspoon baking powder
65 g (2½ oz) plain flour
25 g (1 oz) ground almonds
Chocolate vermicelli
2 tablespoons apricot jam

Soak the cherries in the rum while making the cake mixture. Put the chocolate and sugar in a medium bowl and microwave on High for 2-3 minutes until the chocolate has melted. Do not leave for too long or the chocolate will scorch. Stir thoroughly, then mix in the butter until it melts.

Beat in the egg, vanilla essence and baking powder and, lastly, the flour and almonds. Microwave on High for 1 minute, stir, then cook for a further 2½-3 minutes until the mixture is smooth and just dry on top.

Immediately drain the cherries on to the mixture and add the jam and stir while hot to mix to a soft dough. Leave for a few minutes to cool slightly.

Divide the mixture into 10 pieces and form each into a ball centring a cherry inside. Do not overwork or your hands will become oily and the truffles too smooth to hold the coating.

Half-fill a small curved bowl with chocolate vermicelli, put in the truffles one at a time, swirling the bowl and tossing the truffle round until totally coated. Remove carefully and refrigerate or freeze until firm.
Makes 10

Variations

Substitute barely cooked dried apricot pieces or glacé pineapple for the centres and flavour the mixture with apricot brandy, Grand Marnier or Kirsch.

Easter Gâteau

This is an example of a basic cake recipe which can be cooked as here in 2 × 15 cm (6 in) sandwich cake shapes or in one large container.

100 g (4 oz) butter
100 g (4 oz) icing sugar, sifted
1 rounded teaspoon golden syrup
Few drops orange food colouring
¼ teaspoon almond essence
2 large eggs, beaten
100 g (4 oz) self-raising flour
2 tablespoons fresh orange juice

2 tablespoons apricot jam
4 heaped tablespoons whipped cream
2 tablespoons orange-coloured sugar frosting (page 206)
1-2 tablespoons cocoa

16 ganache balls (see page 211)
2 × 15 cm (6 in) sandwich cake shapes, greased

First make the ganache balls (see following recipe). Toss the balls in sifted cocoa and set aside.
To prepare the cake mixture, beat the butter, icing sugar,

golden syrup, colouring and almond essence together until the mixture is light and fluffy.

Add the eggs slowly, beating vigorously between each addition to avoid curdling.

Mix in the flour and orange juice to a soft dropping consistency.

Divide the mixture evenly between the two dishes, smoothing the surface with a knife. The mixture does not seem to be very much but it rises very well when baked.

Cook the cakes one at a time on High for 1¾-2¼ minutes until the cake is just dry on top and shrinks from the sides of the container. Turn out on to a cooling rack.

Sandwich the cakes with apricot jam and whipped cream. Using a palette knife press the frosting around the sides. Sprinkle the top of the cake with sifted cocoa and place ganache balls in a circle on the cake. If the balls will not stay in place affix them with apricot jam.

Serves 6 to 8.

Variations

Flavour the cake mixture with vanilla essence or add grated orange rind. Fill with the ganache mixture without prior refrigeration. Decorate with fudge icing.

Fill with fresh sliced strawberries and top with whipped cream.

Bake in small paper cases, allowing 20-30 seconds per cake, or in a large container for 4-6 minutes.

Ganache

   75 g (3 oz) plain chocolate, broken up
   1 egg yolk, beaten
   5 g (¼ oz) butter
   1 teaspoon sherry

Put the chocolate in a medium bowl, cover with cling film

and microwave on High for 1-1½ minutes or until melted.
Stir in the egg yolk and butter. As soon as the butter is
melted, add the milk and sherry and beat with a fork until
the mixture thickens.
Refrigerate until cold (or put in the freezer briefly). Roll
into small balls and toss in sifted cocoa.
The mixture will be firm but sticky and messy – but you
should be able to shape it easily.
Makes 16 small balls

Marble Cake

The cake keeps well and is very smooth and moist with a
rich flavour. When the chocolate has set and the cake is
cold, cover with cling film and store in the refrigerator for
up to one week or in the freezer for a month. A fractional
defrost on Low does not affect the chocolate coating.

    150 g (5 oz) plain block cooking chocolate
    100 g (4 oz) unsalted butter
    115 g (4½ oz) caster sugar
    100 g (4 oz) plain flour
    1 level teaspoon baking powder
    2 large eggs, not straight from the refrigerator, beaten
    5 tablespoons single cream
    ½ teaspoon vanilla essence
    1 × 20 cm (2 pint) savarin ring mould, greased

Break up the chocolate, put in a small jug and cover with
cling film. Microwave on High for 1½-2½ minutes until
the chocolate melts. Stir as the sides begin to collapse.
Beat the butter and sugar together until light and fluffy.
If the butter is too hard to blend, put the bowl in the
microwave oven and heat on High for 10-15 seconds.
Sieve the flour and baking powder together.
Stir one tablespoon of the flour into the butter and sugar

mixture. Mix in the beaten eggs a quarter at a time. Add the remaining flour. Stir in the cream and vanilla essence.

Spread one half of the cake mixture evenly in the mould.

Mix just over half the melted chocolate into the remaining mixture. Put on top of the plain mixture, and using a teaspoon, swirl the mixtures slightly together so that there are pockets of chocolate and plain both on the top and bottom of the mould.

Microwave on High for 4½-6 minutes until the cake is just dry on top.

Leave for 5 minutes, then turn out on to a cooling wire.

If the remaining chocolate has started to set, microwave on High for 15 seconds to remelt. Swirl the melted chocolate over the top of the cake, making sure it covers most of the plain mix. Leave to cool.

Serves 6 to 8

Variations

Colour the plain mixture orange or pink and sprinkle chopped jelly decorations on to the chocolate coating while the cake is still warm.

Rich Fruit Cake

Do not overbake this rich mixture or it will harden during standing time while carry-over cooking continues. Fruit becomes very hot during cooking and retains the heat for 30-60 minutes.

    75 g (3 oz) butter, softened
    75 g (3 oz) caster sugar
    2 large eggs
    90g (3½ oz) plain flour
    1 level teaspoon baking powder
    1 level teaspoon mixed spice
    175 g (6 oz) sultanas

75 g (3 oz) currants
5 glacé cherries, chopped
25 g (1 oz) fresh mixed chopped peel
2 tablespoons milk
2 teaspoons coffee essence
1 tablespoon whisky
1 teaspoon orange bitters
50g (2 oz) yellow sugar frosting

Cream the butter and sugar together, then add all the other ingredients except the whisky and orange bitters and beat thoroughly for 3-4 minutes.

Half-fill a round cake shape and make a well the full depth of the mixture in the centre.

Microwave on High for 3 minutes or until the edges of the cake begin to set.

Lower the setting and cook on Low for 10-12 minutes until the mixture is just dry on top and the cake shrinks away from the sides of the dish.

Leave for 5 minutes, then turn on to a plate and reverse on to a cooling wire.

Pierce the surface of the cake in several places and spoon over a mixture of the whisky and orange bitters.

Thickly coat the top and sides of the cake with the yellow sugar frosting.

To store, wrap in cling film, then overwrap in aluminium foil as soon as the cake is cool.

Serves 8 to 12

Variations

Cover the top of the cake with apricot jam and halved glacé cherries. Exchange 50 g (2 oz) sultanas for 50 g (2 oz) chopped dates and add 25 g (1 oz) chopped walnuts.

Upstairs Downstairs Lemon Sponge

During cooking the top sets in a delicious sponge and a creamy lemon sauce forms underneath. Please don't think there is a mistake in the recipe. Only a small amount of flour is required.

2 large eggs, separated
175 g (6 oz) caster sugar
250 ml (8 fl oz) creamy milk
Juice and grated rind of 1 lemon
20 g (¾ oz) plain flour, sifted twice
Pinch salt
1.2 litre (2 pint) shallow pie dish

Whisk the egg yolks and sugar together, using an electric whisk, or set the mixing bowl over a pan half-filled with hot water and whisk with a rotary beater until the mixture is thick and bulky. The mixture is not the same mousse-like consistency that occurs when mixing sponge mixtures.

Stir in the milk, lemon rind and juice, and fold in the flour and salt.

Using clean beaters, whip the egg whites until stiff peaks form.

Do not be tempted to go on after this stage is reached or the egg white will break up and be difficult to mix with the batter. Stir one spoonful of beaten white into the batter, then fold in the remainder, using a metal spoon.

Pour into the prepared dish and microwave on Low for 7-8 minutes, turning the dish from time to time until the mixture sets.

Switch to full power. Microwave on High for 1-2 minutes until the surface of the pudding is firm and a rich lemony sauce has formed underneath. You will be able to see this if you use an ovenglass dish.

Brown under the grill if desired and serve hot or cold.

This pudding can also be cooked on High for 2 minutes, then rest for 2 minutes and continue for a further 2-3 minutes.
Serves 4

Welsh Tarts

Crumb Base
40 g (1 ½ oz) butter, melted
4 large wheatmeal digestive biscuits, finely crushed
2 teaspoons sugar

Filling
225 g (8 oz) Philadelphia cream cheese
1 egg (size 3)
1 teaspoon vanilla essence
50 g (2 oz) caster sugar

Topping
2 tablespoons jam
Shredded coconut
25 g (1 oz) icing sugar

6-8 deep cake paper cases, doubled and put into individual undecorated ramekins or microwave muffin dishes

Combine the crumb base ingredients and press into the bottoms of the paper cases.
Put into the dishes and microwave on High for 1-1 ½ minutes, turning once to set the crust. Individual dishes must be spaced out in a circle and repositioned during cooking.
To make the filling, beat the cheese to soften, then beat in the egg, vanilla essence and sugar.
Spoon into the cake cases and microwave on Medium for

2½-3½ minutes until just set. The mixture does not rise so that the cases may be fully filled.

Chill for one hour for the filling to set completely.

Top each cake with a teaspoon of jam and some shredded coconut.

Mix the sugar to a thin paste with a few drops of warm water and drizzle over the coconut. Leave for a few minutes to set.

Makes 6

BAKED CUSTARDS

For a really thick custard use 4 large eggs to 1 pint of milk. Bring the milk to steaming, but do not let it boil or the eggs will scramble. Stir the milk into the eggs, beating thoroughly, then strain through a sieve into a jug or lipped bowl. Add sweet custard ingredients such as sugar and vanilla essence before straining and savoury quiche ingredients such as bacon and peas after straining.

The pre-heating of the milk gives a boost to the cooking and produces a more even texture from the centre to edge of the dish. Individual custards will cook more uniformly than larger dishes. Microwave on High using a water bath to slow down the cooking or use a combination of High and Low for the best results. Cover the dishes with cling film during the cooking and remember that cooking continues as the custards cool, when the centre will set more firmly.

Custards are sufficiently cooked when the centre is wobbly but not runny. Give large dishes a quarter-turn three times during cooking, and arrange small individual ramekin dishes in a circle on the oven shelf repositioning if necessary two or three times during cooking. If you have an oven fitted with a turntable you can ignore this instruction.

Crème Caramel

Use oven gloves to protect your hands when preparing caramel as sugar syrups are very hot.

Caramel
> 100 g (4 oz) caster sugar
> 4 tablespoons water

Custard
> 600 ml (1 pint) creamy milk
> 4 large eggs, lightly beaten
> 50 g (2 oz) caster sugar
> ½ to 1 teaspoon vanilla essence

> 1.25 litre (2 pint) pie dish or 6-7 individual ramekin dishes

To make the caramel, stir the sugar and water in a large heatproof jug and microwave on High for 5-7 minutes, stirring once during cooking until the the syrup is caramel brown. Inspect every half-minute as the syrup darkens and burns quickly. If foaming occurs stir carefully with a long handled spoon. Have ready a bowl of warm water into which you can dip the base of the jug should the caramel appear to be darkening rapidly.

Pour the syrup equally into the dishes and swirl round the sides to coat. Leave to set while making the custard.

To heat the milk, microwave on High for 2½-3½ minutes until hot to the touch.

Beat the eggs, sugar and vanilla essence together and add the milk, beating until well combined.

Strain through a sieve into a jug or lipped bowl and pour equally into the dish(es). Fill to within 5mm (¼ in) of the rim.

Cover the dishes with cling film and arrange in a circle on the microwave shelf. Microwave on High for 1 minute, then on Low for 7-9 minutes until the custard is just set, repositioning halfway through the cooking period.

Remove the cling film and when cool turn the custards out on to a single serving dish or into individual shallow champagne glasses.

Most of the caramel will have melted to form a sauce around the custard.

Crème caramel can be refrigerated for a day or two before using, but should not be frozen.

Serves 6

Variations

Substitute a tablespoon of strawberry jam for the caramel. Omit the caramel and mix a tablespoon of cocoa into the hot milk for a chocolate custard. Serve in the moulds, topping with a dollop of whipped cream. Omit the sugar and vanilla essence from the custard and substitute chopped cooked bacon for the caramel. Bake the sweetened mixture in a crumb crust for an unusual dessert, sprinkling the surface of the custard with nutmeg as soon as it is removed from the oven.

Theresa's Never Fail Custard

Egg custards are reasonably easy to make in the microwave oven but this one is foolproof. It includes a small quantity of flour to stabilize the sauce. When freshly made, the custard pours like double cream, but on cooling it sets firm enough to use as a pastry filling. Theresa devised the recipe to persuade her children to have their milk.

600 ml (1 pint) milk
40 g (1½ oz) (1 heaped tablespoon) plain flour
40 g (1½ oz) (1 heaped tablespoon) caster sugar
1 large egg
½ teaspoon vanilla essence

In a 1 litre (2 pint) bowl blend 3 tablespoons of the milk with the flour, sugar, egg and vanilla essence.

Stir thoroughly with a wire whisk.

To heat the remaining milk, microwave on High for 2½-3½ minutes until hot to the touch, but not steaming. Use a jug or heat carefully in the fully opened carton, but never in a milk bottle or a Long Life carton.

Pour the milk into the egg mixture and beat thoroughly until smooth. It only takes 3-4 seconds.

Put the bowl in the microwave oven and, without covering, cook on High for 3-3½ minutes, whisking every 30 seconds until the sauce is thick enough to coat the back of a spoon. If you have a clear view into the oven it is time to whisk when you see a thick ridge appearing around the edge of the sauce.

Custard not required immediately should be covered with cling film and refrigerated if possible.

Makes just over 600 ml (1 pint)

Variations

Flavour with almond essence or angostura bitters. Colour green and flavour with crème de menthe. Blend with liquidized soft fruit for a fruit fool.

Chocolate Mousse

Most people like chocolate mousse, it is easy to make in a microwave oven, since it is so simple and quick to prepare. If you wish, make a double quantity and freeze in suitable dishes.

175 g (6 oz) plain chocolate
7 g (¼ oz) unsalted butter
2 teaspoons brandy
2 large eggs, separated

Freshly whipped cream to decorate
4 ramekin dishes or champagne glasses

Break up the chocolate, put into a bowl, cover with cling film and microwave on High for 1½-2 minutes until melted.
Stir in the butter and brandy.
Leave to cool for a few moments – not too long, as the mixture thickens rapidly – and beat in the egg yolks.
Using a clean whisk, beat the egg whites until soft peaks form.
Stir 1 tablespoon of the beaten whites into the chocolate mixture to make it more manageable, then fold in the remainder.
Spoon into individual dishes and refrigerate for 1 hour.
Top with a swirl of freshly whipped cream.
Serves 4

SPONGE PUDDINGS

Sponge puddings, whether made with suet, butter or margarine, are really excellent when they are eaten fresh from the oven. They harden when cool but these puddings should not be eaten cold. Reheat either the whole pudding or just a slice for a bare minute and then add a little extra topping. Use any conventional recipe but if jam or syrup is to be put in the bottom before cooking, be sure to choose an ovenglass or pottery bowl. Preserves, having a high sugar content, become very hot indeed, so leave these puddings to stand for a few moments before serving. Pudding basins should be well-greased and only half-filled with the batter. Cover with cling film but this must not only be loose, but domed above the pudding. If the cling film is too tight it will shrink back on to the top of the pudding, causing it to flatten and become heavy.

My Syrup Sponge Pudding

Much as I like conventional recipes I would urge you to try my perfect syrup pudding.

   100 g (4 oz) self-raising flour
   Pinch salt
   2 large eggs
   100 g (4 oz) best butter (slightly salted)
   100 g (4 oz) soft dark brown sugar
   1 generous teaspoon golden syrup
   ½-1 teaspoon vanilla essence
   2 tablespoons cold milk
   2 generous tablespoons golden syrup
   1 × 1.2 litre (2 pint) pudding basin, greased

Sift the flour and salt together and beat the eggs in a separate bowl.

Cream the butter and sugar together, beating more than usual until the mixture is fluffy.

Stir in the syrup, vanilla essence and one-third of the flour.

Beat in the eggs gradually and, when well-incorporated, fold in the remaining flour.

Gently stir in the milk. The mixture should be a rather wet batter of a dark brown colour.

Spoon the 2 tablespoons of golden syrup into the base of the prepared bowl and pour the batter on top. Cover the bowl very loosely with cling film, pressing it close at the sides but pulling it high above the centre of the pudding.

Microwave on High for 4-7 minutes until the pudding is just dry on top and shrinks away from the sides of the basin.

Remove the cling film carefully and turn out the pudding on to a warm dish and serve within 10 minutes.

Serves 4-6

Variations

Substitute 15 g (½ oz) cocoa powder and 15 g (½ oz) cornflour for 25 g (1 oz) of the flour for a chocolate pudding.

Stir in 50 g (2 oz) raisins or sultanas for a fruit pudding.

Use a mixture of half white and half brown sugar for a paler pudding.

Mix chopped apple into the batter for an apple pudding and bake without jam or syrup adding custard (see page 182) when serving.

Zabaglione

A way of using up left-over egg yolks for a dessert which is so much easier to prepare by microwave.

5 egg yolks plus 1 whole egg, lightly beaten
25 g (1 oz) caster sugar
120 ml (4 fl oz) Marsala wine

Put the wine in a jug and microwave on High for 1½-2½ minutes until just boiling.

Strain the eggs into a medium bowl, stir in the sugar and beat to a foam.

Pour the Marsala on to the egg mixture, beating vigorously. Microwave on High for 1-1½ minutes, beating every 15 seconds until the sauce thickens. Beat once more.

Alternatively, microwave on Low for 2½-4 minutes, then beat vigorously at the end of the cooking time.

Serve at once.

Serves 4

Variations

Use 2 whole eggs and 2 yolks for a less creamy sauce.

Substitute sherry or Madeira for Marsala wine.

Serve as a sauce with fruit instead of a dessert in its own right.

Microwave Cream

When you are desperate for cream in a special recipe and all the shops are closed you can make your own with the aid of your microwave oven. The consistency will depend on the amount of butter you use – must be unsalted. The cream is rich and buttery tasting so it is not really suitable for serving as a topping, but it blends well in cheesecake mixtures, ice-creams, fools and mousses – except chocolate which has too high a fat content.

	Milk	Unsalted Butter
Pouring cream	150 ml (5 fl oz)	110 g (3¾ oz)
Whipping cream	150 ml (5 fl oz)	150 g (5 oz)
Double cream	150 ml (5 fl oz)	190 g (6¼ oz)

Cut the butter into small pieces and put into a bowl with the measured milk.

Microwave on Medium for 3-4 minutes until the butter is melted and the milk just warm. It is better not to use the High setting as even heating is essential.

Pour into the liquidizer and give three 10-second bursts on Medium.

Pour into a clean bowl and refrigerate for a minimum of 2 hours (but preferably overnight) when the cream will thicken further.

Sweeten with 1 rounded teaspoon sugar to 300 ml (½ pint) cream.

Beat with a hand whisk and use as required.

The cream will keep in the refrigerator for 2-3 days.

Makes 150-300 ml (¼-½ pint)

11

Pastry and Yeast Doughs

In the early days of recipe development for microwave ovens I tried to cook every type of food in them. I was so excited that I practically forced myself to prove that everything was possible.

Well: Pastry *is* possible but it is nowhere near as good as when it is baked in a hot conventional oven. If you are going to the trouble of making your own pastry you might just as well go to a bit more and bake it conventionally. Shortcrust and puff are available commercially frozen, and puff, which is time-consuming to make at home, is probably the more successful of the two when baked by microwave. Watching puff pastry rise in the microwave is quite astounding and the beauty of it is that, should it flop when the oven door is open, it will revive to rise as soon as the machine is switched on again. Puff pastry is ready when it holds the risen shape and ceases to shiver. Cooked this way it is crisp, although slightly hard and pale but it can be browned under the grill.

Puff pastry should not be baked 'blind'. Shape as you wish, into strips, crescents or vol-au-vent cases, and microwave on High. As a rough guide, allow 30-60 seconds per 25 g (1 oz) pastry. Cook until the pastry stays risen.

SHORTCRUST PASTRY

There may be times when you have to utilize the microwave oven for making shortcrust pastry, perhaps when your conventional oven is full or possibly broken down, so here is the way to do it.

Make pastry using milk, rather than water, to bind. Roll out and line the dish in the usual way. Cover with a double piece of kitchen paper and put a flat-bottomed undecorated plate on top. Microwave on High for 3 minutes, rotating the dish four times during cooking, unless your oven is fitted with a turntable. Remove the plate and paper at once and you will see that the surface of the pastry is glassy-looking. Continue cooking on High for a further 1½-2 minutes, depending on the diameter and thickness, until flaky bubbles appear and the pastry is opaque. Leave to stand for a few minutes before filling. Sometimes the sides of the pastry case over-cook and, to avoid this, wrap a thin band of aluminium foil over the edges of the dish after the initial baking. Continue baking according to the filling.

A more successful result is achieved if plenty of baking beans are used instead of a plate. Cooking takes a little longer but the heat of the beans cooks and lightens the pastry base.

While unfilled microwave shortcrust pastry does taste doughy, when the filling is added and subsequently cooked, the texture is most acceptable. So, before you decide against microwaving your pastry, try a cooked filled microwaved flan and you will be surprised how palatable it will be. Microwaved shortcrust pastry is palid. To improve the look, brush the edges with beaten egg yolk or add a few drops of yellow food colouring when mixing. Brown the pastry under the grill and, if you are making unfilled pastry cases, the bases can also be browned this way.

To reheat flans and pastry, put the pastry on a double sheet of kitchen paper so that the pastry will remain dry. Reheat only until the filling is hot. Jam fillings can reach boiling point in seconds and if you only require a single slice, wrap in greaseproof paper to prevent the filling from flowing over the edges. Allow about 30 seconds on High for average slices. Custard tarts should be reheated on Medium High so that the mixture does not toughen.

BREAD

Buy fresh yeasty loaves whenever you are passing a particularly appealing baker's shop. Freeze them immediately you get home and you can be assured of fresh bread at any time using your microwave oven for thawing. Leave the bread in its paper bag and seal in a polythene bag. To defrost, just remove the polythene covering, put the bagged loaf in the microwave oven, switch on at High and microwave for 1-2 minutes or until the ends yield to gentle pressure. Large loaves should be turned over halfway through defrosting. You should still feel a hard lump inside the loaf. *Don't* put the bread back for further microwaving. In a very few minutes the heat will equalize and the bread will be thawed. Bread bought without benefit of a paper bag should be wrapped in kitchen paper during thawing. Ice crystals form in the dough during freezing and the moisture created during defrosting is absorbed by the paper and this avoids soggy bread. Bread over-thawed by microwave will start to cook – and then stale more quickly.

For wrapped cut bread, preferably remove the number of slices needed and thaw as above. Separated slices thaw more quickly than a whole loaf. To thaw the whole loaf, remove any metal tags. Puncture the paper or plastic wrapper in several places and thaw as for fresh uncut bread.

Reheat bread rolls in a doily-lined bread basket, provided it has no metal staples, and allow 15-20 seconds per roll on High. Rolls can be thawed and reheated in one go and very little extra time is required. Stale rolls will taste fresh when warmed through by microwave but will not weather a second reheating.

BREAD MAKING

The microwave oven can assist in many ways in yeast bread-making.

To warm the flour in the mixing bowl microwave on High for 30-60 seconds. Heat liquid to blood temperature on High. When the dough is mixed put it back in the bowl (one suitable for microwave of course), three-quarters cover the bowl with cling film and stand it in a dish containing boiling water. Put both into the oven cavity and microwave on Low for 5 minutes. Leave to rest for 10 minutes, then repeat until the dough has doubled in size. On High settings only, completely cover the top of the bowl and, without placing in a water bath, microwave on High for 5-10 seconds followed by a 10-minute rest. Repeat until the dough is risen.

Bread dough can be cooked in a microwave oven but it tends to be more dense with fewer little air holes. The yeast has a lot of hard work to do and the oven 'spring' can only be controlled properly with dry heat at correct temperatures. The carbon dioxide created cannot easily escape from the dough and sometimes, as a result, the bread tastes slightly sour. Microwaved bread does not brown and crispen. Wholemeal bread is acceptable but I can really only recommend microwaved wholemeal *rolls* which are more successful since they have natural colour and their small mass is quickly cooked.

Why not use your microwave oven for hastening the rising time, then bake in a conventional hot oven?

Yeast mixtures containing extra butter and eggs, and more of a batter consistency, do bake well in the

microwave oven; so use this method for savarins, babas
and stollen.

Fruit loaves and tea breads bake satisfactorily and are
delicious sliced and toasted.

SAVARINS

Rum babas and savarins are syrupy, spongy cakes made
from an enriched yeast dough. The microwave oven will
bake the cakes in 4 rather than 40 minutes. Rum babas
were originally made in dariole moulds and often
contained currants, but are better known baked in small
ring moulds. The larger cake, the savarin, is traditionally
baked in a ring which is an ideal shape for cakes baked in
the microwave oven. Use your own recipe or those in other
microwave cook-books.

One of the biggest problems with yeast doughs is that
they take such a long time from start to finish. Use your
microwave oven to warm the milk or water, to hasten the
rising process by giving the covered dough 15 seconds'
(active) microwave energy on Low every 10 minutes. Use
the microwave oven for making the syrups (see page 195),
to make glazes. Baking on High, a small cake takes 2½-3
minutes, a large cake 4-5 minutes. After the cake is ready,
turn it on to a cooling wire set over a tray. Add the liqueur
or sherry to the syrup and spoon on to the upturned cake.
It will absorb more than you think. For glazing, put jam
on an undecorated saucer and microwave on High for 10
seconds until melted but not boiling. To finish, decorate
with chopped pineapple and fill the centre with freshly
whipped cream. Sprinkle with chopped pistachio nuts or
flavour the syrup with rum and decorate the cake with
chopped glacé fruit. To make a ginger savarin use the
syrup from a jar of stem ginger to impregnate the cake.
Chop the ginger and mix with the cream for the filling.

BISCUITS AND COOKIES

Biscuit mixtures baked in one piece and subsequently cut into bars, are delicious, but take care not to over-cook. Biscuits are ready when just dry on top although they may appear under-cooked. Test with a wooden cocktail stick or skewer which should come out clean. When left too long in the oven you may be surprised to find that they are burnt inside. High sugar content items attract the most microwaves and when enclosed, as in the centre of a mixture, with no means of heat escape, burning begins to take place. Since the air in the microwave cavity is cool the outside of the biscuits is not affected.

Rolled out or dropped mixtures are successful but as you can only bake a few at a time you might just as well bake them conventionally.

Bread

Wholemeal breads are more successful than white. Although the results are nowhere near as good as conventionally baked bread, the microwave can be utilized when the conventional oven is busy or in hot weather because the microwave oven does not heat the kitchen. Use your favourite bread recipe, hastening the rising a few times with 15 seconds on Low microwave from time to time. Brush the risen dough with oil, and if you are using a loaf dish this should be greased round the sides and lined with non-stick paper on the bottom. Bake loaves uncovered, turning the dish three times during cooking. Most bread can be microwaved on High for 4-6 minutes. Leave in the dish for a few minutes before turning out on to a cooling rack. Brown all sides under the grill for a crustier finish.

Rolls

Arrange risen rolls 8 at a time in a circle on a lightly greased oven shelf. Microwave on High for 2-3 minutes, repositioning the rolls halfway through the cooking. 450 g (1 lb) flour produces 16 small rolls.

Crumb Bases

These are easier and tastier than microwave pastry for use in sweet dishes. Make up a quantity of crumb base, using crushed biscuits, butter and sugar and vary the types of biscuits and sugar and add ground or chopped almonds for a change.

You need 25 g (1 oz) butter and ½-1 tablespoon sugar to 3 biscuits.

Microwave the butter on High until melted, then stir in the crushed crumbs and sugar.

Press into the dish and then microwave on High for 1-1½ minutes for 6 small tarts or 1½-2 minutes for a large flan.

CHEESECAKE

Make refrigerated cheesecake using the microwave oven to prepare the crumb base and dissolve the gelatine. Baked cheesecake is equally easy to prepare but do not over-cook.

Caramel Cheesecake

Base
  75 g (3 oz) butter
  175 g (6 oz) sweetmeal (digestive) biscuits, grated or finely crushed

Filling

>   225 g (8 oz) natural cottage cheese
>   225 g (8 oz) Philadelphia cream cheese
>   100 g (4 oz) caster sugar
>   1 teaspoon cornflour
>   2 large eggs
>   ½-1 teaspoon vanilla essence
>   25 g (1 oz) sultanas

Topping

>   250 ml (8 fl oz) soured cream
>   25 g (1 oz) caster sugar
>   50 g (2 oz) demerara sugar

Put the butter in a deep 20 cm (8 in) or shallow 23 cm (9 in) flameproof dish. Microwave on High for 1-1½ minutes until melted.

Stir in the biscuit crumbs, mixing thoroughly with a fork, then press evenly into the base and sides of the dish.

Microwave on High for 1½ minutes to set the crust.

Beat the filling ingredients, except the sultanas, together preferably using an electric whisk or food processor.

Pour into the prepared dish, sprinkle with the sultanas and microwave on Low for 8-12 minutes until the sides are well-cooked and the centre just set, giving the dish a quarter-turn three times during cooking.

Combine the soured cream with the caster sugar, pour over the cheesecake and microwave on High for 2-3 minutes, giving the dish a half-turn after one minute.

Chill until firm.

Sprinkle the cake with the demerara sugar and put under the grill until the sugar melts. Chill for 10 minutes before serving.

Serves 6 to 8

Variations

Top with pie filling instead of the demerara sugar. Stir 25 g

(1 oz) melted chocolate unevenly into the filling before cooking. Top cold cake with crushed chocolate flake.

Date and Almond Cookie Bars

I am not greatly in favour of making biscuits in the microwave oven but this recipe really is scrumptious. Bake the mixture in a round or square dish or an oblong loaf shape. The mixture becomes very hot so you may prefer to choose a glass or Vitri-dur. Roast the almonds in the microwave oven on High for 3½-4 minutes.

100 g (4 oz) stoned dates, chopped
50 g (2 oz) grated or finely chopped carrot
15 g (½ oz) caster sugar
1 rounded tablespoon clear honey
4 tablespoons fresh orange juice
1 tablespoon lemon juice
½ teaspoon vanilla essence
50 g (2 oz) blanched almonds, toasted and chopped
100 g (4 oz) soft margarine
75 g (3 oz) soft brown sugar
½ level teaspoon bicarbonate of soda
50 g (2 oz) flour
40 g (1 ½ oz) porridge oats

Combine the dates, carrot, sugar, honey, orange and lemon juices and vanilla essence in a medium glass measuring jug or bowl. Microwave on High for 1-1½ minutes until the mixture is thick.
Stir in the nuts and leave to cool for a few minutes.
Beat the margarine and sugar together until fluffy, then mix in the bicarbonate of soda, flour and oats. Press into the base of the dish and spread the date mixture on top.
Microwave on Medium for 5 minutes, giving the dish a half-turn halfway through cooking.

Raise the setting and microwave on High for 2-2½ minutes, giving the dish a quarter-turn every 45 seconds until the mixture is bubbling rapidly and singing loudly. Although the mixture may look totally uncooked it is ready if the ends come cleanly away from the dish when tipped. *Over-cooking will cause burning inside the mixture.* On cooling, the cookie bars become firm. If they are brittle give less cooking time next time.

Mark into pieces while still warm and separate when cool.

Makes 16-20

Milles Feuilles

This means one thousand leaves but in fact puff pastry can only have as many as 280 separate flaky layers.

> 200-225 g (7½-8 oz) ready-to-roll puff pastry
> Half jar raspberry jam
> 150 ml (¼ pint) confectioner's custard (see page 196)
> 300 ml (½ pint) double cream, whipped
> 175 g (6 oz) icing sugar
> Red colouring
> Cocktail stick or skewer

Roll out the pastry to an oblong 3 mm (⅛ in) thick and cut into 3 equal pieces. Put each on to a sheet of kitchen paper and cook separately. Microwave on High for 2½-3½ minutes until the pastry is full risen and does not flop when the oven door is open.

Trim the pastry with a sharp knife and reserve the trimmings.

Cut each piece in half to form fingers, then split the pastry horizontally and cool on a wire rack. Sandwich each two matching pieces with a layer of jam and confectioner's custard mixed with one-third of the cream. Top with the remaining pastry pieces.

Blend the icing sugar with just enough water to mix to a coating consistency and spoon over the top of the pastries. Before the icing is set, dip the point of the cocktail stick in red colouring and draw through the white icing in a trellis pattern.

Crush the reserved pastry trimmings, spread out on a baking tray and brown briefly under the grill. They brown quickly so take care.

Spread the sides of the pastries with the remaining cream and coat with the browned trimmings.

Makes 6

Sultana Tea Loaf

    1 rounded teaspoon dried yeast granules
    1 level teaspoon sugar
    Pinch Vitamin C powder
    Approx 175 ml (6 fl oz) hand-hot water
    1 tablespoon black treacle
    2 tablespoons malt extract
    1 teaspoon liquid caramel or gravy browning
    15 g (½ oz) butter
    100 g (4 oz) wholemeal flour
    100 g (4 oz) plain white flour, sifted
    ½ teaspoon salt
    3 tablespoons sultanas
    1 tablespoon clear honey
    1 × 25 × 11 × 6 cm (10 × 4¼ × 2½ in) loaf dish

Grease and line the base of the loaf dish. To line, stand the dish on a piece of non-stick paper and draw a line round the base, inserting the pencil underneath the curve. Cut out and reverse when inserting so that the pencil marks are not against the dough.

Stir yeast, sugar and Vitamin C powder into the water and leave until frothy (10-15 minutes).

When yeast mixture is ready combine the treacle, malt extract, caramel and butter in a small searproof bowl and microwave on High for 30-60 seconds to warm and soften. Do not over-heat.

Place flours and salt in a mixing bowl and microwave on High for 30 seconds. Stir.

Add the yeast liquid, treacle mixture and sultanas to the flour and mix to a floppy dough. Add more water if necessary and knead well. Spread evenly into the base of the dish and cover with cling film.

Microwave on Low for 15 seconds. Leave to rise, microwaving for a few seconds on Low from time to time; because this is a rich mixture rising will take at least an hour. To hasten rising in the microwave oven cook on Low for 15 seconds every 10 minutes. You can leave your loaf in much longer if you have a 10% power setting on your oven.

When the cling film balloons and the dough is double in size it is time to cook. Remove the cling film and microwave on High for 4-5 minutes until the bread shrinks away from the sides of the dish and is no longer gooey when pressed.

Turn out on to a cooling rack and pop under the grill to dry off the underside, but do not brown or the bread becomes too crisp.

Turn the loaf over and brush the top of the loaf with honey.

Serve sliced hot with butter or toasted when stale.

Makes 1 loaf

Quiche Lorraine

The first time that you attempt to cook a quiche, choose a filling that fits a 18 cm (7 in) pastry case. With this size there is little likelihood of the centre remaining runny while the outer edge becomes progressively tougher. Quiches must not be made larger than 23 cm (9 in).

    4 bacon rashers, derinded
    75 g (3 oz) Cheddar cheese, grated
    ½ small onion, finely chopped
    175 ml (6 fl oz) evaporated milk
    2 eggs (size 3)
    Pinch salt
    Pinch white pepper
    Pinch Cayenne pepper
    ¼ green pepper cut into strips for garnish
    1 × 18 cm (7 in) pre-baked pastry case

Spread the bacon rashers on a plate and cover with cling film. Microwave on High for 3-4 minutes or until cooked. Drain on kitchen paper.

Using kitchen scissors, snip the bacon into the pastry case. Cover with the cheese and onion.

Put the milk in a small measuring jug and microwave on High for 30-45 seconds until warm. Beat in the eggs and seasonings and pour over the cheese. Microwave on Low for 4-6 minutes, rotating the dish every minute until the custard is set round the edges and just wobbly in the centre.

Leave for 10 minutes to cool by which time the custard will be completely set.

Garnish with pepper strips.

Serves 3 to 4

Variations

Substitute shrimps or chopped ham, and use Lancashire or Cheshire cheese. Garnish with chopped chives.

VOL-AU-VENT

Puff pastry cases can be made in the microwave oven using

home-made pastry, but the ready stamped-out commercially frozen vol-au-vent cases rise more evenly.

Using your microwave oven, you can prepare a supper savoury in moments. Remove from the freezer as many vol-au-vent cases as are required and leave at room temperature for 15-20 minutes until they are no longer rock hard.

If your oven has a turntable, arrange them the right way up on kitchen paper in a circle and microwave on High allowing 1-1½ minutes for each case. Cook three at a time for best results.

In ovens with a non-movable shelf or base, group the vol-au-vent cases close together. It is not easy to re-position the pastry during cooking as puff pastry remains floppy until completely cooked. When the cases are close together they give each other support and rise more evenly.

Vol-au-vent cases may rise unevenly whichever type of oven is used, but it is possible to re-shape them with a palette knife halfway through the cooking period.

Use a fresh piece of kitchen paper for each batch and do not inadvertently leave it in the microwave oven, as it will burn if it becomes too dry.

The pastry cases are cooked when they cease to shiver. They will be pale, but further microwaving will only cause them to burn. If the section near the base seems hard it is because the pastry was insufficiently thawed before cooking.

Brown the tops and bottoms of the vol-au-vent under the grill before filling – or fill and reheat together in a hot oven for a few minutes.

Here are a few suggestions for savoury vol-au-vent.

Use 6 × 6-7.5 cm (2½-3 in) microwaved cases. Make 150 ml (¼ pint) white or Béchamel sauce (see page 186) using 25 g (1 oz) butter, 25 g (1 oz) flour and 150 ml (¼ pint) milk. Flavour as desired, e.g. cheese, tomato purée or anchovy essence.

To fill, use
100 g (4 oz) prawns, partly chopped; mushrooms, chopped or finely sliced; cooked ham, diced with one tablespoon peas, cooked; cooked chicken and a few chopped chives; flaked smoked haddock; canned tuna fish, drained and flaked; canned or fresh salmon, flaked or 2 hard-boiled eggs, chopped and mixed with 4 chopped anchovy fillets.

Puff pastry is equally acceptable when used for sweet dishes. Make your own or buy a block of frozen. Thaw at room temperature, then roll out to a thickness of 3 mm ($\frac{1}{8}$ in) and cut into squares, chips or circles.
Place on kitchen paper and microwave on High until the pastry is well-risen and no longer shivering.
Split horizontally in half and leave to cool.
Trim with a sharp knife. Crush the trimmings or surplus pieces of baked pastry, spread out on a baking tray and brown under the grill and use for decoration.
Allow approximately 1-1½ minutes per 25 g (1 oz) of pastry and be sure not to over-cook.
Recommended maximum quantity to be microwaved at any one time is 100 g (4 oz).
   It is not fatal to open the oven door and have a quick look at the pastry during the cooking period. It may flop, but will rise miraculously again when the cooking continues.

12

Fruit Desserts

Microwaved fruit retains its colour, shape, texture and fresh flavour. Cook all fruit the microwave way unless you require the long slow stewing necessary to extract pectin for jam-making.

Until you had a microwave oven you could not cook a whole orange or grapefruit without the skin sagging, nor extract maximum juice from a hard-skinned lemon. It wasn't possible to have instantly a cold dessert of defrosted fruit, a cooked pudding with fresh firm fruity pieces underneath nor stewed dried fruit without pre-soaking. Just a simple baked apple took almost an hour in a conventional oven and a frying pan was needed to caramelize a handful of apple slices for garnishing. Syrups boiled over or splattered sticky deposits over the hob and crystallized fruit and jellies were complicated to prepare. All these and many other fruit desserts are possible using the microwave oven and they are quicker and easier too.

There are a few rules regarding microwave fruit cookery. Shiny-skinned fruits, such as apples, must be pricked, scored or sliced, otherwise they will burst. Think of the fruit as a completely covered container – the build-up of steam will cause too much pressure inside. When stewing gooseberries, plums, etc. cover the dish or the skins will burst unless the fruit is cooked on a Low setting. Fruit can be cooked from its frozen state but must be stirred, turned or rotated during cooking. Except when defrosting only, always select a cooking container that is large enough to prevent boiling over. Crumbles are the worst culprits as the topping acts as a lid. Three-quarters cover dishes with cling film when stewing so that overspill is avoided, yet stirring can still be carried out.

Thaw on Low or Defrost if you wish to eat the fruit straight. Over-thawing means cooking and you can imagine what that can do to an expensive fruit salad. Both thawing and cooking times are relative to the depth of coldness and this particularly applies to frozen fruit.

DEFROSTING

Place commercially frozen pouches on the oven shelf and pierce once or twice. Microwave on Low for 5-10 minutes until you can move the pieces about when the bag is pressed or flexed. You may not always require an entire packet. Empty the quantity you want into a serving dish – a large shallow one is best – and stir 'sides to middle' as soon as that icy look disappears from the ends.

You can also defrost on a High setting but this involves greater care when stirring. Too much stirring will cause delicate fruit to break up. Remove the fruit from the microwave oven when it is still cold to the touch. Leave at room temperature to complete defrosting.

BAKED APPLES

So many people fail with baked apples that I felt I should write a paragraph about this. The apples must not only be cored but must be scored around the waist so that the skin is completely broken. Any food in a skin is liable to burst. In addition, pair away a thin sliver of apple skin from the top and bottom edges of the cored cavity. If the apples are large, you may find it a good idea to turn them over halfway through the cooking. Do not cover the apple with cling film as this only serves to increase the temperature and cause uneven cooking. You may sometimes have had an apple that partially collapsed while the other half was not cooked. As you watch the apple cooking you will see that the top and bottom sections turn yellow and a gradually diminishing band of green is left in the centre. Remove the apples from the microwave oven when about 1 cm (½ in) or so of the green belt is showing. Now cover the apples with cling film and watch. Within 5 minutes that band of green will have turned yellow and the apple will be cooked perfectly. Should you decide to stuff the apples, you may find it better to bake them in a dish containing a little water, sugar and fruit, pushing the filling into the cavity when the apples are removed from the oven. Sugar is a great microwave attracter and there is a lot of natural sugar in dried fruit, hence there can be an uneven build-up of heat in the centre of the apple. The skin of microwave-baked apples is tougher than those of conventionally baked apples because the skin is at all times in a cooler atmosphere than the rest of the apple. However the tougher skin does hold the apple in shape. As far as timings go, think in terms of 2-3 minutes per apple.

Baked Apple Orange

Here is a variation on the baked apple theme. It is attractive and it is slimming too. The flavour is a combination of soft cooked apple and fresh tangy orange.

    1 large orange
    1 small green dessert apple
    1 glacé cherry

Stand the orange on its more stable end and remove a 2.5 cm (1 in) slice from the top of the orange. Using a grapefruit knife scoop out all the flesh. Chop and set aside. Make decorative zig-zag cuts around the top of the orange.

Core the apple. Insert the apple into the orange so that the top protrudes no more than 1 cm (½ in) and microwave on High for 3-4 minutes covering the top with cling film after 2 minutes. (The apple will take longer to bake than the ordinary baked apple since it is sitting in the orange skin.) There is no need to score it round the waist. When the apple is cooked remove the cling film, fill the cavity with the reserved chopped orange and top with a glacé cherry.

Two apples will take 5-7 minutes; three apples will take 8-11 minutes and four apples will take 10-15 minutes.

Blackcurrant and Banana Fool

Use this basic recipe for any fresh fruit fool.

   450 g (1 lb) blackcurrants, washed and trimmed
   100 g (4 oz) caster sugar
   2 bananas
   300 ml (½ pint) double cream whipped or
   300 ml (½ pint) microwaved double cream

Put the blackcurrants in a large ovenglass bowl with 1 tablespoon water. Three-quarters cover with cling film and microwave on High for 4-5 minutes, stirring occasionally until the fruit is soft.

Stir in the sugar until dissolved, then purée in the liquidizer, adding the bananas, cut into chunks. If you do not possess a liquidizer or food processor, mash the fruit thoroughly and whip with an electric whisk. The fool will be rougher but still very pleasant.

Pour into a chilled bowl and leave to cool.

Fold in the cream and spoon into individual dishes.

Chill in the refrigerator or put into the freezer for 20-30 minutes.

Serves 4 to 6

Caramel Oranges

   4-5 oranges
   300 ml (½ pint) stock syrup (page 195)
   1 tablespoon Curaçao

Using a sharp knife and a good, non-slippery chopping board, remove a thick slice from the top and bottom of the oranges. Stand the oranges one at a time, cut side down, on the board and working from the top edge, cut off the peel and pith vertically, guiding the knife in a curved motion. The orange flesh should now be exposed without any white pithy patches showing.

Slice the oranges horizontally and re-shape so that no one can detect the slices.

Place the orange peel shiny side down on the board and pare away as much of the white pith as you can. As you only require half the peel, you can discard any pieces that are too stubborn.

Finally slice the peel into matchsticks.

Put the shreds into a small jug, just cover with water and microwave on High for 3-4 minutes until these are tender. Drain.

Put the syrup into a large heatproof bowl or jug and microwave on High for 1-3 minutes until boiling. Continue to Microwave on High for 2-3 minutes until the syrup is tobacco-coloured.

Add the Curaçao and shake the bowl to incorporate it.

Stir in the drained orange shreds.

Arrange the oranges in a dish and pour the syrup over.

Baste three or four times so that the oranges absorb some of the syrup.

Leave until cold, basting occasionally.

Serves 4

Variations

Use Grand Marnier or Kirsch and substitute red grapefruit or a mixture of oranges and lemons.

Christmas Fruit Bar

This makes a tasty change from mince pies and has no pastry in the recipe. It is very attractive and has excellent keeping qualities. Serve with sponge fingers and whipped cream.

  1 medium-sized orange
  3 level teaspoons powdered gelatine
  450 g (1 lb) mincemeat
  100 g (4 oz) glacé cherries, chopped
  50 g (2 oz) dried apricots, chopped
  25 g (1 oz) walnuts, chopped
  5 tablespoons sherry
  50 g (2 oz) caster sugar for syrup

Peel the outer layer of peel from the orange so that no pith is attached.
Cut into petal shapes to use as decoration.
Squeeze the orange juice into a bowl and add 1 tablespoon water.
There should now be a total of 4 tablespoons of liquid.
Sprinkle the gelatine over the surface and stir in.
Microwave on High for 1-1¼ minutes until hot, but not boiling.
Stir until fully dissolved, then set aside for the mixture to cool slightly.
Empty the mincemeat into a large bowl and microwave on High for 1-1½ minutes, stirring occasionally until the suet melts.
Add the cherries, apricots, walnuts, sherry and dissolved gelatine. Stir thoroughly.
Pour the mixture into a 600 ml (1 pint) loaf-shaped dish which has been rinsed in cold water.
Chill in the refrigerator until set and cold.
You may find that as the mixture cools some of the liquid

separates and accumulates at one end of the mould, so stir to reincorporate the ingredients.

When the fruit bar is set turn on to a serving dish.

Mix the caster sugar with 4 tablespoons of water in a 600 ml (1 pint) measuring jug and stir well.

Microwave on High for 1 minute, then stir to make sure all the sugar is dissolved.

Continue to cook for 30 seconds or until boiling, then continue microwaving for 1½-2 minutes until a thin syrup forms.

Dip the orange petals in the syrup and arrange decoratively on the top of the fruit bar.

Serves 8-10

Fruit Crumbles

Any conventional recipe can be cooked. Make up crumble mix in bulk and store in the freezer alongside the packets of frozen fruit.

225 g (8 oz) butter or hard margarine
450 g (1 lb) plain or self-raising flour
Pinch salt
100-175 g (4-6 oz) granulated or demerara sugar
(according to the amount of sugar used when cooking the fruit)

Cut up the butter and rub into the sifted flour until the mixture resembles breadcrumbs.

Stir in the sugar.

Allow 225 g (8 oz) crumble mix to 450 g (1 lb) fruit, sweetened to taste.

This quantity serves 4 to 6.

Put the fruit in a deep dish. As the fruit cooks and bubbles, the steam forces its way out causing the syrup to escape round the edges. If the dish is filled to the top, the sticky syrup will ooze over the sides.

Thaw frozen fruit in the dish to make room for the topping. Spread the crumble topping over the fruit and press down lightly. Microwave on High for 12-15 minutes per 450 g (1 lb) combined weight of crumble mix and fruit (15-16 minutes for 675 g (1½ lb) total weight), allowing an extra 4-5 minutes if you are using frozen fruit not previously thawed. Leave to stand for 5 minutes, then brown under the grill. If you do not have time to brown under the grill sprinkle demerara sugar over the mix before microwaving. The sugar crunches up but does not dissolve. A deep round or square dish is the best shape to choose. If you only have a large shallow dish microwave on High for the first half of the cooking time and on Medium for the second half, doubling the microwave minutes on the Medium setting. Turn the dish 90° three times during cooking.

Suggested fillings
Apple
Apple flavoured with orange marmalade
Apple and blackberry
Blackberry
Rhubarb
Rhubarb and apple
Rhubarb with chopped stem ginger flavoured with ginger
   syrup

Gooseberry and Red Currant Grunt

It is essential to use a deep dish as the boiling fruit pushes up the coating lid and may spill over.

Filling
   25 g (1 oz) flour

½ teaspoon ground ginger
¼ teaspoon mixed spice
175 g (6 oz) castor sugar
350 g (12 oz) gooseberries, topped and tailed
100 g (4 oz) redcurrants, de-stalked and trimmed

Topping

40 g (1½ oz) quick porridge oats
75 g (3 oz) wholemeal flour
100 g (4 oz) butter
175 g (6 oz) demerara sugar

Cook the filling first. Put the flour and ginger and mixed spice in a deep round dish and blend in 6 tablespoons cold water.

Stir in the white sugar and the fruit.

Cover the dish loosely with cling film and microwave on High for 3½-4½ minutes until the fruit is softening in a thick syrup. Remove the cling film carefully.

Mix the oats and flour together and rub in the butter to form a crumble mix for the topping. Stir in most of the demerara sugar and sprinkle the remainder on top.

Spread the topping over the filling and microwave on High for 6-8 minutes until crispy on top.

Leave to stand for 5 minutes, then test the topping by inserting a sharp knife – it should come out clean. If not, allow a little longer. The filling is very hot and could burn your tongue.

Serves 4-6

Variations

Plums, apricots, apples and pears all go well with this topping. Dried fruit compôte mixed with 8 tablespoons of its syrup and 25 g (1 oz) flour needs to be brought to boiling point to thicken. Top and microwave as above or use crunchy muesli instead of oats and reduce the demerara sugar.

Lime and Lemon Jelly

This is a recipe that can only be made by microwave as the lemon slices would not be cooked properly any other way.

  1 lime jelly
  1 lemon, thinly sliced

Put the lime jelly in a large measuring jug with 150 ml (¼ pint) water. Microwave on High for 1½-2 minutes until the water is steaming and the jelly beginning to dissolve. Stir until the jelly is melted, then make up to 450 ml (¾ pint) with cold water.

Lay the lemon slices in a circle on a large plate and cover with cling film. Microwave on High for 2-2½ minutes until the lemon rind is tender. Carefully remove the cling film and drain the juice into the jelly. Stir thoroughly, then pour the jelly into a shallow serving dish. Discard the pithy ends of the lemon and float the better slices on top of the jelly. The slices will rise and they can then be easily rearranged before the jelly cools and sets.

Serves 4

Variations

Substitute orange slices and orange jelly or, for a richer jelly, substitute the 150 ml (¼ pint) of water with creamy milk.

Poached Pears Chantilly

Use this basic recipe for a variety of desserts.

  4 large firm pears
  225 g (8 oz) strawberry ice cream
  4 tablespoons strawberry jam, warmed in the microwave
    oven for 20 seconds
  Whipped cream

Peel, halve and core the pears and place cut-side down in a single layer in a shallow dish. Cover with greaseproof paper and microwave on High for 2 minutes. Reposition the fruit, putting the softer pieces in the centre. Re-cover and continue on High for 1½-2 minutes until all the fruit is tooth-tender. Leave to cool for a few minutes.

Place a pear half cut-side up in individual serving dish, put a scoop of ice cream on top and cover with another pear half. Top with the jam and a dollop of whipped cream.
Serves 4

Variations

For Pear Hélène, break up a small bar of plain dessert chocolate and put in a jug with 2 tablespoons of milk, microwave on High for 1½-2 minutes, stirring as soon as the chocolate softens. Pour over the poached pears and serve with whipped cream. Alternatively, substitute peaches for the pears, fill the cavities with chopped stem ginger and pour over a little of the ginger syrup from the jar.

Summer Meringue Pudding

Use any fresh fruit for this dessert. It is more successful if the fruit is not too ripe as too much juice makes the meringue topping weep. Choose from a mixture of bananas, sharp dessert apples, orange segments (still in their skins), halved apricots, sliced peaches, firm strawberries or stoned cherries. Add an oriental touch with lychees or cumquats. For special occasions prepare and serve in individual sundae glasses.

    1 banana, sliced
    1 sharp dessert apple, cored, quartered, but not peeled
    1 small orange, peeled and separated into segments
    6 strawberries, hulled

1 peach, stoned and sliced
1 tablespoon lemon juice
3 egg whites
175 g (6 oz) caster sugar

Mix the fruit and lemon juice together in a large shallow dish. The fruit should only half-fill the dish, allowing room for the meringue to grow.

In a grease-free bowl beat the egg whites until stiff. Add just under half the sugar and continue beating until stiff again. Peaks should form when the beater is lifted.

Fold in the remaining sugar.

Turn the meringue on to the fruit, spreading gently with a spatula so that the meringue touches the edges of the dish.

Microwave on Medium for 7-8 minutes or on Low for 10-12 minutes – until the meringue is firm. Give the dish a 90° turn four times during cooking. Brown for 30 seconds under a grill and serve hot or cold.

Serves 6

The pudding keeps surprisingly well in the refrigerator even though the meringue sometimes flops.

13

Jams and Preserves

I get quite carried away when I think of the delicious variety of jam, jellies and conserves that I can make using my microwave oven. Nearly every type of preserve can be quickly prepared in a microwave oven without the bother of getting out the preserving pan and, later, spending ages cleaning up the stove. Fruit retains its shape, colours remain clear and flavour is saved – all this because of the short cooking time. The longer sugar cooks the darker it becomes, so that with conventional boiling, the jam must to some extent discolour. Compare microwaved gooseberry jam with its conventionally cooked counterpart: one retains the whole gooseberry look and has a green tinge, while the other is mashed and nearly brown.

Use either fresh or frozen fruit, but add less water to the latter. All that you need is a large heatproof bowl and a wooden spoon. Put the fruit into the bowl, partially cover and microwave on High, stirring frequently, or on Low, stirring occasionally, until the fruit is soft. Remember fruit will not soften further once the sugar is added. Some fruits may need extra water and this depends on the kind you choose.

When the fruit is soft, stir in the sugar and, subject to the time factor, either start cooking at once or, better still, leave the mixture for half an hour or so until the sugar is fully dissolved. Add lemon juice, unless the fruit is acid, and water as necessary. Microwaving should now be carried out on High. Only half cover the bowl so that the mixture doesn't boil over and stir only when large bubbles appear around the edges. You must stir up and down as well as round and round or you'll miss the middle.

Test the jam in the usual way, i.e. the thermometer should register 110°C (220°F) (do not forget to remove the thermometer from the bowl before recommencing microwaving); the flake test (when a drop hangs from the side of the spoon); or the wrinkle test when a teaspoonful of jam will wrinkle on a cold saucer in about one minute when pushed with a finger.

Before potting the jam, make sure the jars are sterilized. To heat the jars, quarter-fill them with water and bring to a bubbling boil in the microwave oven. Four jars will take 1½-2 minutes but due to oven 'hot spots' this will not take place simultaneously. Remove each jar as it is ready or you may find the boiling water erupting from the jars. Use oven gloves to remove the jars from the oven and also to pour out the boiling water.

Fill each hot jar to within 2 cm (¾ in) of the rim and cover loosely with cling film or jam pot covers. Microwave on High for 20-60 seconds until you see the cling film balloon up. Immediately open the door and the film will gradually tighten, sinking down to touch the surface of the jam. Seal only one jar at a time so that you can give it your full attention. Should you leave it to its own devices it will probably boil over and then you will have to start again. Microwaved jam returns to the boil during the sealing process but, unlike conventional jam, the fruit should not rise to the top. This is because your microwaved jam is practically all fruit and very little syrup. Just one more word on sealing – it is no good trying to seal a half-filled pot as the cling film is not strong enough to be sucked so far down into the jar. It will only surrender and split.

Apples, blackcurrants, redcurrants, gooseberries and plums are high in pectin, the substance that is required to produce the 'gel'. Pectin is slowly drawn out of fruit by stewing slowly before sugar is added. You can assist this by microwaving on Low or Defrost for a long period or alternatively add liquid pectin which is obtainable at grocers and chemists.

You will be so delighted with your microwave marmalade with its thick syrupy texture that you won't want to go back to the old conventional method. But only three or four jars can be made at a time. If you are the 25 lb every January type you will have to use your usual preserving pan.

For low pectin fruits, which include blackberries, cherries, raspberries and strawberries, either mix in a quantity of 'sharper' fruit, such as cooking apples, or add lemon juice to provide acid, or use the commercial pectin. But for the most delicious raspberry jam you ever tasted, just use sugar and fruit alone. 450 g (1 lb) raspberries only makes 450 g (1 lb) jam and is consequently expensive, but worth every penny. Low pectin fruit turned into jam this way thickens further on storage in the freezer or refrigerator. Leave plenty of head space if it is being frozen or use a heatproof plastic box.

Curds are child's play to make and they keep for 3 weeks in a refrigerator or months in the freezer. Stay close by during the few minutes they take to cook. Pot while they are hot and do not worry if they seem runny. Curds thicken as they cool.

Let your imagination run riot when making Chutney and you can have a different flavour every week. Chutneys improve with keeping as the flavour develops. They must be tightly covered with a non-rusty lid or lid fixed over the cling film and may require a stir before using to provide an even consistency.

Gooseberry Jam

Frozen gooseberries take longer to soften but they cook more quickly than fresh fruit so that the total cooking time will be the same.

1 kg (2 lb) gooseberries

1 kg (2 lb) packet preserving sugar (retained in its packet)

Top and tail the gooseberries and pierce each berry with a sharp knife. This is to allow the pectin to gel quickly without the fruit mashing up.

Put the gooseberries in a large ovenglass bowl and three-quarters cover with cling film. Microwave on High for 4-6 minutes, stirring occasionally until the fruit becomes opaque and begins to soften.

Add 12 tablespoons boiling water (this is a generous 150 ml (¼ pint) and can be boiled in a glass in the microwave oven, taking a minute or so).

Put the packet of sugar (if it is a paper one) in the oven and microwave on High for 1-2 minutes to warm the sugar. Empty the sugar into the gooseberries and stir until completely dissolved.

To encourage obstinate mixtures, microwave on High for 1-2 minutes, followed by further stirring. When the sugar has dissolved, return the bowl to the oven and microwave on High for 15-20 minutes, stirring occasionally until the jam boils.

Continue to microwave on High for 10-20 minutes or until setting point is reached. To test, pour a teaspoon of the syrup on to a refrigerated saucer. The mixture should wrinkle when pushed with the tip of the finger.

Leave to cool a little, then spoon into hot sterilized jars, filling to within 2½ cm (1 in) of the rim.

Seal with jam pot covers or cling film.

Makes 4 jars

Raspberry Jam

Use fresh or frozen raspberries in this recipe but if you choose the frozen variety, thaw them slowly first on Low or Defrost, then drain away the juice, reserving it if you wish for another recipe. Expensive but worth it!

350 g (12 oz) granulated sugar
350 g (12 oz) raspberries

Put the sugar in a large ovenglass bowl and microwave on High for 5-6 minutes until the sugar is warm.
Stir in the raspberries thoroughly and microwave on High for 3 minutes. Stir thoroughly, but do not break up the fruit. Without covering, microwave on High for 12-14 minutes, stirring gently every 3 minutes.
Test for setting – the gel will be fairly weak at this stage but the jam will firm up when cool.
Makes 1 jar

Rhubarb and Grapefruit Jam

Forced rhubarb produces a better colour than the garden variety.

1 kg (2 lb) rhubarb
1 can concentrated grapefruit juice (the kind that makes up to the equivalent of 750 ml (1¾ pint))
1 kg (2.2 lb) packet preserving or granulated sugar

Top and tail the rhubarb and cut into 2½ cm (1 in) chunks. Put into a very large ovenproof bowl with the grapefruit concentrate and 300 ml (½ pint) water. Do not reconstitute the juice first.
Three-quarters cover with cling film and microwave on High for 20-25 minutes, stirring occasionally until the rhubarb is soft and pulpy. Remove the cling film.
Put the bag of preserving sugar in the microwave oven and microwave on High for 1-2 minutes to warm the sugar.
Stir into the rhubarb, mixing thoroughly until the syrup is completely dissolved. Microwave on High for 20-25 minutes until setting point is reached.

Pot, covering with jam pot covers or cling film.
Makes 4 jars

Variations

Stir in 100 g (4 oz) raisins 10 minutes before the end of cooking time. Flavour with 1 teaspoon ground ginger.

Plum Jelly

I made this recipe with a pack of frozen plums which were thawed but had the juice left in, but fresh juicy fruit is equally good. Halve the initial cooking time when using fresh fruit.

   1 kg (2 lb) plums, fresh or frozen
   225 g (8 oz) - 450 g (1 lb) granulated sugar

Put the plums in a large ovenglass bowl, three-quarters cover with cling film and microwave on High for 15 minutes, stirring every 5 minutes until the fruit is very soft. Strain through a nylon sieve into a bowl. Measure the liquid and allow 225 g (8 oz) granulated sugar to 300 ml (½ pint) of plum juice.
Return the juice to the cooking bowl and stir in the sugar. Leave for 30 minutes until cool, then stir if necessary until the sugar is completely dissolved. Three-quarters cover with cling film and microwave on High for 5 minutes. Stir thoroughly, microwave on High for a further 8-10 minutes and test for setting.
Makes 1-2 jars

MARMALADE

Do not try to use ordinary methods when making marmalade in the microwave oven. The pith and pips which contain the gelling agent have to be cooked slowly to extract all the pectin. I have now found the answer. Chop the pips and pith finely and let them boil freely in the given liquid rather than tied in a muslin bag. An efficient chopper such as a food processer is the ideal device but a sharp knife and board can do a pretty good job.

Any fruit combination can be used. Use the quantity of ingredients in any of your favourite recipes, but cut down on the water by about a third. When making lemon marmalade it is a good idea to add a pinch of salt to counteract the acidity. Marmalades will be beautifully clear and retain all the fresh flavour of the tangy fruit.

Three Fruit Marmalade

   1 lemon
   1 grapefruit
   1 orange
   1 kg (2¼ lb) packet preserving or granulated sugar
   Small knob butter

Wash and dry the fruit.
Using a potato peeler, pare away thin strips of peel, starting at the stalk end of the fruit.
Only a thin layer of white pith should be attached to the peel.
Chop the peel or cut into strips as tiny as you wish.
Set aside.
Chop up the fruit including the pith, the flesh and the pips. The pips particularly must be well and truly broken.
Put into a large ovenglass bowl with 450 ml (¾ pint) boiling water.
Without covering, microwave on High for 10-12 minutes.
Pour the mixture through a nylon sieve into another large ovenglass bowl and press the cooked pulp until all the juice is squeezed out. You will find that you are left with a large mound of pulp which you must discard.
Stir in the reserved peel and microwave on High for 10 minutes or until the peel is tender but not soft. Stir once during cooking.

Provided the sugar packet has no metal staples put the entire packet into the oven and microwave on High for 1-2 minutes. This warms the sugar, making it easier to dissolve.

Stir the sugar into the marmalade mixture until dissolved. Microwave on High for 5 minutes then stir in the butter to prevent foaming. Microwave on High for 5 more minutes or until a spoonful of syrup, when put on a refrigerated plate, wrinkles when pushed with the finger.

Pot the marmalade in hot sterilized jars and seal with cling film or jam pot covers.

Makes 3 jars

Lemon Curd

225 g (8 oz) granulated sugar
Juice and grated rind of 3 large lemons
100 g (4 oz) unsalted butter, at room temperature
3 large eggs, beaten

Mix sugar, juice and grated lemon rind in a large bowl. Microwave on High for 3-4 minutes or until the sugar has dissolved. Stir. Add the butter in one piece. Microwave on High for 1 minute, then cut up the butter to hasten melting. Microwave on High for 1-2 minutes until the butter has fully melted. Stir, then leave to cool for 2-3 minutes. The mixture *must* cool down before adding the egg yolks or they will scramble on contact.

Strain in the eggs from a height, beating continuously. Microwave on High for 2-3½ minutes until a band of thickened curd is visible around the edge. Beat lightly to mix, then microwave on High until the curd reappears. Remove the bowl from the oven and beat the mixture thoroughly until the curd thickens. You will notice a resistance to the whisk as you whisk. The lemon curd is cooked when the slightly cooled mixture is thick enough to coat the back of a spoon. The curd will thicken considerably when cool. Remove from the microwave oven with oven gloves. Pour into jars and seal with cling film or jam pot covers.

Makes 575 g (1 ¼ lb)

Variations

Substitute orange juice for 2 of the lemons or use grapefruit instead of lemon juice.

CHUTNEY

Chutney improves with keeping and should be left to mature for several weeks. All kinds can be made in a large ovenglass bowl in the microwave oven without fear of scorching on the bottom, but sweet chutneys with a high sugar content will darken and could burn if they are not stirred frequently. Use a spiced vinegar for pickles which can be prepared well in advance. Although up to 2.75 kg (6 lb) chutney or pickle can be made in the microwave oven at one time I prefer to make a smaller quantity and have a larger variety to choose from. Pickles must be sealed properly or the vinegar will evaporate and dry out.

Tomato Chutney

  1 kg (2 lb) ripe tomatoes, peeled and quartered
  1 medium onion, chopped
  1 teaspoon ground allspice
  1 teaspoon salt
  1 teaspoon Cayenne pepper
  100 g (4 oz) soft brown sugar
  150 ml (¼ pint) malt vinegar

Put all the ingredients into a large ovenglass bowl.
Microwave on High for 15 minutes, stirring occasionally until the mixture thickens and pulps.

Three-quarters cover with cling film to prevent spattering as the bubbles pop, and microwave on High for 15-20 minutes, stirring occasionally until the chutney is thick.

Pour into sterilized jars filling to within 2 cm (¾ in) of the rims.

Cover tightly with cling film.

Put the jars in the microwave oven one at a time and microwave on High for 30-60 seconds until the cling film balloons. Remove the jars remembering to use gloves.

Makes 1.5 kg (3 lb)

Spiced Vinegar

- 1 litre (1¾ pint) malt vinegar
- 2 teaspoons ground mace
- 2 teaspoons ground cinnamon
- 2 teaspoons ground ginger
- 10 cloves
- 1 tablespoon whole allspice, bruised with a rolling pin
- 1 tablespoon white peppercorns, bruised with a rolling pin

Combine all the ingredients in a large ovenglass bowl and microwave on High for 5-7 minutes or until boiling. Cover tightly with cling film and leave for a few days. Strain before using.

Pickled Cabbage

Choose a brightly coloured firm cabbage and discard the outer leaves. Pickled cabbage begins to soften after two months so make only small quantities.

- 1 small red cabbage
- Approx 100 g (4 oz) salt
- 1 litre (1¾ pint) spiced vinegar

Quarter the cabbage and remove the rough stalk. Shred the cabbage finely and layer in a large glass bowl with plenty of salt, the exact amount not being important.

Cover and leave for 24 hours.

Drain through a plastic colander and rinse thoroughly under cold running water. Shake to remove the excess water and leave to stand until all the water has drained away.

Pack the cabbage loosely into cold jars and cover with spiced vinegar.

Seal with waxed discs and tightly fitting lids and leave for 2-3 weeks before using.

450 g (1 lb) cabbage fills approximately one jar.

Pickled Onions

   1 ½ kg (3 lb) pickling onions, peeled
   600 ml (1 pint) spiced vinegar (see page 261)
   225 g (8 oz) coarse salt
   2 litre (4 pints) water

Put the onions in a large bowl or plastic bucket and mix in the salt and cold water. Leave for 2 days.

Rinse in plenty of cold water and drain thoroughly.

Put into 3 clean cold jars and cover with spiced vinegar.

Seal with waxed discs and tightly fitting lids.

Leave for 2-3 weeks before using but not longer than 3 months.

Makes 3 jars

14

Confectionery

Confectionery is simple to make in the microwave oven because there is no direct heat. Sugar is the main ingredient in sweet-making and this is frequently combined with water to form a syrup. The main points to check are that the sugar is fully dissolved before bringing to the boil otherwise the candies will crystallize or be tough and brittle. Do not stir after the syrup comes to the boil and brush down the sides with a wet brush in initial heating. Always use a large heat-resistant glass jug or bowl with a lip so that mixtures can be poured easily.

Expect the containers to become very hot due to the high-temperature mixtures they contain, so first and foremost have an oven glove ready to use both during and after cooking. If you use a jug the handle will stay cool but even slight tipping may cause contact of the sides of the jug with the fingers, so be very careful. Grip a lipped bowl firmly on either side using the oven glove. It is more difficult to pour syrups out of a bowl but gentle rocking from side to side, as pouring takes place, will help to keep the mixtures running centrally.

Never put a hot bowl on to a damp work surface, and protect delicate table tops with a mat. You must not use metal spoons – they are heat conductors and the heat quickly travels up to the tip. Never leave any implement in the cooking container.

Make sweets while you are working in the kitchen so that you can keep a constant watch on the cooking.

It takes quite a long time to reach boiling point and about another ½ minute to reach 105°C (220°F). Then you can expect a rapid rise to reach 115°C (230°F) (soft ball) in a further 30-45 seconds.

A high ratio of sugar to water will take longer to dissolve after which the syrup will thicken rapidly. Conversely, a weak sugar solution, though quick to dissolve, will take longer to thicken. Bear these points in mind should you decide to double quantities.

Always under-boil rather than over-boil. You can always allow a little longer to achieve the density required. Weighing and measuring can be tedious but they are important in sweet-making. Prepare syrups at any convenient time up to a week ahead, bringing them to boiling point. When required, stir before microwaving, then continue cooking to the required temperature.

Of the three testing methods the visual and spoon dip one is probably the best, because you can judge by the size of the bubbles and the colour of the syrup. A smoked glass or pottery bowl would obscure clear inspection and brown sugar syrups cannot be visually tested.

Another test is to drop a teaspoon of syrup into a glass of cold water. Use a hot spoon (first dipped into very hot water) and then the mixture will not solidify on the testing spoon. The mixture will form quite definite shapes when dropped in the water: soft ball, which can be moulded between thumb and finger; hard ball, which has a consistency rather like boiled sweets; and brittle, which forms hair-like strands. Or you can test with a candy thermometer. These must not be left in the microwave oven during cooking and, unless immediately tested, the mixture will either lose or gain heat, thereby bridging the fine dividing line between success and failure.

My recipes are all fairly simple so that with very little practice you will be able to achieve success.

Chocolates are considerably easier to make since melting is simple and many fillings can be dipped. Block cooking chocolate melts evenly and produces a softish coating when set. Chocolate made from this should be kept in a cool place. Left-over chocolate or trimmings can be remelted many times without deterioration. Chocolate will melt more quickly and evenly if covered with cling film, but because over-cooking spoils chocolate and it can even burn, speed may not be your best ally.

Couverture (Chocolate Meunier) is expensive but is true chocolate and has a good biting flavour.

Dessert chocolate, such as made by Cadbury's, Rowntrees, Terry's, etc, melts easily but becomes dull and brittle after dipping and tends to streak when re-used. You will find that plain chocolate of all varieties is easier to work with and runs more freely than milk chocolate, which becomes spongy if over-cooked.

Gelatine is used for Turkish Delight and similar confections and is easy to dissolve in the microwave oven. Just sprinkle the gelatine on to the water and heat on High, stirring once or twice until dissolved. Do not let gelatine boil as it then loses its potency.

Coconut Ice

When boiling the syrup use a large heat-resistant jug or better still a lipped ovenglass mixing bowl. Oven gloves are a must as the syrup is immensely hot. Most glass, plastic or cardboard containers are suitable for setting. If in doubt line them first with non-stick paper.

225 g (8 oz) granulated sugar
Pinch cream of tartar
2 tablespoons water
1 tablespoon milk
½ teaspoon lemon juice or rosewater
50 g (2 oz) desiccated coconut

Pink food colouring
1 × 10 cm (4 in) shallow square container, greased or
lined

Mix the sugar, cream of tartar, water and milk in a large
measuring bowl and microwave on High for 1 minute. Stir
until the sugar is dissolved. Continue on High for 1½-2
minutes until the syrup rises and large bubbles form on
top. To test, a candy thermometer should read 115°C
(230°F) but you should not need to do this as the mixture
can be re-microwaved if it is not thick enough.
Remove syrup from the microwave oven and pour the
lemon juice or rosewater on top. Shake the bowl gently.
This small amount of juice will prevent the syrup from
over-cooking.
Beat in the coconut. If the mixture does not thicken *at all*
when the coconut has been beaten in for at least half a
minute, return to the oven and microwave on High until
the colour lightens. Under-cooked coconut ice is wet
underneath when turned out. Leave it uncovered in a warm
place for 1 hour before despairing.
Pour half the mixture into the prepared dish.
Add a few drops of pink colouring to the remaining
mixture and beat until fairly thick.
Pour the pink on top of the white mixture, smoothing with
a palette knife if necessary. There is no need to wait unduly
for the bottom layer to set. It will be firmer than it looks.
If you wait too long, the two halves separate when the
coconut ice is cut.
Mark when cool and cut when cold either in the mould or
when turned out.
Makes 16 to 20 pieces

Variations
Substitute orange colouring and orange flower water.

Crystallized Grapes

The syrup must be at the correct temperature to achieve a nice 'cracky' finish. Test frequently and as soon as the temperature is reached, dip the base of the jug or bowl in a bowl of warm water to prevent a further temperature rise.

    175 g (6 oz) bunch green or black grapes
    100 g (4 oz) granulated sugar
    1 teaspoon powdered glucose
    5 tablespoons water
    1 sheet non-stick paper
    Candy thermometer or glass of ice cold water and a
        teaspoon

Select only those grapes with stalks attached and make sure that the grapes are clean and absolutely dry. Divide into pairs of earrings.

Mix the sugar, glucose and water in a large heatproof bowl and microwave on High for 1 minute, stir, continue on High without further stirring for 5-6½ minutes or until a candy thermometer registers 150°C (300°F), or test by dropping a teaspoon of the syrup into the cold water. When brittle strands form it is ready. Remove from the microwave oven with oven gloves.

Using a fork hooked between the joined stalks, quickly dip the grapes into the syrup, one pair at a time, to completely coat.

Place on the non-stick paper so that the fruit is not touching and leave for 5-10 minutes until set.

Use within 1-2 hours.

Makes approximately 12 pairs

Variations

You can use cherries or bunches of black or red currants, using the same method.

Date Munchies

Block dates will do very well in this recipe – they are cheaper than the separated stoned kind.

  1 large egg
  150 g (5 oz) caster sugar
  100 g (4 oz) stoned dates, roughly chopped
  ½ teaspoon vanilla essence
  40 g (1½ oz) rice crispies
  Desiccated coconut to coat

Beat the egg until fluffy, then beat in the sugar until the mixture puffs up.

Add the dates, roughly chopped. It does not matter that they are stuck together. They will fall apart during cooking.

Microwave on High for 2½-3 minutes, stirring once during cooking. The dates will now be soft.

Add the vanilla essence and beat thoroughly, then leave to cool for 5 minutes.

Stir in the rice crispies.

Refrigerate the mixture or put in the freezer until cold.

Form the date mixture into walnut-sized balls. It will stick to your fingers but there is no way round this. Toss one at a time in the coconut to coat thoroughly. The best way to do this is to third-fill a small bowl with the coconut and swirl the balls round in it.

Leave uncovered to finish setting.

Makes 25

Variations
Substitute chopped figs or chopped dried apricots and flavour with apricot brandy.

Marshmallows

Here is a recipe devised by one of my students, Kate Hurrell.

300 ml (½ pint) water
225 g (8 oz) granulated sugar
2 level tablespoons powdered gelatine
½ level teaspoon cream of tartar
¼ teaspoon vanilla essence
½ level teaspoon salt
50 g (2 oz) hazelnuts, roughly chopped
1 tablespoon orange flower water or rosewater
4 drops orange or pink food colouring
1 × 13 cm (5 in) square or 15 × 10 cm (6 × 4 in) shallow
  container generously coated with cornflour

Combine the water, sugar, gelatine and cream of tartar in a large heatproof bowl. Microwave on High for 2-3 minutes, stirring occasionally until the sugar and gelatine have dissolved. Microwave on High until the mixture boils, then continue cooking, stirring occasionally for 5-6 minutes until the mixture hangs from the side of the spoon like a thread.

Leave to cool slightly, then divide the mixture into two. To one half add the vanilla essence, half the salt and half the nuts and beat vigorously until the mixture is thick and white. Pour into the prepared container and leave to set for 10 minutes.

Meanwhile, beat the flower water, colouring and remaining salt and nuts into the unflavoured mixture and repeat the beating process.

Pour over the white layer and leave for a few hours to set.

Cut the marshmallow into squares while still in the tin.

Makes 24 squares

Variations

Dip the squares in 100-150 g (4-6 oz) melted dessert chocolate and place on non-stick paper until set.

Substitute green food colouring and peppermint essence for the orange or rosewater, or mix chopped glacé cherries into the pink half and leave 25 g (1 oz) nuts in the white portion.

Marzipan

This marzipan is firm rather than the softer almond paste used for cake-making.

   100 g (4 oz) ground almonds
   50 g (2 oz) caster sugar
   50 g (2 oz) icing sugar
   ¼ teaspoon vanilla essence
   ¼ teaspoon almond essence
   ¼ teaspoon lemon juice
   1-1½ egg whites
   Food colouring if desired

Combine the ground almonds and sugars in a bowl and microwave on High for 5 minutes, stirring every minute.

Lightly beat the egg white, essences, juice, and colouring if used, until a few bubbles appear.

Gradually, add the beaten egg white to the warmed almond mixture, working in each addition with a fork. Use only as much egg as is necessary to bind the mixture.

Knead lightly with the fingertips, then shape and use as required.

The marzipan firms quickly. If not required for immediate use, wrap the block in cling film.

Makes 225 g (½ lb)

Variations

Add liqueur, green colouring and peppermint essence,

pink colouring and rosewater, chopped walnuts, cherries and crystallized ginger, then roll out thinly and cut into discs or form into balls while still warm. Alternatively, leave uncoloured, cut into bars and press halves of walnuts or glacé cherries along the top.

Wrap in silver paper saved from chocolate bars.

Marzipan Chocolates

Use packet or home-made marzipan for this recipe.

    225 g (8 oz) marzipan
    250 g (10 oz) block cooking chocolate
    12 shelled almonds
    Sheet non-stick or waxed paper

Cut the marzipan into 16 or 25 squares.

Spread the almonds out on a piece of paper or plate and microwave on High for 1 minute. While the almonds are still warm, cut in half lengthwise but do not split.

Break up the chocolate and put into a narrow-diameter jug. Cover with cling film and microwave on High for 2-3 minutes or until melted. Watch carefully as even melted chocolate holds its shape. Stir to test. Remaining lumps should melt on stirring as the heat evens out.

Drop the marzipan squares into the chocolate one at a time, flipping them over for even coating. Remove with a skewer or fork and place well spaced out on the non-stick paper.

Top each square with an almond half while the chocolate is still soft, covering the hole left from the skewer.

If the chocolate begins to harden before all the pieces are dipped, microwave on High for 10-20 seconds.

Leave the chocolates to cool, then trim with a sharp knife. The trimmings may be melted down for future use.

Makes 16-25

Variations

Top some of the chocolates with crystallized rose or violet petals, snippets of crystallized ginger or glacé cherries.

Mumbles

Use leftover scraps of marzipan or almond paste for this recipe.

40 g (1½ oz) marzipan or almond paste
25 g (1 oz) plain or block cooking chocolate
15 g (½ oz) raisins
10 almonds or walnuts chopped
4 glacé cherries, chopped
1-2 teaspoons brandy
4 glacé cherries, halved, for decoration

Mix all the ingredients, except the brandy, in a bowl and microwave on High for 1-1½ minutes until the chocolate is melted.
Add the brandy and stir until blended.
Divide the mixture into 8-10 pieces. Form into balls, then flatten slightly with a fork.
Press a halved cherry on top of each mumble.
Makes 8-10

Variations

Substitute sultanas, mixed peel or roughly crushed sweetmeal biscuits, for the raisins, nuts and cherries.

Nut Fudge

A teaspoon of vanilla essence is included in the mixture but check the strength first as some makes are more concentrated than others.

100 g (4 oz) unsalted butter
3 tablespoons milk
1 teaspoon vanilla essence
50 g (2 oz) cocoa powder, sifted
450 g (1 lb) icing sugar, sifted
50 g (2 oz) mixed nuts, finely chopped
1 × 20 cm (8 in) square dish, greased

Put the butter, milk and vanilla essence in a large bowl. Microwave on High for 1-1½ minutes until the butter is melted. To make it even quicker, cut the butter into the milk as soon as it is soft.

Stir in the cocoa and sugar. Microwave on High for 1½-2 minutes or until the mixture boils. This is to make sure that the cocoa does not taste 'raw'.

Stir in the nuts.

Spread the fudge evenly into the dish.

Leave to cool a little, then flatten the fudge with the knuckles if it looks bumpy.

Refrigerate for 1-2 hours before cutting into squares.

Makes 36-64

Variations Add 25 g (1 oz) raisins or substitute 25 g (1 oz) chopped chocolate polka dots for the nuts. For a rum fudge, use rum essence instead of vanilla.

Peanut Brittle

Glucose syrup or Liquid Glucose B.P. is obtainable from larger branches of Boots. It comes in 450 g (1 lb) pots and keeps for a year or two. Powdered glucose is a poor substitute, but could be used if you can't obtain the liquid. Use a wooden spoon for stirring, oven gloves for handling the bowl. Be sure not to over-cook while browning the mixture, as it could burn and fill the oven with acrid smoke.

175 g (6 oz) caster sugar
5 tablespoons glucose syrup
2 tablespoons water
25 g (1 oz) butter or margarine
150 g (5 oz) salted peanuts
1 level teaspoon bicarbonate of soda
¼ teaspoon vanilla essence
1 teaspoon cold water
2 sheets non-stick paper

Put the sugar, glucose syrup and 2 tablespoons of water in a large ovenglass bowl. Microwave on High for 2 minutes. Stir until the sugar is dissolved.

Add the butter or margarine, which will soften on mixing in with the warm syrup. Microwave on High for 1 minute.

Stir in the peanuts and microwave on High for 5-6 minutes until light brown underneath the foam. Do not stir while the peanuts are cooking.

Remove the bowl from the oven with oven gloves and shake gently. You will then be able to see more clearly whether the mixture is sufficiently brown or if it needs another minute's cooking.

Towards the end of the cooking period, blend the bicarbonate of soda, vanilla essence and water in a small bowl.

As soon as the peanut mixture is ready, pour in the blended bicarbonate of soda and beat thoroughly for ½ minute until honeycombed throughout. Insufficient beating will cause a separation of honeycomb and toffee which will not become brittle.

Pour the hot mixture on to a sheet of the non-stick paper and smooth to a depth of 8 mm ($\frac{3}{8}$ in) with a greased pallette knife.

Leave for 3 minutes as at this stage the brittle is too hot to handle.

Cover with a second sheet of non-stick paper and flip over. The mixture will appear flat on this surface.

Leave until cold enough to touch.

Using folded pieces of paper to protect your fingers, pull the brittle from the edges, stretching until the peanuts stand out and the mixture measures 20 × 28 cm (8 × 11 in). You will have to do this in short bursts to give your fingers a rest, taking great care as the mixture is very hot inside.

Leave until cold, then break up and store in an airtight tin. After several weeks the brittle will become tacky but it is so delicious you will not wait that long to finish it up.

Makes 225-350 g (8-12 oz)

Variations

Dip the pieces of brittle into melted chocolate and space out well on non-stick paper until set.

Peppermint and Orange Creams

40 g (1 ½ oz) butter
6 tablespoons milk
Pinch cream of tartar
450 g (1 lb) icing sugar
¼ teaspoon orange flavouring
¼ teaspoon orange colouring
¼ teaspoon peppermint essence
¼ teaspoon green colouring
2 sheets non-stick paper
2.5 cm (1 in) round cutter, greased inside and out

Put the butter and 4 tablespoons of the milk in a large heatproof bowl and microwave on High for 1-1½ minutes until the butter has melted. If the butter was very hard and has not melted by this time a stir will probably do the trick. Stir in the cream of tartar and 225 g (8 oz) of the icing sugar to form a creamy coloured stiff paste. Microwave on High for ½ minute when the mixture will be smooth.

Without putting in too much effort, mix in the remaining 225 g (8 oz) of the icing sugar and microwave on High for 1½ minutes. Stir thoroughly, microwave on High for 1 minute, then beat in the remaining milk.

Work quickly after the mixture is cooked as this is a type of fondant that hardens quickly. Should this occur you can put the mixture back into the microwave for a few seconds to soften. Do not scrape cooked fondant from the sides of the bowl or you will get crunchy bites and not creams.

Divide the mixture into two. Into one half beat the orange flavouring and orange colouring. Colour the remaining mixture green and flavour with peppermint essence.

Pour one mixture on to the non-stick paper as thinly as possible, 5 mm (¼ in) if you can manage it. Cut out discs with the round cutter, regreasing it as necessary.

For easier pouring, put the other half of the mixture in the microwave oven and microwave on High for 10-15 seconds. Pour on to the second sheet of non-stick paper and cut out discs as before.

Makes 20 orange and 20 peppermint creams

Convenience Foods and Menu Planning

CONVENIENCE FOODS

Convenience foods are contained in the cans and packages that we are rapidly coming to rely upon, whether it be a simple vegetable or a more complex main course. You may like to believe that all your cooking starts from basics, but have you never resorted to that can of baked beans?

Convenience foods are exactly what they claim to be – convenient. You should not decry them for they have a valid place in our kitchens today. Convenience foods are useful for the person cooking for one, for the busy worker who has no time to stop, or for the people who have the time, but don't live anywhere near a shop and so cannot live entirely on fresh vegetables. And it goes without saying that the advent of convenience foods has enabled us to have seasonal foods out of season. Both canned and frozen foods are easy to store and their shelf or freezer life is long.

Often a canned food can be added to home-cooked dishes to great effect. The canned tomato or its derivative, tomato paste, is a must in many sauces. Add a few canned or frozen sweetcorn kernels and piquant diced red and green peppers to casseroles or egg dishes at those times that fresh corn and peppers are difficult to obtain.

Of the better known dried or dehydrated foods potato is the most popular and it can be reconstituted speedily in the microwave oven. Cake mixes are much more successful when cooked by microwave and custard powder can be turned into a delicious sauce in seconds. Boil in the bag foods, such as kipper fillets and cod in white sauce, only

CONVENIENCE FOOD COOKING TIMES

Item	Cooking Time After Defrosting	Instructions
Baked beans, 450 g (15.88 oz) can	2½-3 mins	Transfer to dish, cover and stir once during cooking
Beefburgers, 4 frozen	3-4 mins	Place on serving plate, cover with kitchen paper and turn over once
Christmas pudding, 0.5 kg (1 lb)	2¾-3 mins	Remove from container and cook covered
Cornish pasty, 175 g (6 oz)	1½ mins	Heat uncovered on kitchen paper
Fish cakes, 2 × 50 g (2 oz)	1-2 mins	Cook uncovered
Fish fingers, frozen, 10	3-3½ mins	Grease dish and reposition during cooking or pre-heat browning dish (adding small knob butter) and microwave uncovered 1-1½ mins on each side

Fish steaks, frozen 2 × 100 g (4 oz)	2½-3 mins	Cook covered
Pies, individual frozen	2-2½ mins	Remove from foil dish, place on serving dish and brush with milk
Rice pudding, 1 × 439 g (15½ oz) can	3 mins	Cook covered, stir once
Roast beef and gravy, frozen, 350 g (12 oz)	3½-4 mins	Remove from dish and heat on serving plate covered
Sausage rolls, 50 g (2 oz)	15-20 secs	Heat on kitchen paper uncovered
Shepherd's pie, frozen, 400 g (14 oz)	4-5 mins	Remove from foil dish, place on serving dish and cook covered
Soup, 295 g (10½ oz) can	3-3½ mins	Pour into soup bowl, cover and stir twice
Spaghetti, 425 g (15 oz) can	3-3½ mins	Cook covered, stir once
Sponge pudding, 290 g (10½ oz) can	1-2 mins	Place on serving plate and cook covered

Defrost according to directions given in the introduction.

require a slash across the top of the pouch before heating on High. You do not even require a saucepan.

You can make up your own convenience foods. Those who have a kitchen garden are already doing this, turning their produce into a convenience food by blanching, which is a form of par-cooking, before consigning it to the freezer.

Herbs freeze well but you can also dry them in your microwave oven for use at any time. After making sure that they are clean, drain on kitchen paper, removing most of the moisture. Spread out a glassful at a time on a folded sheet of kitchen paper and microwave for 2-3 minutes, shaking the paper every ½ minute. Leave until cold, then crumble them if you wish. It is difficult to tell whether they are sufficiently dry until they cool – it may be necessary to repeat the process.

Make up a batch of crumble mix, freeze microwaved rice, spaghetti sauces, icings and cake mix toppings for convenient use at any time.

When planning menus, give a thought to the food that you have stored in your cupboard, refrigerator or freezer. You may find that you can trim your shopping list quite considerably and reduce your food preparation time.

Fried Crumbs

These are a useful topping for disguising pallid foods. They will also add flavour. Choose the deepest coloured butter that you can buy.

    4 slices bread, crusts removed
    50 g (2 oz) salted butter

Grate the bread finely or whirl in the blender.
Put the butter in a shallow dish and microwave on High for 30-60 seconds until melted.

Sprinkle the crumbs over the entire surface of the dish and microwave on High for 1 minute. This avoids lumpiness.
Stir and continue cooking on High for 1-2 minutes more, stirring frequently.
Makes 100 g-175 g (4-6 oz)

Variations
Use wholemeal or ryebread and add chopped herbs of your choice to the melted butter.

Less Calorie Ratatouille

Use a low calorie can of soup for slimmers, but any soup will do. If there is no left-over chicken in the refrigerator, use a chicken joint, first thawed and cooked in a dish in the microwave oven.

  1 × 285 g (10 oz) can low calorie vegetable soup
  350 g (12 oz) fresh or frozen sliced courgettes
  ½ red pepper, cored, deseeded, sliced
  1 × 210 g (7½ oz) can button or sliced mushrooms, drained (or 100 g (4 oz) fresh mushrooms, sliced)
  175 g (6 oz) cooked chicken, chopped
  25-40 g (1-1 ½ oz) grated Edam or Cheddar cheese

Omit the cheese and combine all the remaining ingredients in a large flameproof casserole.
Without covering microwave on High for 10-15 minutes, stirring occasionally until the vegetables are cooked, the chicken thoroughly heated and the liquid reduced.
The required cooking time depends on whether frozen or fresh ingredients are used.
If, after the dish is cooked, there is still considerable liquid remaining, pour off the surplus and reserve for use as a slimmer's soup.

Sprinkle the cheese over the ratatouille and brown under
the grill.
Serves 4

Variations
Use a can of tomatoes in place of the soup or a cream of
mushroom or lentil soup for non-slimmers. Substitute or
add aubergine, green beans and cauliflower florets.

Pancakes

Keep a stack of pancakes in your freezer and you will be
able to have almost instant starters or desserts. Remove the
required number of pancakes from the freezer. Place one
on top of the other interleaved with greaseproof or non-
stick paper. Thaw in the microwave on Low or Medium
setting for 10-15 seconds per pancake depending on how
cold and thick they are, separating before they are thawed
fully. The thawing will be completed at room temperature
while you are preparing the fillings. Fill and roll up the
pancakes. Place close together in a greased shallow serving
dish and reheat according to the fillings. Do not cover, or
the pancakes will become too soft.
For savoury fillings make up a white or a Béchamel sauce
using half milk and half single cream. 300 ml (½ pint)
sauce is sufficient for 8-10 pancakes depending upon the
size. Mix the filling with the sauce allowing 15-25 g
(½-1 oz) filling for each pancake.

Suggested fillings
Canned asparagus spears; chopped peeled prawns; flaked
smoked haddock; flaked salmon; tuna fish mashed;
chopped hard-boiled eggs and cooked spinach; or chopped
ham or mashed sardines.

Among other suitable sauces for pancake fillings are Bolognese sauce mixed with chopped walnuts flavoured with cheese.

For a more filling pancake, add freshly minced cooked lean beef or pâté.

Either reheat the pancakes as they are or garnish with grated cheese and brown under the grill.

For desserts fill the pancakes with pie filling (but do not over-heat as these fillings become very hot), confectioner's custard (page 196) or freshly chopped fruit.

A whole banana wrapped in a pancake is another idea – the pancake will be warm leaving the banana only just soft. Smother these in microwave-melted chocolate and serve with whipped cream. If you wish to fill cold pancakes with an uncooked filling, such as ice-cream, first thaw the pancakes for a moment or two longer.

Party Salad Ring

Grace your buffet table with this jellied mould or use as a starter or supper dish. The salad can be made with the help of canned, frozen or bottled ingredients.

   3 teaspoons powdered gelatine
   250 g (9 oz) frozen macedoine of vegetables
   1 × 285 g (10 oz) can condensed cream of celery soup
   6 tablespoons bottled salad cream
   225 g (8 oz) cooked turkey, chopped
   Tomato slices and cress for garnish
   1.2 litre (2 pint) ring or oblong mould

Put 4 tablespoons water into a measuring jug or small bowl. Sprinkle the gelatine on top and stir thoroughly. Microwave on High for 1-1¼ minutes until hot but not boiling. Stir and set aside until the mixture clears.

Meanwhile cook the vegetables either in the pouch (first slit) or in a dish covered with cling film. To cook, microwave on High for 5-7 minutes or until tender. Drain.

Mix the soup with the salad cream and stir in the dissolved gelatine thoroughly. Leave until just beginning to thicken.

Fold in the turkey and vegetables. Turn into the ring mould and refrigerate until set.

Turn on to a damp serving dish and garnish with cress and sliced tomatoes.

Serves 6

Variations

Use: Corned beef; chopped ham; cooked chicken (or quickly cook some in the microwave oven); large can of salmon, drained; large can of tuna, drained; condensed mushroom or chicken or tomato soup.

Substitute chopped green and red peppers for some of the vegetables and blanch briefly to soften them in the microwave oven.

MENU PLANNING

Microwave cooking is easy, fast and labour-saving. You cannot cook a meal all at once but you *can* pre-cook the individual dishes and reheat just when you want them. Now that you are a competent microwave cook you will no longer be experiencing cooking problems as such and so can concentrate on producing the best meal in the most suitable way. Don't say to yourself what shall we have for dinner and then try and cook it all by microwave but rather say what shall we eat that can be superbly cooked by microwave.

Food for up to 4 people can be both cooked and

reheated in the microwave oven. For more than this
number you will find that you have to use your microwave
in conjunction with your conventional cooker. No purpose
is served by cooking two pounds of carrots in the
microwave when quicker although no better results are
obtained using a saucepan on the hob. However, quantity
is not necessarily the main criterion since large quantities
of spinach can be easily microwaved in a roasting bag
when, due to its bulk, it would be exceedingly onerous to
cook conventionally as you cannot get all those leaves in a
saucepan at once.

In order to show how best to plan your meals I have
taken four examples to show the range possible.

BREAKFASTS

Breakfast in a bustling household needs some planning to
ensure even tempers and full stomachs. Since you can't all
get into the bathroom at the same time, the family may not
necessarily eat the meal together – in fact, one person may
have to leave the house well before another. The
microwave oven will prove to be an excellent ally in
combating all such problems.

You may find the following items regularly on a
breakfast menu:

Fruit juice or dried or fresh fruit, stewed – the latter can
be prepared by microwave in quantities to last the week
served cold. If preferred hot, all that will be required is a
minute's reheating on High for each portion.

During winter some people like to eat their breakfast
cereal with hot milk. Until you are used to your timings,
heat on Low or Defrost unless you are standing by to catch
it as it boils over. However, the results are more disastrous
when using a saucepan, as boiled-over milk congeals on a

cooker. Provided you use a tall jug, you will be able to microwave on High without mishap. One pint of milk takes about 3-4 minutes to reach steaming point.

Porridge and other hot cereals can be cooked in individual dishes or large bowls and will keep well in the refrigerator for a day or two provided they are covered. Cooking times will depend on the type of cereal used, instant oatmeal taking half the time required for regular porridge oats. It is better to cook porridge in water, adding milk as required when reheating, although if you have a Low setting you will be able to use a mixture or milk alone provided you use a large container to lessen the chances of boiling over.

If breakfast is to be served in relays, decide what you are going to serve as a main dish the night before and put it out on plates covered with cling film. These can be kept in the refrigerator until needed. A kipper or a smoked haddock fillet will take 2 minutes and 2 bacon rashers 1 minute. If you want to cook egg and bacon together, grease the plate, put the egg in the middle and the bacon rashers on the outside, just before cooking pierce through the cling film into the membrane of the egg yolk with a cocktail stick and microwave on Medium for 2-2½ minutes. A firm tomato may be halved and cooked beside the egg, taking no longer.

Scrambled eggs can be par-cooked in advance and reheated on High for 20 seconds as required.

For best results sausages should be cooked in the browning dish but that doesn't mean to say that they can't be cooked on a plate provided they are well-pricked.

If you have chosen to cook bacon, sausage and egg, use the browning dish. Start with the sausages, then add the bacon and only put in the egg at the last minute after the microwave has switched off, quickly clamping down the lid until the egg is done.

Toast will have to be cooked in the conventional way but French toast is very successful made in the browning dish.

BREAKFAST

Fruit Juice

– – –

Porridge

– – –

Bacon and Egg

– – –

Toast
Three-fruit Marmalade

– – –

Tea

Fruit Juice: Keep in refrigerator

Porridge: Prepare to a thin consistency the previous night. Porridge thickens over several hours. Dish in cereal bowls and cover. Reheat while putting on the kettle for tea.

Bacon and Egg: Arrange on a plate the previous night with 2 bacon slices either side of an egg. Cover with cling film. Prick the yolk, re-cover and microwave on Medium while eating the porridge.

Toast: Make in toaster while eating the porridge.

SUNDAY LUNCH

Sunday lunch with the help of your microwave oven becomes a treat rather than a chore. Three-quarters cook the vegetables, then drain them and plunge into a bowl of ice-cold water. Drain again and replace in serving dish until needed. The vegetables will remain in prime condition until it is time to reheat, which should be done for 1-3 minutes when required, remembering to stir once.

SUNDAY LUNCH MENU

Cream of Mushroom Soup

– – –

Roast Beef, Yorkshire Pudding
Roast Potatoes, Cabbage
Carrots

– – –

Blackberry and Apple Crumble

Vegetables: Pre-cook in the microwave oven one at a time in separate serving dishes until crisp-tender, to allow for further softening during reheating as above. Reheat the vegetables while carrying the joint and potatoes to the table.

Potatoes: Put into a roaster bag and par-cook. Transfer to pre-heated conventional oven 20 minutes before serving.

Roast Joint: Three-quarters roast in microwave oven and transfer to conventional oven at same time as the potatoes.

Yorkshire Pudding: Cook in small patty tins on upper shelf in conventional oven at the same time as the joint.

Soup: Make in the microwave oven while the main course is finishing in the conventional oven.

Crumble: Pre-assemble. Microwave while eating main course.

MINITIME SUPPER

Denali Carrot Salad

– – –

Cheese Pancakes with Corned Beef
Less Calorie Ratatouille

– – –

Blackberries and Cream

Denali Carrot Salad: Prepare the previous night and refrigerate.

Cheese Pancakes: Prepare the cheese sauce the previous night and refrigerate, or make fresh using stored pre-grated cheese. Open and chop the corned beef and thaw the pancakes just before the meal. Roll, stuff and cover with the sauce and reheat in the microwave on Low or Medium while eating the salad starter.

Less Calorie Ratatouille: Prepare 2-3 days ahead. Reheat covered before supper in the microwave oven on High for 5 minutes. Wrap in foil to keep warm.

Blackberries and Cream: Thaw on Low setting during main course. Sweeten with stock syrup and serve with fresh or microwave cream made the previous night.

DINNER PARTIES

It is unlikely that you will serve all hot courses at a dinner party, so you may wish to prepare well in advance the cold ones that need cooking in the microwave, especially items such as cold soups which tend to freeze well.

As dinner parties are special and you will choose your best crockery for serving, make sure that it is microwave-proof if you intend to serve in the same dishes you cook in. Also take care if you are going to keep the food hot in the conventional oven on delicate china.

A special menu might consist of: a cold starter, a hot soup, a main course, two vegetables plus potatoes, a choice of two desserts – one hot and one cold, petits fours, cheese, and the usual bread or bread rolls.

Balance the meal so that there is a mixture of crisp and soft foods, plain and rich foods, and a variety of colour. It would not be sensible to serve quiche, a pastry starter, followed by Boeuf en Croûte, a pastry main course and a fruit flan, a pastry dessert. Nor should you follow a tomato soup with a goulash full of tomatoes. The classic example of a meal which tastes good but looks depressing, is one where the colours are the same throughout – potato soup, grilled fish with mashed potatoes and pearl onions followed by rice pudding.

Regular dinner party-givers will not need any advice on menu planning but may need to vary ideas and methods to maximize the benefits of having a microwave oven. Here is an example:

Savoury Salted Almonds

– – –

Canteloupe Melon

– – –

Shrimp and Corn Chowder

– – –

Fillet of Beef in Chasseur Sauce
Lyonnaise Potatoes, Green Salad

– – –

Summer Meringue Pudding

– – –

Mousse au Chocolat

– – –

Cheese, Petits Fours

– – –

Coffee

Almonds:

  50 g (2 oz) salted butter
  ¼ teaspoon ground cardamom
  ¼ teaspoon ground coriander
  ⅛ teaspoon chilli compound powder
  225 g (8 oz) shelled almonds, skinned
  Salt

Put the butter in a large shallow dish with the spices and microwave on High for 1½-2 minutes until melted. Add the almonds and stir to coat well. Microwave on High for 2½-3½ minutes, stirring occasionally, Drain on kitchen paper and sprinkle with plenty of salt while still hot. Store in an airtight container.

Melon: Prepare in advance and refrigerate.

Shrimp and Corn Chowder: Prepare the night before up to the stage before the shrimps are added. Reheat just before dinner, adding extra milk if necessary. Add the shrimps while the first course is being eaten.

Fillet of Beef in Chasseur Sauce: Prepare the sauce and garnishes the previous day. Reheat the sauce in a saucepan and the garnishes in the microwave oven before the meal. Keep hot conventionally. Heat a browning dish and cook the meat while the soup dishes are being cleared away.

Lyonnaise Potatoes: Reheat in microwave oven on High for 5 minutes before dinner and keep hot in the conventional oven.

Green Salad: Prepare in the morning, cover and refrigerate.

Salad Dressing: A convenience food you can make up yourself and keep in the larder.

Summer Meringue Pudding: Prepare earlier the same day.

Mousse au Chocolat: Prepare up to 1 month ahead and freeze. Transfer to the refrigerator 12 hours previously.

Petits Fours: Choose from Marzipan Chocolates, Fudge Squares, which store for months in the refrigerator, and Crystallized Grapes. Prepare 3 hours before the meal and keep in a dry place.

Coffee: Prepare and strain ahead of time. Reheat during the cheese course allowing more time than you think. If in doubt reheat at a Low setting for 2½ times the recommended High setting time.

Irish Coffee: As an extra or alternative to ordinary coffee.

COFFEE

Freshly ground coffee beans and freshly drawn water

produce the finest coffee, which should be drunk as soon as it has infused. Many people use instant coffee granules or coffee bags and are perfectly happy with these. Ideally, coffee should be served as soon as it is made, but it does add to the problems of the busy hostess trying to negotiate her way around a kitchen full of dirty dishes. Make the coffee, therefore, well ahead of time, strain and put into a microwave-proof coffee pot. Leave the lid off in the oven.

HEATING TIMES FROM COLD ON HIGH

Black Coffee	Milk	Coffee & Milk Simultaneously
600 ml (1 pt) 4¼-4¾ mins	300 ml (½ pt) 1-1¼ mins	5½-6½ mins
1.2 litre (2 pt) 7-7½ mins	600 ml (1 pt) 2½-3½ mins	8½-10 mins

Although the coffee and milk may be heated simultaneously, to make certain one or the other does not boil, use the lower recommended times when setting the oven and continue cooking to the maximum time only if necessary.

Irish Coffee

For absolute success whip the cream lightly before spooning over the hot coffee. Makes 750 ml (1¼ pints) coffee for 4 servings. To reheat this amount from cold, microwave on High for 4-5½ minutes.

Freshly made strong black coffee or pre-prepared coffee heated in the microwave oven on High
2-3 tablespoons Irish whiskey per glass
2-3 teaspoons granulated or coffee sugar per glass
1 tablespoon half-whipped double cream per glass

Warm 4 stemmed large wine glasses. Best glasses should be warmed by rinsing in hot water. To heat ordinary uncut wine glasses put 1 cm (½ in) water in each glass and microwave on High until the water starts to bubble. This will take 10-15 seconds for 1 glass and 30 seconds for 4 glasses. Grasp the stems of the glasses and pour away the water. Do not use crystal glasses.

Put the whiskey in the glasses and stir in the sugar.

Space the glasses out on the oven shelf and microwave on High for 10-15 seconds per glass until the whiskey is warm. On no account must it boil or all the alcohol will be driven off.

Stir to completely dissolve the sugar.

Fill the glasses to within 1 cm (½ in) of the rim with piping hot coffee.

Carefully spoon the cream evenly over the surface but do not stir or the cream and coffee will mix.

Serve immediately.

Variations

Substitute Scotch whisky or rum for the Irish whiskey.

For Mocha coffee, stir a tablespoon of powdered drinking chocolate into the coffee when reheating.

Postscript

It is important to remember that although the menus in this chapter are designed so that you can make at least three-quarters of the meal by microwave, if you feel you can do some of the dishes better by cooking them conventionally do so. You should never try to cook by microwave just because you feel you should be using it. This is *not* what successful cooking is about. You and not your microwave is the boss.

Useful Addresses

Mail Order Containers and Cling film suppliers
 Microwave Ovenware Ltd., 70, Church Road, Teddington, Middlesex, TU11 8PY
 Lakeland Plastics, Alexandra Buildings, Station Precinct, Windermere, Cumbria, LA23 1BQ

Microwave Oven and Cookware Stockists
 Tronso Microwaves, 647, Holloway Road, Archway, N19 5SE
 Microwave Kitchen Ltd., 10, Castle Street, Guildford, Surrey, GU1 3UW
 London Microwave Centre, 57, New King's Road, SW6
 Devon Microwave Specialists, 351, Torquay Road, Preston, Paignton, Devon

Manufacturers and Distributors
 Hitachi Sales (UK) Ltd., Hitachi House, Station Road, Hayes, Middlesex, UB3 4DR
 Belling & Co. Ltd., Bridge Works, Southbury Road, Enfield, Middlesex
 Microwave Marketing Ltd. (National Panasonic), Commercial House, 188, Gooch Street, Birmingham, B5 7HE
 Sanyo UK Ltd., 8, Greycaine Road, Watford, Hertfordshire, WD2 4UQ
 AEG Telefunken (UK) Ltd., Bath Road, Slough, Berkshire, SW 4AW

For Other Manufacturers
 The Microwave Oven Association, 16a, The Broadway, London, SW19 1RF

General Enquiries
  International Microwave Power Institute, 3, Bridle Parade, Bridle Road, Shirley, Croydon, Surrey, CR0 8HA
Mechanical Turntables and Cookware
  Anchor Hocking, 10, Wyndham Place, London, W1H 1AS
Flavourings and Colourings (for stockists contact)
  Langdale Ltd., Vulcan Way, New Addington, Croydon, Surrey

Index